GLORIOUS COMPANIONS

August 6, 2003

To Gordon →
May you enjoy reading this
book as much as I enjoyed
writing it. Best wishes, and
may God bless you.
Richard H. Schmidt

GLORIOUS COMPANIONS

Five Centuries of Anglican Spirituality

RICHARD H. SCHMIDT

WILLIAM B. EERDMANS PUBLISHING COMPANY
GRAND RAPIDS, MICHIGAN / CAMBRIDGE, U.K.

© 2002 Wm. B. Eerdmans Publishing Co.
All rights reserved

Wm. B. Eerdmans Publishing Co.
255 Jefferson Ave. S.E., Grand Rapids, Michigan 49503 /
P.O. Box 163, Cambridge CB3 9PU U.K.

Paperback edition 2003

Printed in the United States of America

07 06 05 04 03   7 6 5 4 3 2

ISBN 0-8028-2222-3

www.eerdmans.com

Contents

Contents

Contents

Introduction

The Nature and Purpose of This Book

Thirty years of parish ministry has led to this book. When new adults found a home in parishes I served, it wasn't because they wanted to become Episcopalians. More likely, someone had invited them to church or they had heard something about the congregation that appealed to them. After a few months, however, many became curious about their new church. "Why do we do this? Where did that come from? How do we deal with such-and-such?" Those coming from another denomination asked where their new church stood on issues important to their old church. Former Roman Catholics asked whether Episcopalians have a pope. Baptists wanted to know how we interpret the Bible. Pentecostals inquired about experiences of the Holy Spirit. Lutherans asked to see our doctrinal statements.

These people often sought answers in classes I taught about the Christian faith as understood and lived in the Episcopal Church. For years, I looked for a suitable text, a single volume that would introduce new Episcopalians to the thinkers and spiritual guides who had shaped our church, but the book I needed did not exist. I recommended other books, but none covered all the material I thought important. I photocopied passages from many volumes, often saying something like, "This is out of print, so you'll have to read this photocopy and take my word for the rest of it." I finally decided to write the book myself.

Introduction

This is a book about people. Getting to know people is the best way to learn theology. It was as a person, after all, that God disclosed himself to the world. The people in this book have three things in common: All are Anglicans (or Episcopalians), all love their Lord and seek to live faithfully, and all have produced a literary legacy. Apart from that, they are as different as twenty-nine people could be — men and women, black and white, doers and thinkers, searchers and finders, happy and brooding. You will find here school teachers, housewives, poets, novelists, missionaries, bishops, and martyrs.

Most of the people discussed in these pages were familiar to me from years of reading and parish ministry. When I drew up my initial list of influential Anglicans, the first names that came to mind were mostly ordained English males. There was a reason for that, but I wanted to include in this book some women, lay persons, and people from other parts of the world. When I began rummaging through seminary libraries and asking questions, I was delighted with what I discovered. Some of the most fascinating people in this book were little more than names to me until last year. During the time I was researching and writing this book, I awakened early each morning, conversing in my mind with a challenging and invigorating new friend. It was as if I gained a new soulmate every few days. Each person discussed here has become a glorious companion to me. The title of this book comes from a passage in *Centuries of Meditations*, by Thomas Traherne, one of the authors discussed in these pages. The entire passage reads as follows. It's as good a description of the characters who appear in these pages as I can think of:

> O Jesu, who having prepared all the joys in heaven and earth for me and redeemed me to inherit thy Father's treasures, hast prepared for me the most glorious companions in whose presence and society I may enjoy them: I bless thee for the communion of saints, and for thy adorning the same with all manner of beauties, excellencies, perfections, and delights. O what a glorious assembly is the church of the first born, how blessed and divine! What perfect lovers! How great and honorable! How wise! How sweet and delightful! Every one being the end, every one the king of heaven, every one the son of God in greatness and glory, every one the entire and perfect friend of all the residue, every one the joy of each other's soul, every one the light and ornament of thy kingdom, every one thy peculiar

friend, yet loving every one as thy peculiar friend, and rejoicing in the pleasures and delights of every one! O my God, make me one of that happy assembly. (I, 97)

This book is primarily addressed to the lay person, although I hope it will prove useful to clergy and seminarians as well. Technical words and theological jargon have been avoided. I have my wife to thank for that — she read my draft of each chapter and often said something like, "What does *soteriology* mean? What's a *patristic*?" Then I'd find a "regular" word to convey the same meaning. Each chapter contains an essay on one author, giving enough biographical information to bring the author to life as a real person, discussing his or her thought in the context of its time, and highlighting topics addressed by the author which are still discussed and debated today. A selection of quotations from the author's published work follows. Each chapter concludes with a few questions for reflection and discussion. Chapters may be read in any order; each is written to stand alone. I hope this format will make the book suitable for small study groups.

What Is Spirituality? What Is Anglicanism?

The meaning of the words "five centuries" is, I suppose, clear — but the other two words in the subtitle of this book require some defining.

"Spirituality" is hot these days. Magazines at the supermarket checkout stand contain feature articles about it. Talk show hosts are big on it. Entire aisles in bookstores offer titles on spirituality and sex, spirituality and baseball, spirituality and the cinema. I even saw a book recently on "the spirituality of whole grain diets." There is a vast array of "spiritualities" to choose from — channeling, yoga, monastic retreats, Bible study groups, transcendental meditation, "twelve step" groups. I myself was so caught up in the spirituality craze that I went off a few years ago and got a degree in it.

Spiritualities differ. The word spirituality is a fairly recent one — it was coined around the year 1500 and wasn't widely used until this century. It also lacks a point of reference, inviting each person to supply his or her own. This is dangerous, for you can easily become your own point of reference. Much that is called spirituality today is little more than self-realization, self-assertion, self-obsession, in short, what once would have been recognized as "spiritual pride," the deadliest of the deadly sins. Before the word spirituality assumed center stage, people talked about something else — faithfulness, devotion, obedience, piety, holy living. Those words point beyond themselves. Faithful to *what?* Devoted to *what?* Obedient to *whom?*

When I use the word spirituality, I refer to the search for what is truly important or valuable or beautiful, and to our relationship to it. Although it affects outward behavior, spirituality has a strong interior dimension; the relationship it seeks involves what is often called the "soul." To speak of the soul is to use a religious term. Some spiritualities avoid religious language — they have their reasons for this and I do not fault them for it, having benefitted for years from a group that assiduously refers to its "higher power." Churches and synagogues, however, have been dealing with the soul and the "higher power" for many centuries. Yes, they can be irritating at times — I could testify to that — but their traditions encompass a treasury of spiritual experience and wisdom. If you want a relationship to what is truly important or valuable or beautiful, a church or synagogue is a good place to start looking.

Christians find what is important, valuable, and beautiful in the person of Jesus Christ, but we relate to Jesus Christ in remarkably different ways. I think of the Christian church as a large manor house with many rooms — all of them banquet rooms. The decor, the music, and the conversation vary from room to room, but it is the same house and the lord of the manor presides at every table — it is in fact the same banquet, served in differing venues. Anglicans fill one of the rooms in the house of Christ. (This understanding of the church is, incidentally, a characteristically Anglican understanding — we see ourselves as part of a fellowship extending far beyond us; no Anglican would say that Anglicanism is *the* church.)

But what is Anglicanism? This volume will introduce you to twenty-nine Anglicans. You will discover the answer to that question as you read, and I shall indicate below a few distinctive features of Anglicanism to watch for in the pages that follow. William Countryman, in his *The Poetic Imagination*, has called Anglicanism "a kind of 'family' of churches." This is an apt image. Imagine a large extended family gathered for a holiday dinner. Who belongs to the family? It's not a matter of everyone believing exactly the same things or everyone behaving the same way. Some members of the family may believe things and behave in ways that embarrass or irritate the others. It's not even a matter of everyone being related — one of those gathered may be unrelated to the rest by either blood or marriage, but everyone knows "she's family." A family is a group of people who share a common history. It often comes down to which people the head of the household invites to holiday dinners. Anglicanism is a worldwide family of that sort. The archbishop of Canterbury is head of the Anglican household. Once every ten years, he invites the bishops of various churches around the world to a gathering at his home in England, called a Lambeth Conference (Lambeth is the name of his house). To be an Anglican is to be a member of a church whose bishop is invited to the Lambeth Conference and who chooses to attend. In other words, as Countryman says, an Anglican is anyone "who claims the history and is claimed by the family."

The word Anglicanism is of nineteenth-century origin. It was coined shortly after the American Revolution, when Americans who had been members of the Church of England no longer wanted to belong to a church which required prayers on behalf of the British sovereign, someone they hoped soon to forget. But they appreciated their church in other ways and saw no reason to change much else. So they founded a new, independent church, maintaining the worship, teachings, and ministry of the Church of England. It is now called the Episcopal Church. The archbishop of Canterbury quickly recognized the new American church as being "in communion" with him. Anglicanism today consists of thirty-eight independent churches around the world. They are called "provinces" of the "Anglican Communion." Anglicanism has no central authority. As head of the family, the archbishop of Canterbury acts as convener and host, but only in his own Church of England does he exercise actual authority.

Anglicans differ in many ways, but we share a history. We work and play, eat and pray together. Like members of any family, we occasionally bicker. But we know who we are and we know we belong to each other. We're family.

Anglicanism among the Denominations

It is unusual to describe a church as I have just described Anglicanism, and we Anglicans have often sought further to identify ourselves by defining what we do and how we think in terms of other Christian groups. This has been slightly helpful, sometimes. One way of doing this is to call Anglicanism the *via media*, or "middle way." This phrase was popularized in the nineteenth century by John Henry Newman, to refer to Anglicanism's position between Roman Catholicism on the one hand and Protestantism on the other. We have often said, somewhat smugly, that we are "fully catholic and fully reformed." It's true that Anglicans, following the lead of the Church of England, maintain the scriptures, creeds, worship, and ministry of the historic Christian church, making us "catholic," but decline to recognize the authority of the pope and other peculiarly Roman Catholic doctrines, making us "reformed." We have even referred to ourselves as the "bridge church," fancying that when Romans Catholics and Protestants eventually began to talk to one another, they would find our *via media* just what they'd been looking for. This provided Anglicans with a comfortable and seemingly secure little niche in the Christian scene — so long as the two poles remained fixed. But during the past half century, Rome has accepted many "Protestant" ideas and Protestants have adopted various "Catholic" ways. The two camps have found each other and begun discussing all sorts of things — without benefit of our bridge. The whole idea of *via media* also omits Orthodox and Pentecostal Christians, so perhaps it's time to drop it.

A somewhat more useful attempt to define Anglicanism in terms of other churches is suggested by Harvey H. Guthrie in an essay in *Anglican Spirituality*, edited by William Wolf. Guthrie distinguishes three "manifestations of the church." The first is *confessional*. You become part of a confessional church by "confessing the faith," signing on to a set of doctrines or beliefs. Then there is the *experiential* church, membership in which calls for sharing an experience of some sort, usually a recognizable conversion and subsequent commitment to Christ. Finally, there is the *pragmatic* church, which asks that its members do something — get baptized, receive communion. Anglicans, Guthrie says, are a pragmatic church. Individuals may hold various doctrinal positions and may or may not have had a conversion experience. What makes us part of the church is simply that we do what the church does. This fits well with the definition of Anglicanism as "family" — what makes one part of the family is that one comes to dinner when the family gathers to eat. The usefulness of Guthrie's comparison is limited, however, because most churches, including Anglicanism, contain elements of all three "manifestations," and no such categorization can be absolute.

If we are going to compare ourselves to other Christians, I prefer a comparison based on the major holy days stemming from the life and ministry of Christ. For many Christians, the central event was Christ's death on the cross for the sins of the world. The Roman Catholic Church and most Protestant churches are Good Friday churches. Other Christians see the resurrection of Christ, signifying his victory over Satan and sin, as the central event. The Eastern Orthodox are Easter churches. A third group focuses on Christ's gift of the Holy Spirit as the chief event. These are the Pentecostal churches. Anglicans — and this will become clear to anyone reading the essays in this book — focus on the incarnation of the Son of God, the Word made flesh. Anglican churches are Christmas churches. As in Wolf's comparison, these distinctions are not absolute; all four groups recognize the importance of all four events. But there are unmistakable emphases, and there can be no doubt what theological doctrine vibrates most strongly in the Anglican soul — it is the Incarnation.

Most Anglicans, however, have not defined themselves in terms of someone else. Anglicanism began to develop when the Church of England severed its ties to the pope in the sixteenth century. Those who engineered that break — and it had to do with more than the marital status of Henry VIII, although that was part of it — saw themselves simply as the Christian church in England. There were decisions to be made about various things, but the goal was to fashion the Church of England in such a manner as to bring the citizens of the country to a living faith in Jesus Christ. The essays in this book refer now and then to other Christian groups, especially when dealing with them helped shape Anglicanism's understanding of itself, but the best way to see the development of Anglicanism is to see it as a group of Christians seeking to answer this question: *How do we be the church in this particular place, at this particular time?*

Things to Look For

Several features characterize the Anglican family of churches. One is the freedom granted to individuals to hold differing opinions and behave in different ways (about which I shall say more in a moment). That means that none of the characteristic features of Anglicanism to be discussed below is true of every Anglican, or even of the twenty-nine Anglicans listed in the table of contents of this book. At least one of the subjects of these essays is an exception to everything I am about to say. Moreover, none of the characteristic features of Anglicanism is unique to Anglicans. A Roman Catholic, a Quaker, a Methodist, even a Hindu or a humanist, reading this introduction, might feel moved at some point to say, "That's true of my group as well." No doubt. There is nothing in Anglicanism that cannot be found elsewhere. But every Christian group — every group of human beings, for that matter — has certain values and emphases, a particular slant on things, a way of looking at reality and relating to one another, which, taken together, define its identity. What follows are some of the distinctive features of the Anglican identity, some things to look for in reading the essays in this book.

A favorite, if overworked, image among Anglicans is that of the three-legged stool, which stands only when all three legs are in place, as a visual way to think of the Anglican view of authority. We acknowledge three sources of authority, and we manage not to fall down only when all three are in place. The first and most important of these is **the Bible**. The Articles of Religion, a Reformation-era statement of Anglican views on questions of the day, says that the Bible "containeth all things necessary to salvation," so that nothing not found in the Bible is to be required as an article of faith. That means Christian teaching is to be measured against the Bible. That is our norm, our "canon." But also notice what this statement does *not* say: It does not say that everything found in the Bible is "necessary to salvation" or must be believed. It does not say that the Bible contains no errors. It does not say that God wrote the Bible or dictated it to human authors. The Anglican understanding of biblical authority allows for various ways of understanding the Bible. It acknowledges the human element in the Bible and invites us to engage in dialog with biblical authors. In doing so, we grow in our understanding of what the Bible calls us to be and do. This understanding even allows us to challenge biblical authors, to disagree with them on occasion. None of this diminishes the authority of the Bible in the life of the church — it is simply the Anglican way of entering into the biblical text and appropriating its insights to our lives in a different time and place. It makes no difference, of course, how biblical authority is understood unless we actually read and know the Bible — and I will admit that some Anglicans have done little more than pay lip service to the Bible. The authors discussed in this book have things to say to such persons.

But doesn't this understanding of biblical authority invite all kinds of weird interpretations? I wouldn't say it *invites* weird interpretations, but yes, it does *allow* them, and from time to time, an Anglican has interpreted the Bible in a weird manner. Some do it even today. But it's a risk we feel is worth taking when the alternative is to set up an ecclesiastical tribunal to tell everyone what to think and do. And there are safeguards, which brings us to the second leg of the three-legged authority stool, namely, **reason**. Anglicans have always had a healthy respect for human reason. This is not mere analytical logic, but includes our experience of one another and of the world and our God-given capacity to make sense of our experience. Reason is a gift from God, and our use of it is a response to God. Richard Hooker, writing at the end of the sixteenth century, set a tone which has served Anglicans well for four hundred years. Apart from reason, Hooker said, people would have no way of understanding the scriptures, or anything else. God is active throughout his universe, and that includes God's guiding and informing the human mind. Among other things, this has meant that Anglicans, unlike some other Christians, have usually been quick to accept the insights of secular disciplines like biology, psychology, and physics, even when they challenge traditional understandings of the Bible and Christian teaching. Anglicans perceive God working not merely in the church, but everywhere, and speaking not merely through the Bible, but through many voices. Truth does not conflict with truth, but is one. Our understanding of truth, however, is always growing and changing as God brings new elements of reality to light. This has given to Anglican thinking a flexibility and openness to new understandings not always found among other Christians.

But doesn't this still allow for weird interpretations? Well, yes, it does. The third leg of the stool serves as an additional safeguard. We call it **tradition**. The notion of tradition is often misunderstood. It isn't simply a container full of old customs and doctrines handed down to us. Tradition is the treasury of insights learned by those who have walked this way before us, as they applied the Bible to their lives and used the gift of reason to reflect on their experience. We often fancy that we are the first people ever to ask certain questions or to face certain problems, but this is almost never the case. Those who came before us were not faultless or infallible, any more than we are. They had their "weird" ideas and made their mistakes, and they learned from them. We can learn from them as well, and thereby avoid repeating some of their mistakes. C. S. Lewis expressed the Anglican understanding of tradition in these words:

> Naturally, since I myself am a writer, I do not wish the ordinary reader to read no modern books. But if he must read only the new

or only the old, I would advise him to read the old. . . . Every age has its own outlook. It is specially good at seeing certain truths and specially liable to make certain mistakes. We all, therefore, need the books that will correct the characteristic mistakes of our own period. And that means the old books. . . . Not, of course, that there is any magic about the past. People were no cleverer then than they are now; they made as many mistakes as we. But not the *same* mistakes. . . . Two heads are better than one, not because either is infallible, but because they are unlikely to go wrong in the same direction.

We are guided and informed by tradition, but not bound by it. Tradition is the accumulated experience of the Christian community, and it grows and changes as the community grows and changes. Anglicans have always had a strong sense of being part of a community that extends back through the ages (and forward into the ages). The sixteenth-century English reformers, unlike some of their counterparts on the European continent, had no sense that they were creating something new. Rather, they saw themselves and the English church as part of a continuous stream. The first five centuries of the Christian era, the "primitive church," have always been particularly authoritative for Anglicans, because of their proximity to the New Testament era. John Jewel, Richard Hooker, and Lancelot Andrewes were the first to articulate this understanding of tradition, and their view has informed the Anglican use of tradition ever since.

Despite all this, weird interpretations are still possible. They tend to occur when one of the three legs of the stool is so highly valued that the other two are weakened or discounted. Some of the authors discussed in this book emphasize scripture, reason, or tradition more than the other two, and someone might say that one or another of them comes close to toppling the stool.

Weirdness is easier to recognize in retrospect than at the time it occurs, as illustrated by recent and current debates in the church. In the late twentieth century, women's ordination was a divisive issue. Proponents on both sides claimed to find support in scripture, reason understood as reflection upon human experience, and evolving tradition. Most would now agree, in retrospect, that the opening of the ordained ministry to women, having brought new blessings and vitality to the church, was a legitimate enlarging of Christian tradition, consistent with scripture and reason. As I write these words, Anglicans (and other Christians) are not of one mind as to the place of homosexual persons in the church. Some find passages of scripture which speak, or appear to speak, against homosexuality and hold these to be normative, while others find passages of scripture that urge full inclusion of all persons, which they take to include homosexuals, and hold these to be normative. Reason, including scientific studies of human sexuality, has been cited to support various viewpoints. And although tradition almost unanimously rejects homosexual behavior, some say that the love of Christ, which is the heart of Christian tradition, calls for reconsideration of traditional views. Every Anglican who is concerned about the place of homosexual persons in the church is seeking the proper balance of scripture, reason, and tradition, but it is not easy to determine what that balance is. What is the "weird" view and what is the "not weird" view? In the past, God has often, after due time, made clear the truth on divisive questions. Perhaps God will someday do so on the question of homosexuality. But if not, Anglicans will do as we have done for centuries — continue to pray together and ask for discernment, trusting that God will guide us, even when we disagree and do not see clearly.

The most distinctive feature of Anglicanism is, without doubt, the Book of Common Prayer. It has a unique place in determining Anglican identity. Nowhere else has a book of **worship and prayer** been so definitive in giving shape to a church. A few years ago, I was asked to speak to a group of Lutherans about the differences between their church and the Episcopal Church. "If you ask a typical Lutheran about her church," I said, "she will probably tell you what Lutherans believe and perhaps show you the Augsburg Confession. She *may* say at the end something like, 'and we have a Book of Worship.' But if you ask an Episcopalian about her church, she will tell you of the Prayer Book, the songs she likes to sing, and the sacraments. She *may* add something at the end about Episcopal beliefs." The most heated debates among Anglicans nearly always pertain in some way to worship. The current debate about homosexuality, for example, is being carried out in connection with two worship services, matrimony and ordination.

Worship and prayer are central to Anglicans. Richard Hooker, again, set the standard in the 1590s by presenting his theological positions in the context of discussions about worship. The authors discussed in this book hold different views on worship and prayer, but in nearly every case, worship and prayer lie at the heart of their thought. Anglicans tend to learn scripture not merely in the study, but also, even primarily, by hearing it read in worship. This means Anglicans *pray* the Bible as well as study it; we approach the scriptures with our hearts as much as with our minds. Anglicanism has sometimes suffered from a reputation of not taking theology seriously by "allowing" it to become "mixed up" with worship, and academic theologians from other churches occasionally look down on the Anglican approach to theology for this reason. Anglicans, however, are less interested in a theologian who devises her ideas sitting in a library carrel than in one who devises her ideas on her knees in church.

I have already mentioned the centrality of the **Incarnation** in Anglican spirituality. The word *incarnation* comes from the Latin word meaning *flesh*. Other English words deriving from it are *carnivorous* and *carnal*. To become incarnate is to become enfleshed. To most Anglicans, the union in Christ of God and humanity, spirit and flesh, is the event that provides the clue to understanding everything else. A look at the index of this book will show how central the Incarnation was to most of the thinkers discussed in these pages. The Incarnation tells us not only who Christ is, but who we are, for in uniting himself to human flesh in Jesus, God was uniting himself to all humanity, to *us*.

This understanding of the Incarnation has led to several things in the life of Anglican churches, which can be seen in many of the authors discussed in this book. First, it has kept at bay any tendencies to identify the material world with evil. The material, physical, carnal life of human beings is good, not bad, because God not only made it, but has united himself to it in the person of Jesus Christ. Second, Anglicans find God not only in extraordinary acts of piety and self-denial (although we do find God there), but also in everyday, mundane things — a grain of sand, an apple seed, washing the dishes, balancing a checkbook. Third, God comes to us not only in the good and happy times of our lives, but throughout our lives, even in the grimmest moments. God has, in fact, been there long before us, sanctifying the place with his own sweat and tears. Fourth, because of the Incarnation, Anglicans see the world of secular society, politics, and economics as an arena for Christian witness. We know God cares about the secular world because he has visited it in person. And finally, it is through the Incarnation that we understand the sacraments of the church — God enters our world and our hearts through unlikely material things, like human flesh and blood, represented by a crust of bread and a sip of wine.

Another feature of Anglican spirituality evident in many of the authors discussed in this book is its practical, **pragmatic bent**, already referred to. Few Anglican spiritual masters have been mystics, given to private flights into esoteric realms, and even fewer have been academic professors, writing theology from wood-paneled studies. Even they, however (and a few will be found in these pages), have also possessed a down-to-earth side. Anglican spirituality has typically been concerned with human behavior, morality, conscience, how a Christian lives his faith in day-to-day relationships. It has a certain feet-on-the-ground quality. Repentance is seen as more than sorrow for our sins and failures; it includes transformation, living a new life. Nearly all those discussed in this book called for such transformation, a deeper devotion, a more intentional and focused Christian living in the world. In their zeal, some of them may have overstated the lack of genuine devotion in the church of their day, but even in its best moments, the church needs renewing. I don't know whether Anglicans are uniquely gifted among Christians in our ability to foster a bland, complacent piety — others may grapple with it, too — but it is hardly unknown among us, and the authors discussed in this book attack it head-on.

I have also mentioned the **intellectual freedom** Anglicanism grants to individuals, including the freedom to behave in different ways. Even our spiritual leaders have sometimes distanced themselves from the institutional church and official dogmas. Some of these are represented in the pages that follow. This freedom extends also to member churches of the Anglican Communion, meaning that beliefs and practices in one province do not always coincide with those in another province. While this has occasionally led to awkward situations, it should not surprise us. Richard Hooker allowed great latitude in matters deemed non-essential, which included most disputed questions. What is and what isn't essential is something Anglicans may differ about, but all would agree, following Hooker, that the church in different places must be free to develop its own ways of doing things.

The result is that Anglicans have always tolerated a certain ambiguity, muddiness, and imprecision. We have even at times celebrated it as a virtue. Anglicans have never censured people who ask questions and express doubts. Doubters and questioners are well represented in the pages of this book. Usually, this has not been due to mere intellectual laziness, but to a certain humility, the realization that the human mind cannot grasp the entire truth and some questions can therefore be left unanswered. This is why Anglicans have been content with the historic creeds as our statements of belief, resisting any suggestion that we further define the doctrinal skeleton they afford us, and allowing individuals latitude in interpreting the creeds. Anglicans are comfortable — relatively, usually — in responding to a perplexing doctrinal or moral question by saying, "We don't know; we'll have to pray about it, then wait and see." Anglicans don't expel people who express odd opinions or engage in off-the-wall behaviors, and we continue to worship alongside them. Anglicanism is therefore often called "roomy," "inclusive," "tolerant."

There is of course a down side to this. Anglicans have always been tempted to take no stand on controversial questions because, after all, there is some truth to be found everywhere. Tolerance and inclusiveness can easily become a mere "anything goes" laxity, a moral and intellectual flabbiness. No honest student of the history of Anglicanism will say this has never happened. Some say it is happening today. But we are convinced that the blessings this posture brings to our church far outweigh the dangers. Were Anglicanism a less tolerant communion, we would be less willing to engage the challenges to our understandings which force us to grow and become stronger Christians. Were Anglicanism a less tolerant communion, fewer poets, novelists, and artists would have found a home among us. Were Anglicanism a less tolerant communion, some of the marvelous companions discussed in this book would have departed from us and deprived us of their legacies. Were Anglicanism a less tolerant communion, the glory of God would not have been diminished — I don't think human beings can diminish the glory of God — but it would shine less brightly among us.

Acknowledgments

This book would not have been written without the support and encouragement of the following persons and institutions, to whom I am deeply grateful: *The Episcopal Divinity School,* Cambridge, Massachusetts, which granted me a Procter Fellowship for the fall term, 2000-2001, giving me room and board and access to the faculty and library; *Dr. Fredrica Harris Thompsett* of the Episcopal Divinity School, who graciously gave me many hours of her time and read twenty of these essays, offering helpful suggestions for additions and revisions; *the Virginia Theological Seminary,* Alexandria, Virginia, which granted me a Woods Fellowship for the winter term, 2001, giving me room and board and access to the library and faculty; *Dr. Timothy Sedgwick* of the Virginia Theological Seminary, who advised me in the writing of several of these essays; and *Dr. Robert Prichard, Dr. Richard Jones, Dr. Kathleen Staudt,* and *Drs. Raymond* and *Joyce Glover,* all of the Virginia Theological Seminary, each of whom read and advised me on one or more of these essays. My thanks to them all, and may God bless them as generously as, through them, God has blessed me.

I am especially grateful to my friend and colleague *Dean Mosher* of Fairhope, Alabama, for the splendid illustrations that enhance the pages of this book. From often grainy originals, Dean has produced energetic, expressive likenesses of the subjects of these essays, adding immeasurably to the appeal of the text. I had known it before, but these likenesses confirm again to me that Dean is an illustrator of the highest rank. Thank you, Dean!

Finally, and most importantly, I am grateful to my wife *Pamela,* who spent the better part of six months in a small room, alternately reading and looking at the back of my head as I worked at my keyboard, and who made certain I retained at least some contact with firm ground while my mind traveled to distant places and bygone times. May God bless her, too, although I think it impossible that he could bless her as generously as, through her, he has blessed me.

RICHARD H. SCHMIDT
Daphne, Alabama
March 2001

Chapter 1

THOMAS CRANMER

1489-1556

Father of the Prayer Book

I T IS SHORTLY before noon, Saturday, March 21, 1556. A chill rain is falling in Oxford, where a standing-room-only crowd fills St. Mary's Church. Thomas Cranmer, archbishop of Canterbury until his imprisonment three years ago, stands in the pulpit, clad in a bare and ragged gown, his face stained with tears. He asks for the prayers of the congregation. He urges them to set their minds on God and the world to come, to obey their queen, and to love one another. He bids the rich be generous to the poor. But when he begins to speak in a more theological vein, he cannot complete his address, so great is the uproar. He is pulled down from the pulpit and led outside to the stake which has been erected for him. He briefly kneels to pray, then pulls off his shirt, and prepares to die. He is tied to the stake with an iron chain. When the wood is kindled and the flames begin to leap up around him, he stretches out his right hand into the fire, crying, "This hand hath offended!" Nor does he withdraw his hand from the flame until first it, and then the archbishop himself, are consumed.

How did it come to this? For the answer, we must go back nearly thirty years. Thomas Cranmer never wanted to be archbishop of Canterbury. By 1529, he had been content for twenty-six years as a student and then as a don at Cambridge University, also undertaking occasional diplomatic assignments for King Henry VIII. The king was seeking the annulment of his twenty-year marriage to Catherine of Aragon in 1529. Cranmer was known to favor the king's position, and Henry often relied on Cranmer to write up his side of the case. Three years later, archbishop of Canterbury William Warham died, and since the archbishop of Canterbury would be a key player in the quest for an annulment, Henry named Thomas Cranmer his new archbishop.

Cranmer proved splendidly suited to Henry's purposes. Not only did he grant the annulment and then solemnize Henry's marriage to Anne Boleyn, but he was unwaveringly loyal to his king, in all things, at all times. This was more than personal devotion, though that was part of it. It also arose from a theological conviction difficult for most modern people to grasp: Cranmer believed the king was the rightful head not only of the state, but of the church. Influenced by the new Protestant idea that Christian truth is contained only in the Bible, Cranmer found no reference to a pope in the Bible and little reference to bishops, but he noted that kingship was held in high regard. He made little distinction between the Church of England and the English nation, and believed the king was God's appointed servant to manage both on God's behalf. As a result, Cranmer always deferred to Henry, sometimes expressing his own views, but willingly setting them aside when Henry decreed otherwise.

Religious controversy was in the air. The question at issue was, in modern parlance, "How does one get right with God?" Everyone agreed that sinful human beings had cut themselves off from God and that a sacrifice was necessary to satisfy divine justice — but how was this sacrifice effected? There were gradations of opinion, but two broad camps: The Roman Catholic position was built on scholastic theology, medieval piety, and the authority of the church, embodied primarily in the pope. Catholics believed in "transubstantiation," that in the mass the priest brought about a transformation of the bread and wine into the body and blood of Christ, which was then offered to God, reenacting in a small way the sacrifice of Jesus on the cross and thereby setting sinners right with God. The Protestant position was based on the authority of the Bible, interpreted not by bishops and popes, but by ordinary Christians reading it for themselves. Protestants found in their Bibles the idea that sinners are set right with God by the sacrifice of Jesus on the cross, once and for all, appropriated to believers through faith, understood as a living trust in Christ and his promises. This belief is called "justification by faith." Protestants were also coming to regard the hearts and souls of believers — not the consecrated bread and wine — as the place where Christ was experienced.

As a young man, Cranmer had been a conservative catholic, but he had begun to move towards a more Protestant view as early as 1525. He seems to have shifted his theological ground more than once during his lifetime, perhaps from loyalty to the crown, perhaps because until his dying day, he never stopped trying to sort things out in his own mind. But there can be no doubt that as archbishop, Cranmer was a Protestant on most of the questions at issue. He moved the Church of England in that direction — modestly, within the conservatively catholic bounds set by Henry until the latter's death in 1547, then more extensively under Henry's Protestant son and successor, Edward VI. Cranmer resisted, however, the more radical reforms advocated in Geneva. He had no desire to create a new church. Cranmer embraced Protestant positions because he felt they represented a return to scripture and the practice of the early church.

His chief concern was how to design corporate worship to encourage a lively faith. It was to this question that he devoted his greatest energies and here that he made his most significant contribution. Cranmer was extraordinarily gifted as a liturgical theorist and writer of prayers. His prose has never lacked for enthusiastic, even fawning, admirers. It is routinely described as exalted, golden, classic. But Cranmer did not set out to gain for himself a literary reputation. His goal was to design a program of worship to glorify God and edify the believer. Working with the assistance of other scholars, he took old liturgical forms, sifted and selected from among them, condensed and reconfigured them, and occasionally added something new. The result was the first Book of Common Prayer, published in 1549. A second, revised edition was published in 1552. Cranmer set out to achieve several things:

First, Cranmer wanted to give the people a liturgy in their own tongue rather than in Latin, which failed to reach "the hearts, spirit, and mind" of the people. The Bible had already been translated into English under Henry, and an English litany, composed by Cranmer and virtually the same one found in modern Anglican prayer books, had been authorized in 1544. But Cranmer now sought to provide the Church of England with English language forms for all its services of worship.

Second, he emphasized edification through good preaching and systematic Bible reading. A Book of Homilies was issued to the clergy, containing sermons of sound doctrine authorized to be preached in parish churches. Cranmer wrote several of these homilies. But more important, the new Prayer Book was designed to exercise the people in the whole Bible. Anyone reading the Bible faithfully according to the Prayer Book lectionary would complete the New Testament three times in the course of a year and most of the Old Testament once.

Third, Crammer simplified worship. Medieval worship could require a breviary, missal, manual, pontifical, processional, consuetudinary, ordinal, and Bible. Each of these books contained services of worship, parts of services, or rules for conducting worship. In the Preface to the 1549 Prayer Book, Cranmer remarked that "many times there was more business to find out what should be read, than to read it when it was found out." The new book simplified and combined all these books (except the Bible) into a single volume.

Fourth, the new Prayer Book was to be a means of heightening the involvement of the laity. No longer were they to be mere spectators to semi-secret, mysterious rites performed by a priest at a distant altar in a strange language. The two daily services of Morning and Evening Prayer (condensed from the eight daily services of the Benedictine monasteries) were easy for a lay person to follow, and parish clergy were instructed to read these two services every day in the church and to ring a bell inviting the laity to join them.

Fifth, Cranmer sought a common liturgy throughout England. He hoped the great diversity of liturgical forms which had sprung up during the Middle Ages might be overcome so that a worshiper traveling throughout the realm would feel at home in whatever church he chanced to enter.

Sixth, Cranmer wanted to correct certain theological distortions he felt had crept into the Latin mass. No longer was the Lord's Supper to be seen as a ritual reenactment of Christ's sacrifice on the cross. The communion prayer in the new book explicitly stated that Christ's death was a "full, perfect, and sufficient sacrifice, oblation, and satisfaction, for the sins of the whole world" — repetitively drumming home that no further sacrifice was either necessary or possible. Worshipers did make an offering, but of themselves, "our souls, and bodies, to be a reasonable, holy, and lively sacrifice unto thee." It was a sacrifice "of praise and thanksgiving," not of transubstantiated bread and wine.

The Prayer Book received mixed reviews. But acceptance was growing and there was reason for encouragement — so long as Edward lived. When the young king died in 1553, however, the throne went to his half-sister Mary — a militant papal loyalist. Within weeks, she had Cranmer arrested and imprisoned. Given Cranmer's understanding of royal supremacy, this must have been nearly unbearable for him. Torn between two deeply held beliefs, he wavered. Where was the truth? What did God expect of him? Which was the way to eternal life and which to eternal damnation? Repeatedly humiliated and vilified, Cranmer signed several recantations of everything he had worked to achieve, each more personally degrading than the one before. One last recantation was demanded of him, from the pulpit of St. Mary's, Oxford, on that cold March day in 1556. Cranmer read from the prepared text for several minutes, but then departed from it, recanting his recantations and reasserting his adherence to the Protestant cause. The hand which he held into the fire, the hand that had offended, was the one with which he had signed his several recantations while imprisoned. The sight of their archbishop burning at the stake, holding his hand into the flame, was a horror seared into the memory of English Christians that day — and the collapse of support for the Roman Church in England is usually said to have begun on March 21, 1556.

IN HIS OWN WORDS

Sacraments

For it is not true, as some say, that sacraments confer grace by themselves, without a good movement of heart on the part of their user; for when persons in their reason use the sacraments, the user's faith must be present also, to believe the promises, and receive the things promised, which are conveyed through the sacraments.

"Of the Use of Sacraments" (1538)

The value of scripture

[The Bible] containeth fruitful instruction and erudition for every man; if any things be necessary to be learned, of the holy scripture we may learn it. . . . Here may all manner of persons, men, women, young, old, learned, unlearned, rich, poor, priests, laymen, lords, ladies, officers, tenants, and mean men, virgins, wives, widows, lawyers, merchants, artificers, husband-men, and all manner of persons, of what estate or condition soever they be, may in this book learn all things that they ought to believe, what they ought to do, and what they should not do, as well concerning Almighty God, as also concerning themselves and all other.

Preface to the Bible (1540)

Two kinds of faith

The first entry unto God, good Christian people, is through faith; whereby . . . we be justified before God. . . . There is one faith which in scripture is called a dead faith, which bringeth forth no good works, but is idle, barren, and unfruitful. . . . it consisteth only in believing of the Word of God, that it is true. And this is not properly called faith. . . . Another faith there is in scripture, which . . . as the other faith is called a dead faith, so this may be called a quick or lively faith. And this is not only the common belief of the articles of our faith, but it is also a sure trust and confidence of the mercy of God through our Lord Jesus Christ, and a steadfast hope of all good things to be received at God's hand. . . . This is the true, lively, and unfeigned Christian faith, and is not in the mouth and outward profession only, but it liveth, and stirreth inwardly in the heart. And this faith is not without hope and trust in God, nor without the love of God and of our neighbours, nor without the fear of God, nor without the desire to hear God's word, and to follow the same in eschewing evil and doing gladly all good works.

Homily of Faith (1547)

Faith and works

Faith giveth life to the soul; and they be as much dead to God that lack faith, as they be to the world whose bodies lack souls. Without faith all that is done of us is but dead before God, although the work seem ever so gay and glorious before man. Even as a picture graven or painted is but a dead representation of the thing itself, and is without life or any manner of moving; so be the works of all unfaithful persons before God.

Homily of Good Works (1547)

Ceremonies

Whereas in this our time the minds of men are so diverse, that some think it a great matter of conscience to depart from a piece of the least of their ceremonies (they be so addicted to their old customs:) and again on the other side, some be so new fangled that they would innovate all things, and so do despise the old, that nothing can [please] them but what is new: it was thought expedient not so much to have respect how to please and satisfy either of these parties, as how to please God and profit them both.

"Of Ceremonies, Why Some Be Abolished
and Some Retained," 1549 and 1552 Prayer Books

Prayer for the king

Almighty God, whose kingdom is everlasting, and power infinite: have mercy upon the whole congregation, and so rule the heart of thy chosen servant Edward the sixth, our king and governor, that he (knowing whose minister he is) may above all things seek thy honour and glory: and that we his subjects (duly considering whose authority he hath) may faithfully serve, honour, and humbly obey him, in thee, and for thee, according to thy blessed word and ordinance: Through Jesus Christ our Lord, who with thee, and the Holy Ghost, liveth, and reigneth, ever one God, world without end. Amen.

from the communion service,
1549 and 1552 Prayer Books

Duty of a Christian

Question: What is thy duty towards God? *Answer:* My duty towards God is, to believe in him, to fear him, and to love him with all my heart, with all my mind, with all my soul, and with all my strength. To worship him. To call upon him. To honor his holy name and his word, and to serve him truly all the days of my life.

Question: What is thy duty towards thy neighbor? *Answer:* My duty towards my neighbor is, to love him as myself. And to do to all men as I would they should do unto me. To love, honor and succor my father and mother. To honor and obey the king and his ministers. To submit myself to all my governors, teachers, spiritual pastors and masters. To order myself lowly and reverently to all my betters. To hurt nobody by word nor deed. To be true and just in all my dealing. To bear no malice nor hatred in my heart. To keep my hands from picking and stealing, and my tongue from evil speaking, lying and slandering. To keep my body in temperance, soberness, and chastity. Not to covet nor desire other men's goods. But learn and labor truly to get mine own living, and to do my duty in that state of life, unto which it shall please God to call me.

from the catechism printed in the
1549 and 1552 Prayer Books

Collect for Advent I

Almighty God, give us grace, that we may cast away the works of darkness, and put upon us the armor of light, now in the time of this mortal life, in which thy son Jesus Christ came to visit us in great humility; that in the last day when he shall come again in his glorious majesty to judge both the quick and the dead, we may rise to the life immortal; through him who liveth and reigneth with thee and the Holy Ghost, now and ever. Amen.

> This collect is one of several original compositions of Cranmer
> which continue to appear in modern Anglican prayer books.

The eucharist

And all doctrine concerning [the eucharist] . . . which is not grounded upon God's word, is of no necessity, neither ought the people's heads to be busied, or their consciences troubled with the same. So that things spoken and done by Christ, and written by the holy Evangelists and St. Paul, ought to suffice the faith of Christian people, as touching the doctrine of the Lord's Supper, and holy communion or sacrament of his body and blood.

> *Defence of the True Catholic Doctrine of the Sacrament* (1550)

The body and blood of Christ

This spiritual meat of Christ's body and blood, is not received in the mouth, and digested in the stomach (as corporal meats and drinks commonly be), but it is received with a pure heart and a sincere faith. And the true eating and drinking of the said body and blood of Christ, is with a constant and a lively faith to believe, that Christ gave his body and shed his blood upon the cross for us, and that he doth so join and incorporate himself to us, that he is our head, and we his members, and flesh of his flesh, and bone of his bones, having him dwelling in us, and we in him.

> *Defence*

Sacrifice of the mass

The offering of the priest in the mass . . . cannot merit and deserve, neither to himself, nor to them for whom he singeth or sayeth, the remission of their sins. . . . For if only the death of Christ be the oblation, sacrifice, and price, wherefore our sins are pardoned, then the act or ministration of the priest cannot have the same office.

Defence

The intent of sacraments

Our Savior Christ hath not only set forth these things most plainly in his holy word, that we may hear them with our ears, but he has also ordained one visible sacrament of spiritual regeneration in water, and another visible sacrament of spiritual nourishment in bread and wine, to the intent that, as much as is possible for man, we may see Christ with our eyes, smell him at our nose, taste him with our mouths, grope him with our hands, and perceive him with all our senses. For as the word of God preached putteth Christ into our ears, so likewise these elements of water, bread, and wine, joined to God's word, do after a sacramental manner put Christ into our eyes, mouths, hands, and all our senses.

Answer to Stephen Gardiner (1551)

Last words

And now I come to the great thing that so much troubleth my conscience, more than any thing that ever I did or said in my whole life; and that is, the setting abroad of writings contrary to the truth; which now here I renounce and refuse, as things written with my hand, contrary to the truth which I thought in my heart, and written for fear of death, and to save my life, if it might be; and that is, all such bills and papers which I have written or signed with my hand since my degradation; wherein I have written many things untrue. And forasmuch as my hand offended, writing contrary to my heart, my hand shall first be punished therefore; for, may I come to the fire, it shall be first burned.

> Cranmer's words before going to the stake,
> as reported by John Foxe (1556)

FOR REFLECTION AND DISCUSSION

Where did ultimate authority lie for Cranmer? Compare Cranmer's view of authority to your own.

In a sentence, how do you "get right with God"? Avoid using common religious phrases in your answer.

Why are sacraments important? What do they do?

On the basis of Cranmer's liturgical goals, how would you evaluate the liturgy of today's church?

For what did Cranmer die? Would you die for it?

Chapter 2

JOHN JEWEL

1522-1571

First Anglican Apologist

D ISPUTES AMONG Christians, even today, are usually about what to do or what to believe. When the Reformation rocked the Western church in the sixteenth century, a host of such questions were at issue. What to do: Should priests be permitted to marry? In what language should worship be conducted? Should lay people be allowed to read the Bible? And what to believe: How is God's forgiveness attained? What happens to the bread and wine on the altar? What is the church? But another issue, then as now, usually underlies disputes about practice and belief. It is the question of authority: How does one know what to do and believe? Where is the truth found? Who decides?

Feelings about what to do and believe are often so hotly argued that the deeper question of authority is not openly addressed. In the sixteenth century, however, it was on the table and often became *the* subject of debate. All parties accepted the authority of the Bible — but what did the Bible mean, and who was to say what it meant? Two main camps emerged: The Roman Catholics held to the medieval belief that the church, through its ordained leadership and especially through the pope, determined what the Bible meant and therefore what was to be done and believed. Anything else, they thought, would result in chaos. Protestants, on the other hand, held a range of views (the fear of chaos was not unfounded), but most Protestants believed that individual Christians or Christian communities, by reading the Bible under the guidance of the Holy Spirit, could know what the Bible meant and thereby determine what they should do and believe.

When John Jewel was ordained (probably in 1551), it was this fluid, confusing theological scene that greeted him. He studied under the great continental reformer Peter Martyr, professor of divinity at Oxford, and received his theological degree from Oxford in 1552. The next decade would see two ecclesiastical revolutions in England, as the country was swept into the arms of Rome by Queen Mary, beginning in 1553, then out again following Mary's death and the accession of Elizabeth in 1558. During Mary's short and violent reign, Protestants either converted to Rome, laid low, fled the country, or were burned at the stake. In 1554, Jewel attended the trial of Protestant bishops Thomas Cranmer and Nicholas Ridley, acting as notary for them. Shortly thereafter, he did something he regretted the rest of his life. Whether out of duty to his new queen, to save his skin, or "for the sake of quietness" (as one biographer speculates), Jewel signed a series of articles agreeing to the main body of Roman Catholic teaching, an act for which he later publicly repented, but which theological opponents would use against him. Despite this action, however, Jewel still felt unsafe with Mary on the throne and fled to the continent in 1555, resuming his studies there under Peter Martyr, who had left earlier.

To understand the controversies of sixteenth and early seventeenth century Europe, one must first understand that partisans on all sides perceived truth as absolute, uniformity as essential, religious systems as complete and unnegotiable, and compromise as a mark of weakness or infidelity. When Mary died in 1558, Jewel and his Protestant friends (who had obviously forgiven him for signing his name to the wrong paper in 1554) returned to England to resume the reformation begun under Edward VI. The Council of Trent, an effort by the Roman Catholic Church to reassert papal authority and traditional teachings, had been meeting sporadically since 1545 and was still going strong, attacking the Church of England and its newly revived Protestant ways as innovation and heresy.

On November 26, 1559, at Paul's Cross, an outdoor gathering place next to London's St. Paul's Cathedral, John Jewel counterattacked in a wily sermon known as his "Challenge Sermon." In it he detailed over two dozen "abuses" of the Roman church. Most of these related to the mass (that priests celebrated the mass in private, that only the bread was distributed to lay communicants, that the consecrated bread was elevated and worshiped in an idolatrous fashion, et al.), but Jewel also challenged the claim by the pope to be head of the universal church, the prohibition of Bible reading by lay people, and the conduct of worship in an unknown tongue. Jewel carefully chose only practices and teachings which he knew could not be supported by citations from the Bible, the general councils, or the writings of theologians from the first six centuries of the Christian era — and then challenged his opponents to justify their practices from precisely these sources. In so doing, Jewel turned the debate upside-down, putting the Roman Catholics on the defensive — it was they, he said, who were guilty of innovation and heresy. If one of his opponents could produce even a single passage from those ancient sources in support of his views, Jewel said, he would "yield and subscribe to him, and he should depart with the victory."

Jewel's sermon, preached a second and third time within a year, produced a stir, but a more thorough and systematic defense of the position of the Church of England was needed. William Cecil, chief advisor to the new queen, asked Jewel, who had been consecrated bishop of Salisbury in January, 1560, to prepare such a defense. He then produced the work for which he is chiefly remembered, *An Apology of the Church of England*, written in

1561 and published a year later — in Latin, since it was primarily addressed to Roman Catholic theologians who conducted their business in that tongue. The word apology is used not in its modern sense, meaning an expression of regret, but in its older sense, meaning a defense of something that has been questioned. Two English translations appeared within three years, and the *Apology* was a sensation. Jewel proved himself a learned, clever, incisive, and outspoken apologist, the brightest light of the first generation of Elizabethan church leaders. The *Apology* is a short, crisp, lively work, but its appearance sparked a series of long, tedious rebuttals and rebuttals to rebuttals, some of them answering an opponent's most recent publication paragraph by paragraph. It became known as "the Great Controversy." The primary disputants were Jewel and one Thomas Harding, representing a group of Roman Catholic exiles living in Belgium.

Jewel's *Apology* is the first substantive statement of the beliefs and practices of the Church of England. It builds on themes first articulated in the Challenge Sermon. Pope Pius IV had condemned many faithful English Christians without grounds, Jewel began, and since he granted them no audience, it was necessary to plead their case in writing. Jewel said the validity of practices in the Church of England could be demonstrated from the Bible and the writings of the early church fathers, who had based their writings on the Bible. Those who cannot justify their views from scripture prefer their "cold inventions" to the truth, which they have defaced and corrupted, Jewel said.

Jewel then outlined the Christian faith as practiced in the Church of England, basing his discussion on the historic creeds and then addressing the three-fold ordained ministry. According to scripture and ancient witness, he said, no bishop is superior to any other, nor is any "worldly creature" to set himself up as head of the whole church, as the bishop of Rome had presumed to do, surrounded by his "parasites [who] flatteringly sing in his ears." Jewel then defended the Church of England's position on the marriage of priests, eucharistic doctrine and practices, and liturgical customs.

If new and divisive ideas were introduced into the church, Jewel said, it was done in Rome, not in England. The English had, in fact, *restored* ancient practice. If the English were schismatics for having left Rome, what, he asked, were the Romans for having left the ancient church? Jewel concluded the *Apology* by defending, again on the basis of ancient practice, the right of the church in England to reform itself by means of a regional synod, convened by the secular authority.

The question of authority lay at the heart of the Challenge Sermon, the *Apology,* and the controversy they sparked. Jewel agreed with other Protestants in affirming that scripture was the ultimate authority for church doctrine and practice and that neither the pope nor any other bishop was entitled to decide what the scripture meant. But Jewel differed from some of his Protestant colleagues in that he did not believe the meaning of scripture was always clear. That is where his appeal to the councils and fathers of the early church came in. When the meaning of scripture is uncertain, look back to those who lived nearest to the time of Christ, Jewel advised, and ask what sense they made of scripture. The test of any teaching or practice in the church, he said, is not whether the medieval church had accepted it — that church had, in fact, introduced "sundry horrible enormities" — but whether it can be supported by appeal to the Bible and the earliest Christian understanding of the Bible.

Later Anglican apologists all built — and still build — on the foundation laid by John Jewel. Cranmer and others before him had appealed to scripture and the writings of the early church and relied upon reason and sound learning, but it was Jewel who first articulated these principles and made them the norm for the Church of England. Richard Hooker, the great thinker who, a generation later, would write what became the classic Anglican theological text, studied under Jewel. So influential did the *Apology* become that archbishop of Canterbury Richard Bancroft provided in 1610 that a copy be placed in all English churches. As late as the twentieth century, copies of the *Apology* could still be found in some English parishes and cathedrals, chained to the lectern.

IN HIS OWN WORDS

Judge for yourselves

Now, good people, judge ye in your conscience indifferently us both, which of us bringeth you the better and sounder arguments. We bring you nothing but God's holy word, which is a sure rock to build upon, and will never flee or shrink. And therefore are we able truly to say with St. Paul, "We have delivered unto you the same things that we have received of the Lord."

"Challenge Sermon" (1559)

Empty claims

[Some people] stand this day against so many old fathers, so many doctors, so many examples of the primitive church, so manifest and so plain words of the holy scriptures; and yet have they herein not one father, not one doctor, not one allowed example of the primitive church, to make for them. . . . Of all the words of the holy scriptures, of all the examples of the primitive church, of all the old fathers, of all the ancient doctors, in these causes they have not one.

"Challenge Sermon"

Appeal for unity

O that our adversaries, and all they that stand in defense of the mass this day, would content themselves to be judged by this rule! O that, in all the controversies that lie between us and them, they would remit the judgment unto God's word! So should we soon agree and join together: so should we deliver nothing unto the people but what we have received at God's hand.

"Challenge Sermon"

"A wilderness of superstition"

We found everywhere the people sufficiently well disposed towards religion, and even in those quarters where we expected most difficulty. It is however hardly credible what a harvest, or rather what a wilderness of superstition, had sprung up in the darkness of the Marian times. We found in all places votive relics of saints, nails with which the infatuated people dreamed that Christ had been pierced, and I know not what small fragments of the sacred cross.

from a letter to Peter Martyr, after his first
visitation of the Diocese of Salisbury (1560)

Homeless truth

It hath been an old complaint, even from the first time of the patriarchs and prophets, and confirmed by the writings and testimonies of every age, that the truth wandereth here and there as a stranger in the world, and doth readily find enemies and slanderers amongst those that know her not. . . . Wherefore we ought to bear it more quietly, which have taken upon us to profess the gospel of Christ, if we for the same cause be handled after the same sort; and if we, as our forefathers were long ago, be likewise at this day tormented and baited with railings, with spiteful dealings and with lies; and that for no desert of our own, but only because we teach and acknowledge the truth.

An Apology of the Church of England (1562)

Eucharist

In the Lord's Supper there is truly given unto the believing the body and blood of the Lord, the flesh of the Son of God, which quickeneth our souls, the meat that cometh from above, the food of immortality, grace, truth, and life; and the Supper to be the communion of the body and blood of Christ, by the partaking whereof we be revived, we be strengthened, and be fed unto immortality, and whereby we are joined, united, and incorporate unto Christ, that we may abide in him, and he in us.

Apology

Eucharistic presence

For, although we do not touch the body of Christ with teeth and mouth, yet we hold him fast, and eat him by faith, by understanding, and by the spirit.

Apology

Whose teaching is new?

There can nothing be more spitefully spoken against the religion of God
than to accuse it of novelty, as a new comen up matter. For as there can be
no change in God himself, no more ought there to be in his religion. . . . no
man can now think our doctrine to be new, unless the same think either
the prophets' faith, or the gospel, or else Christ himself be new. And as for
their religion, if it be of so long continuance as they would have men ween
it is, why do they not prove it so by the examples of the primitive church,
and by the fathers and councils of old times? Why lieth so ancient a cause
thus long in the dust destitute of an advocate? Fire and sword they have
had always ready at hand; but as for the old councils and the fathers, all
mum, not a word.

Apology

A valid departure

It is true we have departed from them [Roman Catholics], and for so doing
we both give thanks to Almighty God, and greatly rejoice on our own behalf. But yet for all this, from the primitive church, from the apostles, and
from Christ, we have not departed. . . . Let them compare our churches
and theirs together, and they shall see that themselves have most shame-
fully gone from the apostles, and we most justly have gone from them.

Apology

Peter and the Pope

Tell us, hath the Pope alone succeeded Peter? And wherein, I pray you? In
what religion? In what office? In what piece of his life hath he succeeded
him? What one thing (tell me) had Peter ever like unto the Pope, or the
Pope like unto Peter? Except peradventure they will say thus; that Peter,
when he was at Rome, never taught the gospel, never fed the flock, took
away the keys of the Kingdom of Heaven, hid the treasures of his Lord, sat
him down only in his castle in St. John Lateran, and pointed out with his
finger all the places of purgatory and kinds of punishments, committing

some poor souls to be tormented, and other some again suddenly releasing thence at his own pleasure, taking money for so doing; or that he gave order to say private masses in every corner; or that he mumbled up the holy service with a low voice, and in an unknown language; or that he hanged up the sacrament in every temple and on every altar, and carried the same about before him whithersoever he went, upon an ambling jennet, with lights and bells; or that he consecrated with his holy breath oil, wax, wool, bells, chalices, churches, and altars; or that he sold jubilees, graces, liberties, advowsons, preventions, first-fruits, palls, the wearing of palls, bulls, indulgences, and pardons; or that he called himself by the name of the head of the church, the highest bishop, bishop of bishops, alone most holy. . . . These things, no doubt, did Peter at Rome in times past, and left them in charge to his successors, as you would say, from hand to hand; for these things be nowadays done at Rome by the popes, and be so done, as though nothing else ought to be done.

Apology

Conclusion

In conclusion, we have departed from him to whom we were not bound.

Apology

FOR REFLECTION AND DISCUSSION

Is truth absolute?

Do you agree that "as there can be no change in God himself, no more ought there to be in his religion"?

How is the question of authority an issue in today's ecclesiastical disputes?

When the meaning of scripture is unclear or disputed, how should its meaning be determined?

Under what circumstances, if any, may the church depart from the words of scripture?

Chapter 3

RICHARD HOOKER

1554-1600

Definitive Anglican

M OST RELIGIOUS GROUPS point with pride to the great leader whose teachings identify them in a world of many faiths. Lutherans have their Luther, Presbyterians their Calvin, Roman Catholics their Aquinas. But to whom do Anglicans point?

Richard Hooker is the name. Although that name is hardly a household word in most Anglican homes, Anglicans the world over owe Richard Hooker a great debt. Hooker did not set out to construct a theological *summa* touching every dot on the doctrinal map, nor did he offer dazzling new insights on disputed points. Our debt to Hooker is less for his theology as such than for the way he arrived at it.

Religious freedom and pluralism are modern ideas. In the sixteenth century, religion was viewed not as an individual matter, but as part of a nation's identity. Church and state were distinct, but closely connected. It was rather like the way citizens in many modern countries regard education: The state is expected to maintain an educational system, and while citizens may differ over what sort of education that should be, few would deny that education is a responsibility of the state. Similarly, in sixteenth-century England, the question was not whether there should be a national church, but what kind of church it should be.

Richard Hooker lived at the end of a century of heated religious controversy. The Church of England had begun to distance itself from Rome in 1532, and the next three decades saw Roman Catholics and Protestants in an often violent struggle for the soul of the nation, as England lurched between Catholicism and Protestantism with each new king or queen. The politically astute Elizabeth I assumed the throne in 1558, following the death of the brittle and unpopular Catholic Queen Mary. Under Elizabeth, Roman sympathy waned, and Anglicanism as we know it began to take shape. But its position was hardly secure — a strident, confident form of extreme Protestantism was on the rise.

Elizabeth appointed Hooker as Master of the Temple Church in London in 1585, making him pastor to dozens of lawyers. At the Temple Church, Hooker engaged in frequent debate with Protestant partisans. These Protestants wanted to purify the Church of England (hence their nickname "Puritans") from every tinge of Roman thought and practice, including sacramental theology, liturgical vestments, ceremonial customs, naming churches after saints, use of written prayers, feast days, and the office of bishop. They sought not only to require that biblical commands be obeyed, but that practices not commanded in the Bible be forbidden, "that nothing be done . . . but that which you have the express warrant of God's word for." Moreover, they charged the state with the responsibility to enforce this discipline. The most radical of the Puritans wanted to model every aspect of English society, civil as well as ecclesiastical, along biblical lines. It was a dreary, humorless conformity to the Bible — as interpreted by the Puritans, and only by the Puritans.

In 1595, Hooker was appointed to a parish in Bishopsbourne, near Canterbury, where he moved with his family. There Hooker had the leisure to devote to a monumental, eight-volume book he had begun writing while in London. It is this book for which he is chiefly remembered. Apparently unconcerned with catchy titles, Hooker named his work *Of the Laws of Ecclesiastical Polity.* An appropriate subtitle might have been *How to Build and Run a National Church.*

Hooker set out to defend the ideas and practices the Church of England had retained from its catholic past, primarily questions of church government (or "polity," hence the book's name) and worship. But the *Polity* manages to address many other questions as well. Reading Hooker's great work is like rowing a boat along a lengthy coastline, touching shore at many an inlet and island along the way, exploring each in turn, while never quite losing sight of the destination. To the modern reader, Hooker's writing style may seem dense in places, but he writes with absolute clarity. Every word is carefully chosen; every sentence is a masterpiece of grammatical construction.

Not until Book V of the *Polity* does Hooker get around to defending the specific customs at issue. In Books I-IV, he lays his groundwork — thoroughly, carefully, brilliantly. The *Polity* begins with a discussion of law. Hooker sees a universe governed by various kinds of law. As Hooker uses the word, a "law" is not something imposed by an outside force, but anything "which doth appoint the form and measure of working," "any rule or canon by which actions are framed." That is to say, a law is simply the way something works, whether it's the rotation of a planet, the regulation of commerce, or the government of the church. All law originates with God as an implanted directive, inherent in the universe and governing all its operations. God himself, Hooker says, moves within the law he has determined for himself. Laws are patterns by which things tend to their perfection, and some are eternal while others may be changed. Laws governing human societies, such as churches, may be changed, even if they are laid down in the Bible, when the circumstances which called for them no longer exist.

Christians had been debating about authority for nearly a century, and that debate lies at the heart of the *Polity*. Hooker disputed the claim of the radical Puritans that the Bible should be the only authority in every area of life. Hooker looked for guidance from several sources — the Bible, the works of nature, human experience (both one's own and that of older and wiser persons preserved by tradition), and reason (which included "intuitive beholding" and "invincible demonstration"). It should be noted that unlike the Enlightenment thinkers who lived a century later, Hooker never saw human reason as autonomous or absolute. Reason, like the Bible and other sources of guidance, was God's gift and subject to God's authority.

The Bible, Hooker wrote, contains everything needed for the salvation of humanity that is not apparent to reason, but one must not "make the bare mandate of sacred scripture the only rule of all good and evil in the actions of mortal men." In no way is the Bible demeaned by recognizing that there are some matters it does not address, some helpful things it does not say. Hooker observed that church government and ceremonial are among the topics on which the Bible is largely silent, and he felt that even the few things the Bible does say on those matters are not binding on all people at all times. Hence any form of church government found to be useful and any ceremonial found to be edifying may be embraced — and changed when circumstances call for something different.

But the church should move cautiously in casting aside ancient practices, Hooker warned. Admitting that ceremonies and forms once edifying had been abused in the pre-Reformation church, Hooker urged that they not be discarded, but restored to their original use and retained for the good of the church. "A knife may be taken away from a child, without depriving them of the benefit thereof which have the years and discretion to use it." This high regard for tradition made Hooker an essentially conservative thinker; it was the Puritans who were the radical innovators.

Hooker is at his best in discussing the much debated topic of sacraments. The key is his idea of *participation,* which he defines as "that mutual inward hold which Christ hath of us and we of him," each possessing the other "by way of special interest, property, and inherent copulation." God the Father loves God the Son eternally, and because the Son joined himself to human flesh, we too "participate" in that love. "We are therefore adopted sons of God to eternal life by participation of the only-begotten Son of God, whose life is the well-spring and cause of ours." This participation is manifest in two forms, *imputed* participation, a status freely given to all, and *infused* participation, a gradual growth in Christlikeness. Participation in God is God's gift to us, called "grace." Sacraments both teach us about God's grace and serve as instruments by which God bestows grace to us. On the heated question of how this works, and especially what occurs to the bread and wine when the priest consecrates them, Hooker is intentionally silent: "I wish that men would more give themselves to meditate with silence what we have by the sacrament, and less to dispute of the manner how. . . . this heavenly food is given for the satisfying of our empty souls, and not for the exercising of our curious and subtle wits."

Hooker's writing is marked by a gracious, conciliatory spirit unusual in the theological debates of the day. Other Christian controversialists lambasted their opponents in vivid, colorful language and were quick to consign them to the fires of hell. But Hooker called John Calvin, the theologian whose writings inspired the Puritans, "the wisest man that ever the French Church did enjoy." He never questioned the integrity of his opponents and made clear that he regarded them as fellow members of the Body of Christ. One might even find heretics (persons holding views contrary to church teaching) in heaven alongside true believers, Hooker allowed. This humility of spirit, looking for the good in one's opponents and willingly joining hands with them, has always characterized Anglicanism at its best. It is Richard Hooker whom we have to thank for this gift.

Scholar A. S. McGrade does not exaggerate when he writes that Hooker's work "remains the one systematic and intelligible justification of the whole range of Anglican belief and worship."

IN HIS OWN WORDS

Note: All quotations are from *Of the Laws of Ecclesiastical Polity*.

Sharpness of wit

There will come a time when three words uttered with charity and meekness shall receive a far more blessed reward than three thousand volumes written with disdainful sharpness of wit.

Preface 2.10

Revelation and reason

There are but two ways whereby the Spirit leadeth men into all truth: the one extraordinary, the other common; the one belonging but unto some few, the other extending itself unto all that are of God; the one, that which we call by a special divine excellency "revelation," the other "reason."

Preface 3.10

To the Puritans

A very strange thing sure it were, that such a discipline as ye speak of should be taught by Christ and his apostles in the word of God, and no church ever have found it out, nor received it till this present time; contrariwise, the government against which ye bend yourselves be observed every where throughout all generations and ages of the Christian world, no church ever perceiving the word of God to be against it.

Preface 4.1

Persuading a multitude

He that goeth about to persuade a multitude, that they are not so well governed as they ought to be, shall never want attentive and favourable hearers.

I.1.1

Law

That which doth assign unto each thing the kind, that which doth moderate the force and power, that which doth appoint the form and measure of working, the same we term a *Law*. So that no certain end could ever be attained, unless the actions whereby it is attained were regular; that is to say,

26

made suitable, fit and correspondent unto their end, by some canon, rule or law. Which doth first take place in the works even of God himself.

I.2.1

Nature

Now if nature should intermit her course, and leave altogether, though it were but for a while, the observation of her own laws; if those principal and mother elements of the world, whereof all things in this lower world are made, should lose the qualities which now they have; if the frame of that heavenly arch erected over our heads should loosen and dissolve itself; if celestial spheres should forget their wonted motions, and by irregular volubility turn themselves any way as it might happen; if the prince of the lights of heaven, which now as a giant doth run his unwearied course, should as it were through a languishing faintness begin to stand and to rest himself; if the moon should wander from her beaten way, the times and seasons of the year blend themselves by disordered and confused mixture, the winds breathe out their last gasp, the clouds yield no rain, the earth be defeated of heavenly influence, the fruits of the earth pine away as children at the withered breasts of their mother no longer able to yield them relief: what would become of man himself, whom these things now do all serve? See we not plainly that obedience of creatures unto the law of nature is the stay of the whole world?

I.3.2

Nature and scripture

It sufficeth therefore that nature and scripture do serve in such full sort, that they both jointly, and not severally either of them, be so complete, that unto everlasting felicity we need not the knowledge of any thing more than these two may easily furnish our minds with on all sides; and therefore they which add traditions, as a part of supernatural necessary truth, have not the truth, but are in error.

I.14.5

Misuse of scripture

For whereas God hath left sundry kinds of laws unto men, and by all those laws the actions of men are in some sort directed; they [the Puritans] hold that one only law, the scripture, must be the rule to direct in all things, even so far as to the "taking up of a rush or straw."

II.1.2

The insolent mind

A man whose capacity will scarce serve him to utter five words in sensible manner blusheth not in any doubt concerning matter of scripture to think his own bare *Yea* as good as the *Nay* of all the wise, grave, and learned judgments that are in the whole world: which insolency must be repressed, or it will be the very bane of Christian religion.

II.7.6

The Puritans' tenuous case

The most which can be inferred upon such plenty of divine testimonies is only this, that *some things* which they maintain, as far as *some men* can *probably conjecture,* do *seem* to have been out of scripture *not absurdly* gathered.

II.7.9

Use of scripture

We must likewise take great heed, lest in attributing unto scripture more than it can have, the incredibility of that do cause even those things which indeed it hath most abundantly to be less reverently esteemed.

II.8.7

Heretics

We must acknowledge even heretics themselves to be, though a maimed part, yet a part of the visible church. If an infidel should pursue to death an heretic professing Christianity, only for Christian profession's sake, could we deny unto him the honor of martyrdom?

III.1.11

Nature and grace

Nature hath need of grace, whereunto I hope we are not opposite, by holding that grace hath use of nature.

III.8.6

All knowledge precious

There is in the world no kind of knowledge, whereby any part of truth is seen, but we justly account it precious . . . to detract from the dignity thereof were to injure even God himself, who being that light which none can approach unto, hath sent out these lights whereof we are capable, even as so many sparkles resembling the bright fountain from which they rise.

III.8.9

Reason interprets scripture

Unto the word of God, being in respect of that end for which God ordained it perfect, exact, and absolute in itself, we do not add reason as a supplement of any maim or defect therein, but as a necessary instrument, without which we could not reap by the scripture's perfection that fruit and benefit which it yieldeth.

III.8.10

Harmless customs

Customs once established and confirmed by long use, being presently without harm, are not in regard of their corrupt original to be held scandalous.

IV.12.4

Advice to preachers

Preachers may better bestow their time, than in giving men warning not to abuse ceremonies.

IV.12.8

Religion and justice

So natural is the union of religion with justice, that we may boldly deem there is neither, where both are not. For how should they be unfeignedly just, whom religion doth not cause to be such; or they religious, which are not found such by the proof of their just actions?

V.1.2

Prayer

When we are not able to do any other thing for men's behoof, when through maliciousness or unkindness they vouchsafe not to accept any other good at our hands, prayer is that which we always have in our power to bestow, and they never in theirs to refuse.

V.23.1

The Incarnation

[Since] God hath deified our nature, though not by turning it into himself, yet by making it his own inseparable habitation, we cannot now conceive how God should without man either exercise divine power, or receive the glory of divine praise. For man is in both an associate of Deity.

V.54.5

Partakers of Christ

It pleaseth [Christ] in mercy to account himself incomplete and maimed without us. But most assured we are that we all receive of his fulness, because he is in us as a moving and working cause; from which many blessed effects are really found to ensue, and that in sundry both kinds and degrees, all tending to eternal happiness.

V.56.10

Sacraments

It pleaseth Almighty God to communicate by sensible means those blessings which are incomprehensible.

V.57.3

Holy Communion

Let it therefore be sufficient for me presenting myself at the Lord's table to know what there I receive from him, without searching or inquiring of the manner how Christ performeth his promise; let disputes and questions, enemies to piety, abatements of true devotions, and hitherto in this cause but over-patiently heard, let them take their rest; let curious and sharp-witted men beat their heads about what questions themselves will ... what these elements are in themselves it skilleth not, it is enough that to me which take them they are the body and blood of Christ, his promise in witness hereof sufficeth, his word he knoweth which way to accomplish; why should any cogitation possess the mind of a faithful communicant but this, *O my God, thou art true, O my soul thou art happy*?

V.67.12

Government by bishops

O nation utterly without knowledge, without sense! We are not through error of mind deceived, but some wicked thing hath undoubtedly bewitched us, if we forsake that government, the use whereof universal experience hath for so many years approved, and betake ourselves unto a regiment neither appointed of God himself, as they who favour it pretend, nor till yesterday ever heard of among men.

VII.1.4

Expectations of bishops

As for us over whom Christ hath placed them [bishops] to be the chiefest guides and pastors of our souls, our common fault is that we look for much more in our governors than a tolerable sufficiency can yield, and bear much less than humanity and reason do require we should. Too much perfection over rigorously exacted in them, cannot but breed in us perpetual discontentment, and on both parts cause all things to be unpleasant.

VII.24.16

FOR REFLECTION AND DISCUSSION

What justification might be given for an officially established national church, as envisioned in sixteenth-century England? Compare the advantages and disadvantages of an established church to the separation of church and state found in many Western countries today.

In what areas of life are biblical norms binding and in what areas may Christians disregard them?

What did Hooker mean by "reason"? How does that compare to the modern use of the term?

How do you see the relationship between the Bible and human reason as sources of truth? How does reason help interpret the Bible? What are the dangers in subjecting the Bible to human reason?

What, if anything, do you find helpful in Hooker's discussion of sacraments?

What group of people do you find it most difficult to accept in church? List the good things about these persons. Share your list with a friend, and remember it the next time you have occasion to speak of or to these persons.

Hooker allows that heretics may be found within the visible church and is apparently not greatly disturbed by this. How do you feel the church should deal with heresy?

Chapter 4

LANCELOT ANDREWES

1555-1626

Private Devotions

Y EARS AGO I was rummaging through the stacks of a library looking for
something else when my eye fell upon a slender volume entitled *The
Private Devotions of Lancelot Andrewes.* My first thought was to wonder
what sort of mother would name her boy Lancelot, a name which even in
the sixteeth century was likely to incite the catcalls of jeering schoolboys. I
pulled the book off the shelf and leafed through it. Within moments I realized I had discovered a new friend from across a distance of four centuries.
For over thirty years now, I have returned again and again to the *Private
Devotions of Lancelot Andrewes* in my own prayer life.

Andrewes was bishop, in succession, of the English dioceses of
Chichester, Ely, and Winchester. He was a man of prayer (his normal routine was to spend five hours each day in private prayer and meditation),
but his chief reputation was as a preacher and a scholar. Although
Andrewes was a frequent and popular preacher at the court of King
James I, his sermons are little read today. He preached in the "witty" or
"metaphysical" style of the time, which rarely referred to personal matters
or current concerns, but strictly confined itself to the exploration of a biblical idea. Andrewes dissected his biblical texts minutely, including etymo-
logical analyses of Hebrew and Greek words. He relied on puns, allitera-
tions, and sophisticated plays on words. King James was educated in
theology, as were many members of his court, but most modern readers
find Andrewes' sermons heavy going. Even T. S. Eliot, who loved them, said
that Andrewes "takes a word and derives the world from it; squeezing and
squeezing the word until it yields a full juice of meaning which we should
never have supposed any word to possess," and that the sermons of
Andrewes are "only for the reader who can elevate himself to the subject"
— which few modern readers will or can do.

Andrewes was a linguistic and biblical scholar second to none. He spent
the better part of two decades at Cambridge, first as a student and then as a
don, where he undertook to master a new language every year, eventually
gaining fluency in no fewer than fifteen of them, both ancient and modern.
This extraordinary erudition served him well when he became one of the
chief translators of the Authorized (King James) Version of the Bible, chair-
ing the committee which translated the first twelve books of the Old Testament. A contemporary once remarked that had Andrewes been alive at the
time, he might "almost have served as an interpreter-general at the confusion of tongues." So at home was Andrewes with a variety of languages that
he said his prayers in three languages — none of them his native English.

He wrote the *Devotions* for his own personal use, not for publication, and when the text was first published, twenty years after his death, it had first to be translated into English from the original Greek, Latin, and Hebrew.

Andrewes is often mentioned with Richard Hooker as one of the leading minds in the development of a distinctive Anglican theological stance. His theology was catholic, "neither pared away on the one hand nor embellished with questionable deductions on the other," as F. E. Brightman has said in the introduction to his excellent translation of the *Devotions*. Or, as Andrewes himself said in one of his sermons, "One canon [the Bible] reduced to writing by God himself, two testaments, three creeds, four general councils, five centuries, and the series of fathers in that period — the centuries, that is, before Constantine, and two after, determine the boundary of our faith." That has been the norm for Anglican theologizing ever since. However loudly Anglicans of a later time may squabble about the issues of their day, always the appeal, by both sides, is to the authority of the scriptures, creeds, and writings of the early Christian era. Andrewes was the first to articulate this norm.

The appeal to ancient tradition also illustrates Andrewes' hunger for order. He is often contrasted with his younger contemporary, John Donne. If one of them is the photograph, the other is the negative image. Donne's poetry, devotions, and sermons (which *are* still read today) reveal a volatile, earthy, and perhaps not always respectable personality, and he fought hard against his call to ordination. Andrewes' life, theology, sermons, and devotions all reveal balance, order, and planning. His interior life, like his outward life, knew few ups and downs, manifesting a steady, focused growth from youth to old age. Andrewes knew early in his life that he would seek ordination and never questioned his call. But neither did he seek to advance his career, turning down two bishoprics as an act of protest over Elizabeth's appropriating of church funds for the crown, before accepting the appointment to Chichester from James, following Elizabeth's death. In a royal court noted for its sleaze, greed, and back-stabbing, Lancelot Andrewes, with his five hours a day in prayer and his biblically-based sermons, sailed like a steady clipper ship over the churning deep.

So averse was Andrewes to controversy and politics that he passively acquiesced in the execution of two heretics in 1612 — the last time anyone was burned in England on account of religion. However Andrewes may have felt about this means of resolving doctrinal differences, there can be no doubt that he saw heretical opinions as a great danger. The last minute thwarting of the Gunpowder Plot seven years earlier, in which a group of radical Roman Catholics had nearly succeeded in blowing up the House of Lords, had left a profound impression on Andrewes and his contemporaries. Order and uniformity, to which Andrewes naturally inclined, were also the values championed by those around him; freedom of belief was an idea whose time would not come for another century.

Andrewes' chief legacy, however, is his *Private Devotions*. Not surprisingly, the work is carefully ordered. The heart of the *Devotions* is a set of seven exercises, one for each day of the week. The themes follow the six days of Creation. All seven daily devotions are structured identically, with six sections: a brief introduction, followed by a confession, prayer for grace, profession of faith (often based on the Creed), intercessions, and a concluding act of praise. These are, clearly, the prayers of a man who prayed regularly and methodically.

There is virtually nothing in the *Devotions* that Andrewes wrote himself. Nearly everything was borrowed, a great deal of it from the Bible (especially the Psalms), but also from the many sources Andrewes had encountered in his wide reading. These include not only the Prayer Book, but the sermons of the Greek and Latin church fathers, ancient pagan philosophers, classical liturgies of the Eastern and Western churches, and contemporary writers, both Protestant and Catholic. Andrewes would select a sentence from one source, splice it to a phrase from another source, and then add a few words from a third and fourth source, producing a set of lines that reads as if they were from a single hand. One might think of the *Devotions* as a splendid mosaic or patchwork quilt. Archbishop Cranmer sometimes drew upon such sources in his composition of *The Book of Common Prayer,* and Brightman has observed that Andrewes' *Devotions* are for private prayer what the Prayer Book is for the church's public worship.

The modern reader of the *Devotions* will quickly realize he is reading something written centuries ago, and almost certainly by an Englishman. Andrewes' intense penitence will seem overdrawn to many in this day of breezy spirituality, especially if they know the words come from one noted for his saintly otherworldliness, and Andrewes' reverence for the monarchy and the nobility will sound old-fashioned, and very English. But these features should not inhibit today's reader from appreciating the profound depth of the *Devotions,* nor need they pose an obstacle to adopting them as a model for contemporary prayer.

If Andrewes' sermons rarely made reference to his personal life, his prayers often do. He never mentions names (except the names of dioceses and parishes), but a reader easily imagines the faces of his friends, colleagues, and kindred. The *Devotions* are remarkable in that they refer to specific persons, places, situations, and concerns, yet have about them a sense of universality and timelessness. Andrewes takes common, everyday things and imbues them with a sense of the holy. The sensitive reader can feel that she, along with all the mundane, seemingly insignificant little items of her daily life, is transported to the outskirts of heaven.

One should read the *Devotions* slowly, in small pieces, searchingly, and with a hungry soul. Each day's prayers could easily be read straight through in ten minutes, but it is better to let a word or phrase sink in and filter through the mind. Fredrica Thompsett has suggested reading the *Devotions* while walking a labyrinth, reading one line with each deliberate step towards the center. The language and the topics referred to will sometimes (but by no means always) seem archaic, but the modern reader can easily make connections with her own life.

It appears that Andrewes himself used the *Devotions* in something like this way. Richard Drake, one of the earliest translators of the *Devotions,* said, when he came into possession of Andrewes' own copy, "Had you seen the original manuscript, happy in the glorious deformity thereof, being slubbered with his pious hands and watered with his penitential tears, you would have been forced to confess, that book belonged to no other than pure and primitive devotion." The copy to which Drake referred no longer survives. But a copy of the *Devotions* may always be found in London's Southwark Cathedral, at the tomb where Andrewes is buried and where to this day pilgrims pause to pray the prayers Lancelot Andrewes prayed.

IN HIS OWN WORDS

Note: The following citations are from the 1840 translation of the *Private Devotions* by John Henry Newman.

From an Order for Morning Prayer

Glory be to thee, O Lord, glory to thee.
Glory to thee who givest me sleep to recruit my weakness,

and to remit the toils of this fretful flesh.
To this day and all days,
a perfect, holy, peaceful, healthy, sinless course,
Vouchsafe, O Lord.

Teach me to do the thing that pleaseth thee,
for thou art my God;
Let thy loving Spirit lead me forth into the land of righteousness.
Quicken me, O Lord, for thy name's sake,
and for thy righteousness sake bring my soul out of trouble;
remove from me foolish imaginations,
inspire those which are good and pleasing in thy sight.
Turn away mine eyes lest they behold vanity;
let mine eyes look right on,
and let mine eyelids look straight before me.
Hedge up mine ears with thorns lest they incline to
      undisciplined words.
Give me early the ear to hear,
and open mine ears to the instruction of thy oracles.
Set a watch, O Lord, before my mouth,
and keep the door of my lips.
Let my word be seasoned with salt,
that it may minister grace to the hearers.

From an Order for Evening Prayer

The day is gone, and I give thee thanks, O Lord.
Evening is at hand, make it bright unto us.
As day has its evening so also has life;
the even of life is age,
age has overtaken me, make it bright unto us.
Cast me not away in the time of age;
forsake me not when my strength faileth me. . . .
Abide with me, Lord,
for it is toward evening,
and the day is far spent of this fretful life.
Let thy strength be made perfect in my weakness.

Confession

Merciful and pitiful Lord,
Long-suffering and full of pity,
I have sinned, Lord, I have sinned against thee;
O me, wretched that I am,
I have sinned, Lord, against thee much and grievously,
in attending on vanities and lies.
I conceal nothing: I make no excuses.
I give thee glory, O Lord, this day,
I denounce against myself my sins;
Truly I have sinned before the Lord
and thus and thus have I done.
I have sinned and perverted that which was right,
and it profited me not.
And what shall I now say?
Or with what shall I open my mouth?
What shall I answer, seeing I have done it?
Without plea, without defense, self-condemned, am I.
I have destroyed myself.
Unto thee, O Lord, belongeth righteousness,
but unto me confusion of face,
because thou art just in all that is come upon me;
for thou hast done right,
but I have done wickedly.
And now, Lord, what is my hope?
Truly my hope is even in thee,
if hope of salvation remain to me,
if thy loving-kindness cover
the multitude of my iniquities.

Prayer for Grace

Hedge up my way with thorns,
that I find not the path for following vanity.
Hold thou me in with bit and bridle,

lest I fall from thee.
O Lord, compel me to come in to thee.

Two things have I required of thee, O Lord,
deny thou me not before I die;
remove far from me vanity and lies;
give me neither poverty nor riches,
feed me with food convenient for me;
lest I be full and deny thee and say, who is the Lord?
Or lest I be poor and steal,
and take the name of my God in vain.
Let me learn to abound, let me learn to suffer need,
in whatsoever state I am, therewith to be content.
For nothing earthly, temporal, mortal, to long nor to wait.
Grant me a happy life, in piety, gravity, purity,
in all things good and fair,
in cheerfulness, in health, in credit,
in competency, in safety, in gentle estate, in quiet;
a happy death,
a deathless happiness.

May thy strong hand, O Lord, be ever my defense;
thy mercy in Christ, my salvation;
thy all-veritable word, my instructor;
the grace of thy life-bringing Spirit, my consolation
all along, and at last.

Profession

Godhead, paternal love, power,
providence:
salvation, anointing, adoption,
lordship;
conception, birth, passion,
cross, death, burial,
descent, resurrection, ascent,
sitting, return, judgment;

Breath and Holiness,
calling from the Universal,
hallowing in the Universal,
communion of saints, and of saintly things,
resurrection,
life eternal.

Intercession

Grant to our population to be subject unto the higher powers,
not only for wrath, but also for conscience-sake.
Grant to farmers and graziers good seasons;
to the fleet and fishers fair weather;
to tradesmen, not to overreach one another;
to mechanics, to pursue their business lawfully,
down to the meanest workman,
down to the poor.
O God, not of us only but of our seed,
bless our children among us,
to advance in wisdom as in stature,
and in favor with thee and with men.

I commend to thee, O Lord,
my soul, and my body,
my mind, and my thoughts,
my prayers, and my vows,
my senses, and my limbs,
my words, and my works,
my life, and my death;
my brothers, and my sisters,
and all their children;
my friends, my benefactors, my well wishers,
those who have a claim on me;
my kindred, and my neighbors,
my country, and all Christendom.
I commend to thee, Lord,
my impulses, and my startings,

my intentions, and my attempts,
my going out, and my coming in,
my sitting down, and my rising up.

Let us pray God
for the whole creation;
for the supply of seasons,
healthy, fruitful, peaceful;
for the whole race of mankind;
for those who are not Christians;
for the conversion of atheists, the ungodly;
Gentiles, Turks, and Jews;
for all Christians;
for restoration of all who languish in errors and sins;
for confirmation of all who have been granted truth and grace;
for succor and comfort of all who are dispirited, infirm, distressed, un-
settled,
men and women;
for thankfulness and sobriety in all who are hearty, healthy,
        prosperous, quiet,
men and women;
For the catholic church, its establishment and increase;
for the eastern, its deliverance and union;
for the western, its adjustment and peace;
for the British, the supply of what is wanting in it,
the strengthening of what remains in it;
for the episcopate, the priesthood, Christian people. . . .
For those who have a claim on me from relationship,
for brothers and sisters, that God's blessing may be on them,
and on their children;
or from benefits conferred,
that thy recompense may be on all who have benefitted me,
who have ministered to me in carnal things;
or from trust placed in me,
for all whom I have educated, all whom I have ordained . . .
for all who love me, though I know them not;
or from Christian love, for those who hate me without cause,
some, too, even on account of truth and righteousness;

or from neighborhood, for all who dwell near peaceably and harmlessly;
or from promise, for all whom I have promised to remember
      in my prayers;
or from mutual offices, for all who remember me in their prayers,
and ask of me the same;
or from stress of engagements, for all who on sufficient reasons fail
      to call upon thee;
for all who have no intercessor in their own behalf;
for all who at present are in agony of extreme necessity or deep
      affliction;
for all who are attempting any good work
which will bring glory to the name of God
or some great good to the church;
for all who act nobly either towards things sacred or towards the poor;
for all who have ever been offended by me either in word or in deed.

Praise

Up with our hearts;
we lift them to the Lord.
O how very meet, and right, and fitting, and due,
in all, and for all,
at all times, places, manners,
in every season, every spot,
everywhere, always, altogether,
to remember thee, to worship thee,
to confess to thee, to praise thee,
to bless thee, to hymn thee,
to give thanks to thee,
maker, nourisher, guardian, governor,
preserver, worker, perfecter of all,
Lord and Father,
King and God,
fountain of life and immortality,
treasure of everlasting goods,
whom the heavens hymn,
and the heaven of heavens,

the angels and all the heavenly powers,
one to other crying continually, —
and we the while, weak and unworthy,
under their feet, —
Holy, Holy, Holy
Lord the God of Hosts;
full is the whole heaven,
and the whole earth,
of the majesty of thy glory.
Blessed be the glory of the Lord out of his place,
For his Godhead, his mysteriousness,
his height, his sovereignty, his almightiness,
his eternity, his providence.
The Lord is my strength, my stony rock, and my defense,
my deliverer, my succor, my buckler,
the horn also of my salvation and my refuge.

Wherefore day by day
for these thy benefits towards me, which I remember, —
wherefore also for others very many which I have let slip
from their number, from my forgetfulness,
for those which I wished, knew and asked,
and those I asked not, knew not, wished not, —
I confess and give thanks to thee,
I bless and praise thee, as is fit, and every day,
And I pray with my whole soul,
and with my whole mind I pray. . . .
now, in this day and hour,
and every day till my last breath,
and till the end of the world,
and for ages upon ages.

O Lord, my Lord,
for my being, life, reason,
for nurture, protection, guidance,
for education, civil rights, religion,
for thy gifts of grace, nature, fortune,
for redemption, regeneration, catechising,

for my call, recall, yea, many calls besides;
for thy forbearance, long-suffering, long long-suffering to me-ward
many seasons, many years, up to this time;
for all good things received, successes granted me, good things done;
for the use of things present,
for thy promise, and my hope of the enjoyment of good things to come;
for my parents honest and good,
teachers kind,
benefactors never to be forgotten,
religious intimates congenial,
hearers thoughtful, friends sincere, domestics faithful,
for all who have advantaged me,
by writings, homilies, conversation, prayers, patterns, rebukes, injuries;
for all these, and all others
which I know, which I know not,
open, hidden, remembered, forgotten,
done when I wished, when I wished not,
I confess to thee and will confess,
I bless thee and will bless,
I give thanks to thee and will give thanks,
all the days of my life.

FOR REFLECTION AND DISCUSSION

How does your spirituality compare to that of Andrewes? What in his
prayers do you find it easiest to identify with? What do you find hardest to identify with?

Do you find Andrewes' penitence overdrawn, or do you feel he sounds a
note today's Christians need to hear?

Where in today's world — or in your own life — do you feel a greater sense
of balance and order is needed?

Write your own form of intercession, using Andrewes as a model.

Chapter 5

JOHN DONNE

1573-1631

He Dueled with Death

JOHN DONNE is almost certainly the most anthologized author in Anglican history. Excerpts from his works routinely appear in collections of poetry and devotional readings, as well they should. But there is a danger: Because Donne wrote so often about death, those who dip only superficially into his writings may think of him as a depressing, morose author. There are many passages in Donne from which a few sentences, lifted out of context, can give this impression, but that is to misread him.

It is true that Donne was fascinated by death. One might say he was obsessed by it, especially by his own death. It is as if he stalked death, walked around it, examined it from every angle, at every time of day, recording his most minute observations of it, analyzing it, challenging it. And he did have his gloomy moments — but that is hardly surprising, when his wife and six of his twelve children predeceased him and the average life expectancy of English males born in 1573 was just twenty-nine years. Even so, though, the note that rings most clearly in Donne's sermons, devotions, and religious poetry is not gloom, but the mercy and goodness of God.

John Donne did not intend to become a priest or theologian. As a young adult, he studied law in London, where he was well known to bartenders and theater owners, had a way with women, and wrote bawdy poetry. He was in military service for a time and traveled abroad. In 1601, Donne fell in love with Ann More, the daughter of a prominent family at the court of Queen Elizabeth. When Ann's father refused to consent to the marriage, the two eloped, and the bride's father had Donne thrown into prison because Ann was a minor. After Donne was released, the marriage was declared valid and the couple began their life together, poor but happy.

Donne was ambitious, but his efforts to curry favor with the wealthy and powerful gained him little advantage. He began to dabble in theology. A friend urged Donne in 1607 to seek ordination, but Donne refused because of past sins which he felt disqualified him and because he realized his motive would have been to gain a career, not to promote God's glory. But as his theological writings were favorably received, others, including King James, pressed Donne to seek holy orders. He finally agreed and was ordained in 1615. The death of his wife two years later plunged Donne into a spiritual crisis, deepening his sense of priestly vocation and bringing focus to his recurring ruminations about human mortality. Still ambitious, Donne sought preferment in the church — and received it. He was appointed chaplain to the king following his ordination, then professor of divinity at Cambridge, and in 1621, dean of St. Paul's Cathedral, London.

Donne is often compared to Lancelot Andrewes. They were the two most celebrated preachers of their day. Each was an intellectual giant. The two knew and apparently respected each other, but they could hardly have been more different temperamentally or in the pulpit. Whereas Andrewes valued order and a learned detachment, both in his life and in his preaching, Donne was passionate, moody, and volatile. Andrewes' sermons are rarely quoted today, whereas editors of modern anthologies (to say nothing of today's preachers) may choose from hundreds of passages in Donne's sermons, any of which will speak to a modern reader as powerfully as it did to a seventeenth-century congregant, of a robust, extremely personal love of God.

This is not to say that many people read John Donne's sermons straight through. Some do, but early seventeenth-century sermons, exemplified both by Donne and Andrewes, were long (typically an hour or more) and intellectually demanding. Donne, however, mingled passages of poignant personal revelation among those of more daunting academic prose. We meet a turbulent soul, grieving over his sins, questioning his faith, pondering his mortality, wrestling with God, striving for humility — and in the end, soaring with thankfulness and praise.

In addition to his sermons, Donne is remembered today for his poetry and his *Devotions*. Donne began writing poetry long before his faith matured, and much of his early poetry is lively and enjoyable — though hardly something one would choose for devotional reading. He is perhaps the foremost among a group of poets of the day whom Samuel Johnson later dubbed the "metaphysical poets" (he meant the term derisively, implying an arrogant display of intellectual prowess and wit) and which also included George Herbert, Andrew Marvell, and Henry Vaughan. Both Donne's secular and his religious verse are of this type. It's not the sort of poetry one skips lightly through. Metaphysical poetry is characterized by concise, concentrated expression, heavy rhythms, and a certain deliberate roughness. Demands are made on the reader; difficulty is almost considered a virtue. The genre has been called sinewy, strenuous, masculine; a metaphysical poem is typically brief but densely packed. It will often contain what are called "conceits," that is, comparisons which work in the context of the poem but which would normally be thought inappropriate or unlikely. Every word in a John Donne poem is there for a reason, and it often carries several nuances of meaning, pointing in more than one direction. The reader should proceed slowly, pause after each word or phrase, read the poem more than once. The more time you spend with a poem from Donne, the more you will discover in it.

Donne's early secular poetry was earthy, even erotic, and some of his later religious poetry is the same. It has been said that his early love poems and his later religious poems interpret each other, and even (this is an exaggeration, I believe, but with a shred of truth) that Donne didn't change all that much after his religious faith matured, but merely transferred his feelings from women to God. It has also been said (more truthfully, I think) that Donne affirmed the earthy and elevated it to the heavenly. His poetry has been called "incarnational" — a word which derives from the Latin *carnalis,* consisting of flesh. Although he possessed a brilliant intellect, Donne's relationship to God was centered not in the mind, but in the heart, one might even say in the gut — and his poems attest to it.

Donne's themes in his poems are the same as those in his sermons. Penitence is perhaps the dominant note, often linked with passages on human mortality, and always leading to the joy of knowing a loving, forgiving God. The uneasy coexistence of opposites pervades Donne's poetry and other writings: ambition versus humility, flesh versus spirit, death versus life, time versus eternity, fear versus faith, rebellion versus submission. It is these polarities which give his writing much of its power and energy.

Late in 1623 and continuing into 1624, Donne was struck by a violent illness that has been called "relapsing fever," from which the sufferer seemed to improve, only to experience a relapse. This illness lasted several weeks. Donne experienced insomnia and prostration, but was mentally alert. Thinking his death was at hand, Donne reflected at length on the same themes that had commanded his attention before, but now with a more focused intensity. When his strength began to return, he wrote one of his most compelling works, *Devotions Upon Emergent Occasions.* In it he traces the progress of his illness, relating his experiences at each stage, including visits from physicians, ingestions of medicines, inability to eat, even the sounds outside his bedroom window. The devotions draw a parallel between the body's illness and recovery and the soul's progress from sin to redemption and are written in twenty-three chronological chapters, each containing three sections: Meditation, Expostulation, and Prayer.

Donne recovered from his "relapsing fever," but his health was never again robust. A gradual physical decline set in until, by the spring of 1631, he was exceedingly frail. He told his closest confidants that far from fearing death, he longed for it. Donne was appointed to preach at St. Paul's Cathedral on the First Friday in Lent, 1631. His health was now failing rapidly and it is said his flesh barely covered his bones. Those in the congregation that day wondered whether he could deliver his sermon. But deliver it he did. Entitled "Death's Duel," it is perhaps his best-known sermon. Donne then retired to his home where he prepared to die.

The next day, a friend asked him, "Why are you sad?" Donne replied, "I am not sad; but most of the night past I have entertained myself with many thoughts of several friends that have left me here, and are gone to that place from which they shall not return; and that within a few days I also shall go hence, and be no more seen. . . . I was in serious contemplation of the providence and goodness of God to me. . . . And though of myself I have nothing to present to him but sins and misery, yet I know he looks not upon me now as I am of myself, but as I am in my Savior, and hath given me, even at this present time, some testimonies by his Holy Spirit, that I am of the number of his elect: I am therefore full of inexpressible joy, and shall die in peace."

John Donne died on March 31, 1631. After his burial, someone wrote this epitaph with a coal on the wall over his grave:

Reader! I am to let thee know,
Donne's body only lies below;
For, could the grave his soul comprise,
Earth would be richer than the skies!

IN HIS OWN WORDS

Prayer for forgiveness

O Lord, thou hast set up many candlesticks, and kindled many lamps in me, but I have either blown them out or carried them to guide me in . . . forbidden ways. Thou hast given me a desire of knowledge, and some means to it, and some possession of it, and I have armed myself with thy weapons against thee. Yet, O God, have mercy upon me, for thine own sake have mercy on me. Let not sin and me be able to exceed thee, nor to defraud thee, nor to frustrate thy purposes: But let me, in despite of me, be of so much use to thy glory, that by thy mercy to my sin, other sinners may see how much sin thou canst pardon.

Essays in Divinity (1611-1614)

The hand of God

Let me discern that [what] is done upon me is done by the hand of God, and I care not what it be: I had rather have God's vinegar than man's oil, God's wormwood than man's manna, God's justice than any man's mercy. . . . Even afflictions are welcome, when we see them to be his.

Sermon on Psalm 90:14

The limits of reason

We may search so far and reason so long of faith and grace, as that we may lose not only them but even our reason too, and sooner become mad than good.

Sermon on John 1:8

The coming of God

If some king of the earth have so large an extent of dominion in north and south, as that he hath winter and summer together in his dominions, so large an extent east and west, as that he hath day and night together in his dominions, much more hath God mercy and judgment together: he brought light out of darkness, not out of a lesser light; he can bring thy summer out of winter, though thou have no spring; though in the ways of fortune, or understanding, or conscience, thou have been benighted till now, wintered and frozen, clouded and eclipsed, damped and benumbed, smothered and stupefied till now, now God comes to thee, not as in the dawning of the day, not as in the bud of the spring, but as the sun at noon, to illumine all shadows, as the sheaves in harvest, to fill all penuries. All occasions invite his mercies, and all times are his seasons.

Sermon on Isaiah 7:14

Distractions in prayer

But when we consider . . . the manifold weakness of the strongest devotions in time of prayer, it is a sad consideration. I throw myself down in my chamber, and I call in and invite God and his angels thither, and when they are there, I neglect God and his angels, for the noise of a fly, for the rattling of a coach, for the whining of a door; I talk on, in the same posture of praying, eyes lifted up, knees bowed down, as though I prayed to God; and if God or his angels should ask me when I thought last of God in that prayer, I cannot tell. Sometimes I find that I had forgot what I was about, but when I began to forget it, I cannot tell. A memory of yesterday's pleasures, a fear of tomorrow's dangers, a straw under my knee, a noise in mine ear, a light in mine eye, an anything, a nothing, a fancy, a Chimera in my brain, troubles me in my prayer. So certainly is there nothing, nothing in spiritual things, perfect in this world.

Sermon on John 11:21

Holy Sonnet No. 7

At the round earth's imagined corners, blow
Your trumpets, angels, and arise, arise
From death, you numberless infinities
Of souls, and to your scattered bodies go,
All whom the flood did, and fire shall o'erthrow,
All whom war, dearth, age, agues, tyrannies,
Despair, law, chance, hath slain, and you whose eyes
Shall behold God, and never taste death's woe.
But let them sleep, Lord, and me mourn a space,
For, if above all these, my sins abound,
'Tis late to ask abundance of thy grace,
When we are there; here on this lowly ground,

Teach me how to repent; for that's as good
As if thou hadst sealed my pardon, with thy blood.

Holy Sonnet No. 10

Death be not proud, though some have called thee
Mighty and dreadful, for thou art not so,
For those whom thou think'st thou dost overthrow
Die not, poor death, nor yet canst thou kill me.
From pleasure, than from thee, much more must flow,
And sooner our best men with thee do go,
Rest of their bones, and souls delivery.
Thou art slave to fate, chance, kings, and desperate men,
And dost with poison, war, and sickness dwell,
And poppy, or charms can make us sleep as well,
And better than thy stroke; why swell'st thou then?
One short sleep past, we wake eternally,
And death shall be no more; death, thou shalt die.

Holy Sonnet No. 14

Batter my heart, three-personed God; for you
As yet but knock, breathe, shine, and seek to mend;
That I may rise, and stand, o'erthrow me, and bend
Your force to break, blow, burn, and make me new.
I, like an usurpt town, to'another due,
Labor to'admit you, but oh, to no end,
Reason, your viceroy in me, me should defend,
But is captived, and proves weak or untrue.
Yet dearly'I love you, and would be loved fain,
But am betrothed unto your enemy:
Divorce me, untie, or break that knot again,
Take me to you, imprison me, for I
Except you'enthrall me, never shall be free,
Nor ever chaste, except you ravish me.

A Hymn to God the Father

Wilt thou forgive that sin where I begun,
    Which is my sin, though it were done before?
Wilt thou forgive those sins through which I run,
    And do run still, though still I do deplore?
        When thou hast done, thou hast not done,
            For I have more.

Wilt thou forgive that sin by which I've won
    Others to sin? And made my sin their door?
Wilt thou forgive that sin which I did shun
    A year or two, but wallowed in a score?
        When thou hast done, thou hast not done,
            For I have more.

I have a sin of fear, that when I have spun
    My last thread, I shall perish on the shore;
But swear by thy self, that at my death thy Sun
    Shall shine as he shines now, and heretofore;
        And having done that, Thou hast done,
            I have no more.

Prayer in infirmity

O most mighty and most merciful God, who, though thou have taken me off of my feet, hast not taken me off of my foundation, which is thyself; who, though thou have removed me from that upright form in which I could stand and see thy throne, the heavens, yet hast not removed from me that light by which I can lie and see thyself; who, though thou have weakened my bodily knees, that they cannot bow to thee, hast yet left me the knees of my heart, which are bowed unto thee evermore; as thou hast made this bed thine altar, make me thy sacrifice, and as thou makest thy Son Christ Jesus the priest, so make me his deacon, to minister to him in a cheerful surrender of my body and soul to thy pleasure, by his hands.

Devotions Upon Emergent Occasions, III (1624)

John Donne

Time and eternity

Eternity is not an everlasting flux of time, but time is a short parenthesis in a long period; and eternity had been the same as it is, though time had never been.

Devotions, XIV

The bell tolls

Here the bells can scarce solemnize the funeral of any person, but that I knew him, or knew that he was my neighbor: we dwelt in houses near to one another before, but now he is gone into that house into which I must follow. . . . Who bends not his ear to any bell which upon any occasion rings? But who can remove it from that bell which is passing a piece of himself out of this world? No man is an island, entire of itself; every man is a piece of the continent, a part of the main. If a clod be washed away by the sea, Europe is the less, as well as if a promontory were, as well as if a manor of thy friend's or of thine own were: any man's death diminishes me, because I am involved in mankind, and therefore never send to know for whom the bell tolls; it tolls for thee.

Devotions, XVI, XVII

Into thy hands

As death is the wages of sin it is due to me; as death is the end of sickness it belongs to me; and though so disobedient a servant as I may be afraid to die, yet to so merciful a master as thou I cannot be afraid to come; and therefore into thy hands, O my God, I commend my spirit, a surrender which I know thou wilt accept, whether I live or die.

Devotions, XVII

A prayer

As I acknowledge that my bodily strength is subject to every puff of wind, so is my spiritual strength to every blast of vanity. Keep me therefore still,

O my gracious God, in such a proportion of both strengths, as I may still have something to thank thee for, which I have received, and still something to pray for and ask at thy hand.

Devotions, XXI

A prayer

O eternal and most gracious God, the God of security, and the enemy of security too, who wouldst have us always sure of thy love, and yet wouldst have us always doing something for it, let me always so apprehend thee as present with me, and yet so follow after thee, as though I had not apprehended thee.

Devotions, XXII

FOR REFLECTION AND DISCUSSION

Do you find Donne depressing and morose, or do you find him joyful and triumphant? Or both?

Do you agree that Donne's spirituality is "incarnational" or "gutsy"? Do you see any connection between an incarnational spirituality in someone like Donne and the Incarnation of God in Jesus Christ?

Describe Donne's experience of God. Where does Donne's experience of God make contact with your own?

With what can you identify in Donne's comment on "Distractions in prayer"? What remedies are there for such distractions?

List the violent verbs in Holy Sonnet No. 14. How do you respond to the sexual imagery in this poem? Can you think of other ways to express the point Donne is making?

Chapter 6

GEORGE HERBERT

1593-1633

Poet Parson

G EORGE HERBERT has two sets of admirers. Literary enthusiasts esteem him as a poet. Herbert was one of a group of English poets in the early seventeenth century which also included his older friend, John Donne. Metaphysical poetry, as their work is called, is tightly written and packed with surprising concrete images and comparisons. Herbert was among the best of the metaphysical poets and his reputation as a poet is secure.

Herbert's other set of admirers esteem him as a saintly priest and pastor. His reputation for saintliness is also secure, but the matter is not so simple as some would have it. That reputation derives in part from the delightful biography of Herbert by Izaak Walton, published four decades after Herbert's death. Walton cannot be faulted for underplaying his subject's sanctity. He portrayed Herbert as an up-and-coming man of the world who turned his back on a career at court to embrace the life of a scholar and country parson. That much is true, but the decision did not come easily or quickly for Herbert. He had thought of ordination as early as 1616, but resisted it. Herbert wrote to his stepfather in 1620 with thinly veiled pride at his appointment as public orator at Cambridge University, a post from which others had sprung to prominent positions at the court of James I, and he later said that he had "ambitiously thirsted for" such preferment. He managed to win election to Parliament and served there in 1624, but made no great mark. When two influential friends died that year and the king himself died a year later, Herbert's prospects for advancement at court grew dimmer. He seems to have struggled with his vocation until 1626, when he suddenly proceeded with his long-contemplated ordination to the diaconate. He delayed his ordination to the priesthood until 1630, then accepted appointment as rector of the small parish in Bemerton, then a rural area just outside Salisbury, where he served for just three years until, after a short illness, he died in 1633, a month before his fortieth birthday.

Herbert's reputation for sanctity rests on more than Walton's adoring biography, however. His own writing testifies to his genuine holiness of life. His one prose work, *A Priest to the Temple; or, The Country Parson,* written during his time at Bemerton, provides a classic if idealized picture of the rural parish priest, teaching both by precept and by example, leading his flock in the regular round of corporate worship services, ever firm yet ever gentle. Herbert makes no claim to have measured up to the standard spelled out in *A Priest to the Temple,* but says he was setting a goal to aim at, since "he shoots higher that threatens the moon, than he that aims at a tree." It is reliably reported, however (Walton is not the only source here), that Herbert virtually epitomized the ideal of which he wrote.

A Priest to the Temple is a "how to" manual for the country parson, with an emphasis on the inner life of the parson himself. It may seem to the modern reader naive or sanctimonious in places (as when Herbert suggests that when checking into a hotel, the parson invite the other guests to join him for public prayers in the lobby), but most of the book contains sound advice for a parish priest, any time, anywhere. Herbert counsels patience, "neither being greedy to get, nor niggardly to keep," and keeping one's word. He writes of the parson's domestic life, of his concern for both his parishioners' temporal and their spiritual needs, and of the commonsense humility with which the parson mediates conflict in the parish.

The conduct of worship was foremost in Herbert's understanding of parish ministry, as seen not only in *A Priest to the Temple* but in his poetry as well. His goal was a praying church, leading to the conversion of hearts. To that end, Herbert taught the liturgy to his parishioners at Bemerton and read Morning Prayer at 10:00 am and Evening Prayer at 4:00 pm every day in the church, with a small congregation always joining him and (according to Walton) laborers in nearby fields pausing at their plows to bow their heads when they heard the church bell ring. Herbert's advice on the conduct of worship is, typically, of the practical sort: "[The country parson's] voice is humble, his words treatable [distinct], and slow; yet not so slow neither, as to let the fervency of the supplicant hang and die between speaking, but with a grave liveliness, between fear and zeal. . . ."

His poems, however, are Herbert's chief claim to renown. They include a stunning variety of arresting images, some drawn from external sources, but many originating, apparently, in Herbert's own imagination. This imagery soars one moment to the outskirts of heaven, then quickly reverts to the earthy. The composite is a rich stew of word pictures and actions.

Herbert saw the hand of God everywhere, in everything, in "fish and flesh; bats, bird and beast; sponges, nonsense and sense; mines, th' earth and plants," in the vast expanse of the heavens as well as in the simplest daily task. The two poems which open with the following lines have become popular hymns:

> Let all the world in every corner sing,
>   *My God and King.*

The heav'ns are not too high,
His praise may thither fly:
The earth is not too low,
His praises there may grow.

"Antiphon (I)"

Teach me, my God and King,
  In all things thee to see,
And what I do in anything,
  To do it as for thee.

"The Elixir"

Most of Herbert's poems were published a few months after his death in a collection entitled *The Temple*. Herbert had written the poems over several years, but arranged them while in Bemerton according to a scheme loosely based on the architecture of a church building. His poems are very religious, explicitly Christian, often specifically liturgical, with titles like "Church Music," "Confession," "The Pilgrimage," and "Good Friday." Although Herbert saw the hand of God everywhere, his first love was the church and he focused on the church as the theater of God's activity — its scriptures, teachings, liturgies, holy days, and seasons. It is hard to imagine a more specifically *ecclesiastical* collection of poems than *The Temple*. And yet, Herbert's poetry is also extremely personal, providing an intimate look into his soul in a way *A Priest to the Temple* does not — "a divine soul in every page," as Walton put it. Herbert cries out to Christ — in penitence, in petition, in praise — and often resorts to the device of a dramatic dialogue between Christ and himself. Although sophisticated as poems, these dialogues are lively and direct, like spontaneous conversations.

The struggle between willfulness and submission, vanity and humility, human sin and divine grace is a recurring theme in Herbert's poetry, leaving no doubt that his decision to accept appointment to an obscure country parish signaled a real and hard-won conversion of the heart:

How know I, if thou shouldst me raise,
  That I should then raise thee?
Perhaps great places and thy praise
  Do not so well agree.

61

Wherefore unto my gift I stand;
   I will no more advise:
Only do thou lend me a hand,
   Since thou hast both mine eyes.

                          "Submission"

    Joy is the distinguishing mark of Herbert's poetry, but this is not to say that every line is joyful — his sense of his own unworthiness always precedes his acceptance of God's love, and his words on that theme can be striking:

I read, and sigh, and wish I were a tree;
   For sure then I should grow
To fruit or shade: at least some bird would trust
Her household to me, and I should be just.

                          "Affliction (I)"

I know it is my sin, which locks thine ears,
   And binds thy hands,
Outcrying my requests, drowning my tears;
Or else the chillness of my faint demands.

                     "Church Lock and Key"

But the final note of Herbert's poetry is joyful praise, not human sin:

   My God, thou art all love.
   Not one poor minute scapes thy breast,
   But brings a favor from above;
And in this love, more than in bed, I rest.

                          "Evensong"

But as I raved and grew more fierce and wild
   At every word,
Me thoughts I heard one calling, *Child:*
And I replied, *My Lord.*

                        "The Collar"

    At first glance, some of Herbert's poems may seem to offer transparent insights, but Herbert is not, on the whole, an easy read. None of the metaphysical poets had the slightest interest in writing "light verse." Yet Herbert remains popular, not merely among the handful of persons who read serious poetry for pleasure, but for ordinary people as well. Is it his disarming humility? Is it his unexpected but telling images? Is it his spiritual honesty? Is it the joy that shines through his words? All of that, probably, but I think more than anything else, it is Herbert's glimpses, one after another after another, of heaven on earth. For George Herbert, heaven was not merely a distant or future reality, but an immediate, present reality, piercing and hallowing the mundane.

IN HIS OWN WORDS

Note: All prose quotations are from *A Priest to the Temple; or, The Country Parson*, first published in 1652.

God's revelation

God in all ages hath had his servants, to whom he hath revealed his truth, as well as to him; and that as one country doth not bear all things, that there may be a commerce; so neither hath God opened, or will open all to one, that there may be a traffic in knowledge between the servants of God, for the planting both of love, and humility.

Chapter 4

Good sermons

The country parson preacheth constantly, the pulpit is his joy and his throne. . . . the character of his sermon is holiness; he is not witty, or learned, or eloquent, but holy. . . . it is gained first, by choosing texts of devotion, not controversy, moving and ravishing texts, whereof the scriptures are full. Secondly, by dipping, and seasoning all our words and sentences in our hearts, before they come into our mouths, truly affecting, and cordially expressing all that we say; so that the auditors may plainly perceive that every word is heart-deep. Thirdly, by turning often, and making many apostrophes [direct addresses] to God, as, "O Lord, bless my people, and teach them this point," or, "Oh my Master, on whose errand I come, let me hold my peace, and do thou speak thyself; for thou art love, and when thou teachest, all are scholars."

Chapter 7

Know when to stop

The parson exceeds not an hour in preaching, because all ages have thought that a competency, and he that profits not in that time, will less afterwards, the same affection which made him not profit before, making him then weary, and so he grows from not relishing, to loathing.

Chapter 7

Scholars' temptation

Curiosity in prying into high speculative and unprofitable questions is another great stumbling block to the holiness of scholars.

Chapter 9

Labor

But then [the parson] admonisheth [the congregation] of two things: first, that they dive not too deep into worldly affairs, plunging themselves over head and ears into carking and caring; but that they so labor as neither to labor anxiously, nor distrustfully, nor profanely. . . . They labor anxiously when they overdo it, to the loss of their quiet and health: then distrustfully when they doubt God's providence, thinking that their own labor is the cause of their thriving, as if it were in their own hands to thrive, or not to thrive. *Then they labor profanely when they set themselves to work like brute beasts, never raising their thoughts to God, nor sanctifying their labor with daily prayer; when on the Lord's day they do unnecessary servile work, or in time of divine service on other holy days, except in the cases of extreme poverty, and in the seasons of seedtime, and harvest.* Secondly, he adviseth them so to labor for wealth and maintenance, as they make not that the end of their labor, but that they may have wherewithal to serve God the better and to do good deeds.

Chapter 14 [italics Herbert's]

To whom the preacher preaches

For in preaching to others, he forgets not himself, but is first a sermon to himself, and then to others; growing with the growth of his parish.

Chapter 21

The priest at communion

Especially at communion times he is in a great confusion, as being not only to receive God, but to break, and administer him. Neither finds he any issue in this, but to throw himself down at the throne of grace, saying, "Lord, thou knowest what thou didst, when thou appointedst it to be done thus; therefore do thou fulfill what thou didst appoint; for thou art not only the feast, but the way to it."

Chapter 22

Old customs

The country parson is a lover of old customs, if they be good, and harmless; and the rather, because country people are much addicted to them, so that to favor them therein is to win their hearts, and to oppose them therein is to deject them. If there be any ill in the custom, that may be severed from the good, he pares the apple, and gives them the clean to feed on.

Chapter 35

Prayer before sermon

Lord Jesu! Teach thou me, that I may teach them: Sanctify and enable all my powers; that in their full strength they may deliver thy message reverently, readily, faithfully, and fruitfully. Oh, make thy word a swift word, passing from the ear to the heart, from the heart to the life and conversation: that as the rain returns not empty, so neither may thy word, but accomplish that for which it is given. Oh Lord, hear, Oh Lord, forgive! Oh Lord, hearken, and do so for thy blessed Son's sake, in whose sweet and pleasing words, we say, Our Father, &c.

Redemption

Having been tenant long to a rich Lord,
   Not thriving, I resolved to be bold,
   And make a suit unto him, to afford
A new small-rented lease, and cancel the old.
In heaven at his manor I him sought:
   They told me there, that he was lately gone
   About some land, which he had dearly bought
Long since on earth, to take possession.

I straight returned, and knowing his great birth,
   Sought him accordingly in great resorts;
   In cities, theaters, gardens, parks, and courts:
At length I heard a ragged noise and mirth

   Of thieves and murderers: there I him espied,
   Who straight, "Your suit is granted," said, and died.

Easter (II)

I got me flowers to strew thy way;
I got me boughs off many a tree:
But thou wast up by break of day,
And brought'st thy sweets along with thee.

The sun arising in the east,
Though he give light, and th' east perfume;
If they should offer to contest
With thy arising, they presume.

Can there be any day but this,
Though many suns to shine endeavor?
We count three hundred, but we miss:
There is but one, and the one ever.

Matins

My God, what is a heart?
Silver, or gold, or precious stone,
Or star, or rainbow, or a part
Of all these things, or all of them in one?

My God, what is a heart,
That thou shouldst it so eye, and woo,
Pouring upon it all thy art,
As if that thou hadst nothing else to do?

Teach me thy love to know;
That this new light, which now I see,
May both the work and the workman show:
Then by a sunbeam I will climb to thee.

Trinity Sunday

Lord, who hast formed me out of mud,
And hast redeemed me through thy blood,
And sanctified me to do good;

Purge all my sins done heretofore:
For I confess my heavy score,
And I will strive to sin no more.

Enrich my heart, mouth, hands in me,
With faith, with hope, with charity;
That I may run, rise, rest with thee.

The World

Love built a stately house: where *Fortune* came,
And spinning fancies, she was heard to say,
That her fine cobwebs did support the frame,
Whereas they were supported by the same:
But *Wisdom* quickly swept them all away.

Then *Pleasure* came, who liking not the fashion,
Began to make *Balconies, Terraces,*
Till she had weak'ned all by alteration:
But reverend *laws,* and many a *proclamation*
Reformed all at length with menaces.

Then entered *Sin,* and with that sycamore,
Whose leaves first sheltered man from drought and dew,
Working and winding slyly evermore,
The inward walls and sommers cleft and tore:
But *Grace* shored these, and cut that as it grew.

Then *Sin* combined with *Death* in a firm band
To raze the building to the very floor:
Which they effected, none could them withstand.
But *Love* and *Grace* took *Glory* by the hand,
And built a braver palace than before.

The Flower

Who would have thought my shriveled heart
Could have recovered greenness? I was gone
    Quite underground; as flowers depart
To see their mother-root, when they have blown;
        Where they together
        All the hard weather,
    Dead to the world, keep house unknown.

    And now in age I bud again,
After so many deaths I live and write;

I once more smell the dew and rain,
And relish versing: Oh my only light
    It cannot be
    That I am he
On whom thy tempests fell all night.

These are thy wonders, Lord of love,
To make us see we are but flowers that glide;
    Which when we once can find and prove,
Thou hast a garden for us, where to bide.
    Who would be more,
    Swelling through store,
Forfeit their paradise by their pride.

Love (III)

Love bade me welcome: yet my soul drew back,
    Guilty of dust and sin.
But quick-eyed Love, observing me grow slack
    From my first entrance in,
Drew nearer to me, sweetly questioning
    If I lacked anything.

"A guest," I answered, "worthy to be here."
    Love said, "You shall be he."
"I, the unkind, ungrateful? Ah, my dear,
    I cannot look on thee."
Love took my hand, and smiling did reply,
    "Who made the eyes but I?"

"Truth, Lord, but I have marred them; let my shame
    Go where it doth deserve."
"And know you not," says Love, "who bore the blame?"
    "My dear, then I will serve."
"You must sit down," says Love, "and taste my meat."
    So I did sit and eat.

FOR REFLECTION AND DISCUSSION

Reflect upon a time in your life when ambition and faithfulness seemed to conflict. What did you learn from the experience? How did your resolution of it compare to Herbert's decision to be ordained and accept the call to Bemerton?

How would you describe Herbert's understanding of parish ministry? How does it compare to your understanding?

If an aspiring priest today were to ask you about *The Country Parson* as a manual for the priestly office and George Herbert as a role model, what would you say?

Look up the poems by George Herbert contained in the hymnal your church uses. What do these hymns say to you and what about them do you think led the hymnal editors to include them?

Write a few sentences about one of the poems of George Herbert and what it says to you.

Chapter 7

JEREMY TAYLOR

1613-1667

Loyalist

J EREMY TAYLOR was tall, handsome, bright, tolerant, likeable, happily married, gifted with words, and in love with God. But he was not exempt from the political and ecclesiastical upheavals of his age or from personal tragedy. He was in, then out of favor with those in power, and although admired by many in his own lifetime, Taylor died grieving and far from home.

The son of a Cambridge barber and churchwarden, Taylor studied at Cambridge University and was ordained before his twenty-first birthday. When a scheduled lecturer at St. Paul's Cathedral in London was unable to fulfill his assignment, the young Taylor was asked to fill in. News that a brilliant young preacher had arrived in town reached archbishop of Canterbury William Laud, always eager to serve as patron to clergy of the right sort. Sharing the archbishop's love of beauty and order in worship, Taylor was of the right sort. Laud arranged for Taylor to study at Oxford, a university where the archbishop's high church views were more in favor than at the more evangelical Cambridge. Taylor remained at Oxford for three years, then took a parish at Uppingham, near London. Laud also arranged for Taylor to be named one of the chaplains to King Charles I. Taylor married in 1639. His future seemed assured.

But the fierce winds blowing through the English church and state meant nothing was assured. The repressive policies of King Charles, who refused to convene Parliament for eleven years before 1640, together with the high-minded and high-handed churchmanship of Laud, infuriated the extreme Puritan party. They demanded an end to both the monarchy and church government by bishops. Civil war ensued. Parliament sent Laud to the Tower in 1641. He was executed in 1645, and the king in 1649. Bishops and the Prayer Book were abolished; Parliament now ruled England, and bickering parties among the Puritans in Parliament vied for control.

What of Jeremy Taylor and other Anglican loyalists? The middle two decades of the seventeenth century were dangerous ones for them. Taylor published a book in 1642 maintaining the divine origin of the office of bishop, which further alienated him from the Puritans. He was briefly imprisoned. But Taylor fared better than many loyalists. He found himself in south Wales in 1645 and was taken in by the earl of Carbery, at whose home, Golden Grove, he spent eight years and did much of his best writing. His wife, Phoebe, died there in 1651. Eventually, Taylor's political views resulted in a second imprisonment, for a year. Following his release, probably in 1656, Taylor remarried, providing a mother for his several children, but struggled through a time of poverty and wandering.

With the restoration of the monarchy and historic church in 1660, Taylor might have expected to be named bishop of an English diocese, but some of his writings had raised theological suspicions, even among Anglicans, and he was given instead a poor diocese in northern Ireland, inhabited largely by resolute Presbyterians who wanted nothing to do with Jeremy Taylor or any other bishop. He spent the final years of his life struggling against dogged opposition on the outskirts of the church he had loved and served. When Taylor received news that twenty-four-year-old Charles, his only living son (he had already buried six sons), had died in London, he fell ill himself and died a few days later, on August 13, 1667.

Jeremy Taylor was a gifted and prolific writer. His confidence in the goodness of the divine order did not waver, and his prose sometimes rises to luminous heights. Taylor wrote the first biography of Jesus in English, *The Great Exemplar,* an enormous book — it runs to nearly a thousand pages — in which he wove together gospel stories, meditations, theological discourses, and prayers of his own composition. While *The Book of Common Prayer* was outlawed, he composed prayers and alternative worship services in the spirit of the forbidden book.

Taylor's two most popular titles were — and remain — books of practical advice on the spiritual life, *The Rule and Exercises of Holy Living* (1650) and *The Rule and Exercises of Holy Dying* (1651). Both books embody a balanced, ordered devotion, stressing temperance and moderation — remarkable in a time of such heated controversy. Their conception of the Christian life is one of gradual growth in holiness. The latter book came six months after the death of his beloved Phoebe. Its brooding tenderness and vigorous faith have drawn readers to it for 350 years.

The blend of spiritual insight and practical application is the most distinctive feature of Taylor's writing. He could discuss theoretical issues with the brightest minds of his day, but his interest always gravitated towards the everyday lives of Christians: Does a theological idea result in a more civil and humane society? What effect does an idea have on the actual lives of people? What ideas help a Christian believer develop a deeper relationship with God? It was this practical bent and the questions it led Taylor to ask that raised eyebrows and probably led to his being denied an English bishopric after 1660.

Taylor's first book written at Golden Grove was *The Liberty of Proph-*

esying, published in 1646. It marked a shift in Taylor's thought away from Laudian rigidity, towards a religious tolerance, within broad bounds. He proposed the Apostles' Creed as a sufficient statement of Christian belief, allowing "a charitable and mutual permission to others that disagree from us and our opinions" on the interpretation of the creed and other matters "not fundamental," so long as believers did not resort to treason or sedition. Taylor pointed out that for nearly four hundred years, the early church had not buttressed its teaching by the authority of the state. This plea for toleration was based on practical considerations: Persecution, Taylor said, does not lead to holiness of life, either on the part of the persecuted or of the persecutors. Toleration was an idea whose time would not arrive until the end of the century, however, and *The Liberty of Prophesying* was not widely welcomed.

Taylor was also accused of Pelagianism. Pelagius was a British monk who lived and wrote in Rome around 400 A.D. He had said that while the active power of God, or grace, is essential for human salvation, human beings are free to take the initial steps towards salvation on their own, without benefit of grace. His theological opponent, St. Augustine, held that apart from divine grace working in the soul, human beings cannot turn to God at all. Augustine's view depended on the doctrine of "original sin," the belief that the human will is corrupted and that every human being, from the moment of conception, is trapped in a web of sin and powerless to do anything about it. To put the matter in pictorial terms, imagine yourself hanging over a cliff, clinging to a branch high above a deep abyss. Are you rescued when you cry for help and someone responds? Or does your rescue depend solely on the initiative of your rescuer? Pelagius took the former position; Augustine, the latter position.

Augustine's view had carried the day in the fifth century and became the orthodox position. But the question did not stay settled. The sixteenth-century Protestant reformers accused the medieval church of reintroducing Pelagianism by selling indulgences (a remission by the church of the penalty due to human sin) and other practices relying on human initiative. They called the church to abandon this false trust in human merit and return to relying on the grace and sovereignty of God alone. By Jeremy Taylor's day, the Reformation position, in a form based on the teaching of John Calvin and emphasizing the "total depravity" of humankind, had gained wide acceptance in England, not only among Puritans, but among Anglicans as well. It appeared in the Articles of Religion, adopted by the

English Parliament in 1571, which referred to "the fault and corruption of the nature of every man" and "this infection of nature." The Articles further affirmed that human beings cannot, solely on their own strength, turn to God and that everything depends on the merit of Christ.

Taylor's concern was, typically, practical: If people are powerless to turn to God and if everything depends on the power and grace of God, then of what use is repentance? Why try to change? Why do the right thing? Taylor held that a person is not guilty until he *chooses* evil (that is, he is not born into it) and that while sinners need God's grace, they are capable of asking for that grace. In his book *Unum Necessarium*, published in 1655, he held that the one necessity was repentance. If people are incapable even of repenting, Taylor said, then the life of holiness might as well be preached to a wolf as to a human being. He emphasized that Christian faith is more than believing the truth — it also includes doing the truth, living a Christlike life. This teaching, Taylor maintained, is consistent with the Articles of Religion.

It is well to remember Taylor's historical context. A book like *Unum Necessarium* would not have been written in 1500, but by 1655, a shift had occurred in the thinking of English Christians. Some had come to see human beings as passive, almost inert creatures, merely acted upon by God. Jeremy Taylor provided a needed balance in affirming that, even amidst desolating personal trials, one can grow in grace — and that to do so requires a decision.

IN HIS OWN WORDS

Reason

Scripture, tradition, councils, and fathers, are the evidence in a question, but reason is the judge.

The Liberty of Prophesying (1646)

Faith and charity

Faith supplies charity with argument and maintenance, and charity supplies faith with life and motion; faith makes charity reasonable, and charity makes faith living and effectual. . . . For to think well, or to have a good opinion, or an excellent or a fortunate understanding, entitles us not to the love of God and the consequent inheritance; but to choose the ways of the Spirit, and to relinquish the paths of darkness, this is the way of the kingdom, and the purpose of the gospel, and the proper work of faith.

"Discourse on Faith" in *The Great Exemplar* (1649)

The faith of devils and the faith of Christians

The faith of the devils hath more of the understanding in it, the faith of Christians more of the will; the devils in their faith have better discourse, the Christians better affections; they in their faith have better arguments, we more charity. So that charity or a good life is so necessary an ingredient into the definition of a Christian's faith, that we have nothing else to distinguish it from the faith of devils; and we need no trial of our faith but the examination of our lives.

"Discourse on Faith"

Honesty and dishonesty

The same things are honest and dishonest: the manner of doing them, and the end of the design, makes the separation.

Holy Living (1650)

God's presence

God is present by his essence; which, because it is infinite, cannot be contained within the limits of any place; and as the sun, reflecting upon the mud of strands and shores, is unpolluted in its beams, so is God not dishonored when we suppose him in every one of his creatures, and in every part of every one of them.

Holy Living

God's love of order

God is, by grace and benediction, specially present in holy places, and in the solemn assemblies of his servants. . . . God's love of order, and the reasonable customs of religion, have in ordinary, and in a certain degree, fixed this manner of his presence; and he loves to have it so.

Holy Living

Who walks with God

He walks as in the presence of God that converses with him in frequent prayer and frequent communion; in all his necessities, in all doubtings; that opens all his wants to him; that weeps before him for his sins; that asks remedy and support for his weakness; that fears him as a Judge; reverences him as a Lord; obeys him as a Father; and loves him.

Holy Living

When Taylor was deprived of his living

Let me look about me. They have left me the sun and moon, fire and water, a loving wife, and many friends to pity me, and some to relieve me, and I can still discourse; and unless I list, they have not taken away my merry countenance, and my cheerful spirit, and a good conscience: they still have left me the providence of God, and all the promises of the Gospel, and my religion, and my hopes of heaven, and my charity to them too; and still I sleep and digest, I eat and drink, I read and meditate, I can walk in my neighbor's pleasant fields, and see the varieties of natural beauties, and delight in all that in which God delights, that is, in virtue and wisdom, in the whole creation, and in God himself. And he that hath so many causes of joy and so great, is very much in love with sorrow and peevishness, who loses all these pleasures, and chooses to sit down upon his little handful of thorns.

Holy Living

Prayer for a contented spirit

O Almighty God, Father and Lord of all the creatures, by secret and undiscernible ways bringing good out of evil; give me wisdom from above; teach me to be content in all changes of person and condition, to be temperate in prosperity, and in adversity to be meek, patient, and resigned; and to look through the cloud, in the meantime doing my duty with an unwearied diligence, and an undisturbed resolution, laying up my hopes in heaven and the rewards of holy living, and being strengthened with the spirit of the inner man, through Jesus Christ our Lord. Amen.

Holy Living

Our true dwelling place

Since we stay not here, being people but of a day's abode, and our age is like that of a fly and contemporary with a gourd, we must look somewhere else for an abiding city, a place in another country to fix our house in, whose walls and foundation is God, where we must find rest, or else be restless for ever . . . we must carry up our affections to the mansions prepared for us above, where eternity is the measure, felicity is the state, angels are the company, the Lamb is the light, and God is the portion and inheritance.

Holy Dying (1651)

Prayer for a holy life

O do unto thy servant as thou usest to do unto those that love thy name; let thy truth comfort me, thy mercy deliver me, thy staff support me, thy grace sanctify my sorrow, and thy goodness pardon all my sins, thy angels guide me with safety in this shadow of death, and thy most holy spirit lead me into the land of righteousness, for thy name's sake, which is so comfortable, and for Jesus Christ his sake, our dearest Lord and most gracious Savior. Amen.

Holy Dying

Marriage

[Marriage] hath in it the labor of love, and the delicacies of friendship, the blessing of society, and the union of hands and hearts; it hath in it less of beauty, but more of safety, than the single life; it hath more care, but less danger; it is more merry, and more sad; is fuller of sorrows, and fuller of joys; it lies under more burdens, and it is supported by all the strengths of love and charity, and those burdens are delightful.

Sermon, "The Marriage Ring" (1653)

The wrong questions

It is a very great fault amongst a very great part of Christians, that in their inquiries of religion, even the best of them ordinarily ask but these two questions, "Is it lawful? Is it necessary?" If they find it lawful, they will do it without scruple or restraint; and then they suffer imperfection, or receive the reward of folly: for it may be lawful, and yet not fit to be done. . . . And as great an error is on the other hand in the other question. He that too strictly inquires of an action whether it be necessary or no, would do well to ask also whether it be good: whether it be of advantage to the interest of his soul? . . . If a Christian will do no more than what is necessary, he will quickly be tempted to omit something of that also.

Unum Necessarium (1655)

A prayer of confession

O eternal God, gracious and merciful, the fountain of pardon and holiness, hear the cries and regard the supplications of thy servant. I have gone astray all my ways, and I will for ever pray unto thee and cry mightily for pardon. . . . I humbly confess my sins to thee, do thou hide them from all the world; and while I mourn for them, let the angels rejoice; and while I am killing them by the aids of thy spirit, let me be written in the book of life, and my sins be blotted out of the black registers of death; that my sins being covered and cured, dead and buried in the grave of Jesus, I may live to thee my God a life of righteousness, and grow in it till I shall arrive at a state of glory.

Unum Necessarium

The good person

He is a truly charitable and good man, who when he receives injuries, grieves rather for the malice of him that injures him, than for his own suffering; who willingly prays for him that wrongs him, and from his heart forgives all his faults; who stays not, but quickly asks pardon of others for his errors or mistakes; who sooner shows mercy than anger; who thinks better of others than himself; who offers violence to his appetite, and in all things endeavors to subdue the flesh to the spirit.

The Golden Grove (1657)

The judgment that matters

Take not much care what, or who is for thee, or against thee. The judgment of none is to be regarded, if God's judgment be otherwise. Thou art neither better nor worse in thyself for any account that is made of thee by any but by God alone: secure that to thee, and he will secure all the rest.

The Golden Grove

Taylor's purpose

My purpose is not to dispute, but to persuade; not to confute anyone, but to instruct those that need; not to make a noise, but to excite devotion.

The Worthy Communicant (1660)

The test of true religion

The way to judge of religion is by doing of our duty; and theology is rather a divine life than a divine knowledge. In heaven indeed we shall first see, and then love; but here on earth we must first love, and love will open our eyes as well as our hearts, and we shall then see and perceive and understand.

Sermon, "Via Intelligentiae" (1662)

The things of God

There is in the things of God to them which practice them a deliciousness that makes us love them, and that love admits us into God's cabinet, and strangely clarifies the understanding by the purification of the heart.

"Via Intelligentiae"

The Trinity

No man can be convinced well and wisely of the article of the holy, blessed, and undivided Trinity, but he that feels the mightiness of the Father begetting him to a new life, the wisdom of the Son building him up in a most holy faith, and the love of the Spirit of God making him to become like unto God.

"Via Intelligentiae"

FOR REFLECTION AND DISCUSSION

Religious tolerance has become the norm in the Western world since Taylor's day. Should there be limits to religious tolerance?

Can a person turn to God prior to receiving divine grace, or is the act of turning to God evidence of grace already at work? What in your personal experience supports your view? What biblical support can you cite for your position?

Have you ever felt like an exile in your own land? How did you deal with the experience?

Read and reflect upon the prayers of Jeremy Taylor included in the quotations above. How does his spirituality inform or challenge your own?

Chapter 8

THOMAS TRAHERNE

1637-1674

Champion of Felicity

THE LITERARY WORKS of Thomas Traherne have had a strange history. Traherne published a book on forgeries by the Roman Catholic Church in 1673; a text on Christian ethics appeared two years later. Neither book made a major impact, and within a few decades, the name of Thomas Traherne was forgotten. "The centuries had drawn their curtains around him," said Bertram Dobell in 1906. The words are from Dobell's introduction to a book of Traherne's poems. The autograph copy of the poems and a prose manuscript now known as *Centuries of Meditations* were bought for a few pence at a second-hand bookshop in London in 1896, shortly before they would likely have been tossed into the rubbish. Neither text bore the name of an author. A painstaking investigation by Dobell finally revealed them to be the works of the long-forgotten Traherne. Dobell arranged for the publication of both works. Nor does the tale end there. Another Traherne manuscript was identified in 1964, and yet a fourth — longer than all the others combined — was pulled from a burning rubbish heap in South Lancashire in 1967. These works await publication.

The two Traherne works currently in print are not likely to be forgotten again. He is now recognized as one of the great poets of his era, and *Centuries* has become a devotional classic. The work consists of a series of just over four hundred brief meditations. When Traherne had written a hundred of them, he drew a line across the page and started again — hence the name *Centuries of Meditations*. The work has a rhythmic, almost hypnotic quality. Its mysteriously suggestive images linger in the mind — and soothe the troubled soul. It has been called a jewel and "one of the finest prose-poems in our language."

Traherne's writing brims with *felicity* — that is his usual word; he also calls it *blessedness* and *happiness*. It is a surprising theme coming from a man of Traherne's background. Little is known of his life, but it is clear his youth was a time of deprivation and turmoil. Traherne's father was a poor shoemaker in the rolling farm country of Hereford, a few miles from the Welsh border, and it seems his parents died when Thomas and his brother Philip were young. While still a youth, Thomas wrote, "How can I believe that [God] gave his Son to die for me who having power to do otherwise gave me nothing but rags?" He grew to maturity during a time of plague, civil war, and religious polemics — but Traherne seems to have steered his way fairly well through these swirling currents. First ordained to the Puritan ministry and appointed to a parish in Credenhill, near Hereford, he was reordained an Anglican priest after the restoration in 1660, and retained his parish. Perhaps his early experiences of adversity had taught him to seek felicity elsewhere than in controversy. In any case, when he left Credenhill in 1667 to take a chaplaincy in London and began to write his poems and *Centuries,* he not only desired felicity but had, it seems, found it. Thankfulness and joy radiate from every page. "I came into this world only that I might be happy," he wrote in *Centuries.* "And whatsoever it cost me, I will be happy. A happiness there is, and it is my desire to enjoy it." Traherne died suddenly in 1674, at the age of thirty-seven, happy but still poor — his last will and testament lists little but books.

Traherne discovered felicity in his sense of the unity of all created things with God. He was undeniably a Christian writer (his meditation on the cross is particularly striking — the cross is the "abyss of wonders, the center of desires, the throne of love"), but he does not dwell on the person of Christ. All created things point to their Creator; everything, therefore, from the smallest grain of sand to the largest heavenly body, is clothed in glory. For Traherne, the world was not, as for the Puritans, a wilderness fraught with dangers and temptations, but "the beautiful frontispiece of eternity," a theater manifesting the wonders of God, a school offering lessons in joy and delight:

How easily doth nature teach the soul!
How irresistible is her infusion!

My senses were informers to my heart,
the conduits of his glory, power, and art.

. . . in God's works are hid the excellence
of such transcendent treasures.

Traherne has been called a neo-Platonist. A group known as the Cambridge Platonists were in the forefront of English philosophical thinking at the time. They saw reason as the key to religious discernment. But Traherne had little interest in reason, nor was he a neo-Platonist if by that term is meant a view of reality that sharply distinguishes the seen from the unseen. Traherne was keenly conscious of the unseen world, but for him, the visible world was drenched in the invisible; it was almost as if the glitter of that other world had been sprinkled over this world, giving to even the most mundane object a sparkle not its own. Traherne relished the common things of everyday life, not primarily for their own sake, but as pointers to God and indications of God's love. He had little use for diamonds and pearls, gold and silver, those things "being the very refuse of nature, and the worst things in God's kingdom," though good in their proper place. For Traherne, God was far more delightfully manifest in common things — "every spire of grass," "every stone and every star," "heaven in a wild flower" — but most of all, in human beings who bear God's image and therefore partake of God's delights — "God's treasures be our treasures, and his joys our joys."

For all his appreciation of the glories manifest in the world and in human beings, however, Traherne was not oblivious to human sin. To see him as "facilely optimistic," as one commentator has done, is to misread him. An easy optimism would have been impossible for one who had experienced Traherne's childhood deprivations and the violence of the Puritan Commonwealth. He defined a Christian as "an oak flourishing in winter." He saw human beings as fallen creatures, struggling with sin, but his sense of sin was individual, not corporate. The fall was not something that occurred to the human race in some earlier age, but an event in the life of everyone now living. Traherne remembered his childhood, despite its hardships, as a time when God had walked and talked with him. Infancy for him was a time of "innocent clarity," when "all things were spotless and pure and glorious." This innocence was only later eclipsed by customs and manners, "which like contrary winds blew it out." Traherne had no use for the self-abasement which the Puritans called for. Sin was not for him a pervasive stain afflicting the human race, but "lack of sense" which causes people "to shrivel up into nothing who should be filled with the delights of ages." Release from the power of sin is within the reach of anyone who will become like a little child once more, delighting in the goodness and glory of God evident throughout the world to anyone with open eyes.

The love of God underlies everything Traherne wrote. Traherne saw all things as created by a loving God for the pleasure of human beings, and so strong was his sense of the love of God in his own life that he sometimes wrote as if the entire universe had been created specifically for him. But he never thought of himself apart from other people — if God made the universe for the pleasure of Thomas Traherne, no less had God made it for the pleasure of everyone! The love of God is so delightful that "God infinitely rejoiceth in himself for being love." God is present by love. By love is God great and glorious. By love God lives and feels in other persons. By love he is pleasing to himself. The love of God extends to all objects and creatures. The wonder of God's love is that "among innumerable millions, it maketh every one the sole and single end of all things: It attaineth all unattainables and achieveth impossibles."

Human beings not only receive this divine love, but partake of it. The love of God, being infinite, can "do infinite things for an object infinitely valued." We are "prone to love, as the sun is to shine, it being the most delightful and natural employment of the soul of man." It is here, in the love of God and the love which it elicits in return from human beings, that Traherne found the felicity he sought. When a human soul loves, it enjoys the contemplation of its own being and delightfully communicates the goodness of God to others. Love forbears and forgives. Three things, Traherne said, come to pass when a soul loves: a glorious spirit abides within, a glorious spirit flows as in a stream, and a glorious spirit resides in the one loved. Human love, though delightful in itself, is most delightful because it communicates the goodness of God.

With two unpublished Traherne manuscripts still to come, it is likely that the twenty-first century will come to an even greater appreciation of Traherne than the twentieth century. In particular, his sense of the unity of creation, of humanity as part of a larger natural order under the loving sovereignty of God, may prove a needed corrective in a world where landfills and parking lots are increasingly replacing forests and meadows and where species are dying to feed human consumption. The words of one who saw in a drop of water, a grain of sand, not something to be used, but a creature possessing "infinite excellencies," may be precisely the words which the world of a later day needs to hear.

IN HIS OWN WORDS

The Circulation

All things do first receive that give.
    Only 'tis God above,
  That from and in himself doth live,
    Whose all sufficient love

Without original can flow
And all the joys and glories show
Which mortal man can take delight to know.
He is the primitive eternal spring,
the endless ocean of each glorious thing.
The soul a vessel is,
A spacious bosom to contain
All the fair treasures of his bliss
Which run like rivers from, into the main,
And all it doth receive returns again.

Desire

For giving me desire,
An eager thirst, a burning ardent fire,
A virgin infant flame,
A love with which into the world I came,
An inward hidden heavenly love,
Which in my soul did work and move,
And ever ever me inflame
With restless longing, heavenly avarice,
That never could be satisfied,
That did incessantly a paradise
Unknown suggest, and something undescried
Discern, and bear me to it; be
Thy name for ever praised by me.

Note: The following quotations are from *Centuries of Meditations*.

The purpose of human life

The end for which you were created is that by prizing all that God hath done, you may enjoy yourself and him in blessedness.

I, 12

Loving God

The laws of God, which are the commentaries of his works, show them to be yours: because they teach you to love God with all your soul, and with all your might, whom if you love with all the endless powers of your soul, you will love him in himself, in his attributes, in his counsels, in all his works, in all his ways, and in every kind of thing wherein he appeareth, you will prize him, you will honor him, you will delight in him, you will ever desire to be with him and to please him. For to love him includeth all this. You will feed with pleasure upon every thing that is his. So that the world shall be a grand jewel of delight unto you, a very paradise, and the gate of heaven. It is indeed the beautiful frontispiece of eternity, the temple of God, the palace of his children.

I, 20

Enjoying the world

You never enjoy the world aright till the sea itself floweth in your veins, till you are clothed with the heavens, and crowned with the stars and perceive yourself to be the sole heir of the whole world: and more than so, because men are in it who are every one sole heirs, as well as you. Till you can sing and rejoice and delight in God, as misers do in gold, and kings in scepters, you never enjoy the world.

I, 29

Heaven and hell

To have blessings and to prize them is to be in heaven; to have them and not to prize them is to be in hell, I would say upon earth: To prize them and not to have them is to be in hell.

I, 47

Heir of the world

Love has a marvelous property of feeling in another. It can enjoy in another, as well as enjoy him. Love is an infinite treasure to its object, and its object is so to it. God is love, and you are his object. You are created to be his love and he is yours. He is happy in you when you are happy, as parents in their children. He is afflicted in all your afflictions. And whosoever toucheth you toucheth the apple of his eye. Will not you be happy in all his enjoyments? He feeleth in you, will not you feel in him? He hath obliged you to love him. And if you love him you must of necessity be heir of the world, for you are happy in him. All his praises are your joys, all his enjoyments are your treasures, all his pleasures are your enjoyments. In God you are crowned, in God you are concerned. In him you feel, in him you live, and move and have your being. In him you are blessed. Whatsoever therefore serveth him serveth you and in him you inherit all things.

I, 52

"All the world is yours"

The sun is but a little spark of his infinite love. The sea is but one drop of his goodness. But what flames of love ought that spark to kindle in your soul; what seas of affection ought to flow for that drop in your bosom! The heavens are the canopy and the earth is the footstool of your throne, who reign in communion with God, or at least are called so to do. How lively should his divine goodness appear unto you, how continually should it rest upon you, how deeply should it be impressed in you. Verily, its impressions ought to be so deep as to be always remaining, always felt, always admired, always seen and rejoiced in. You are never truly great till all the world is yours, and the goodness of the donor so much your joy that you think upon it all day long.

II, 14

Love

We are made to love, both to satisfy the necessity of our active nature and to answer the beauties in every creature. By love our souls are married and soldered to the creatures, and it is our duty like God to be united to them all. We must love them infinitely, but in God, and for God, and God in them, namely, all his excellencies manifest in them. When we dote upon the perfections and beauties of some one creature, we do not love that too

90

much, but other things too little. Never was anything in this world loved too much, but many things have been loved in a false way, and all in too short a measure.

II, 66

True satisfaction

The very end for which God made the world was that he might manifest his love. Unless therefore we can be satisfied with his love so manifested, we can never be satisfied.

II, 87

Loving all things properly

Suppose a river or a drop of water, an apple or a sand, an ear of corn or an herb. God knoweth infinite excellencies in it more than we. He seeth how it relateth to angels and to men, how it proceedeth from the most perfect lover to the most perfectly beloved, how it representeth all his attributes, how it conduceth in its place, by the best of means to the best of ends. And for this cause it cannot be beloved too much. God the author and God the end is to be beloved in it; angels and men are to be beloved in it; and it is highly to be esteemed for all their sakes. O what a treasure is every sand when truly understood! Who can love anything that God made too much? His infinite goodness and wisdom and power and glory are in it. What a world would this be, were every thing beloved as it ought to be!

II, 67

The source of misery

Our misery proceedeth ten thousand times more from the outward bondage of opinion and custom, than from any inward corruption or depravation of nature. And it is not our parents' loins so much as our parents' lives that enthralls and blinds us.

III, 8

The glory of God

The best of all possible ends is the glory of God, but happiness was what I thirsted after. And yet I did not err, for the glory of God is to make us happy.

III, 39

Common things

God being, as we generally believe, infinite in goodness, it is most consonant and agreeable with his nature that the best things should be most common, for nothing is more natural to infinite goodness than to make the best things most frequent, and only things worthless scarce. Then I began to inquire what things were most common: air, light, heaven and earth, water, the sun, trees, men and women, cities, temples, etc. These I found common and obvious to all. Rubies, pearls, diamonds, gold, and silver, these I found scarce, and to most denied. Then began I to consider and compare the value of them, which I measured by their serviceableness, and by the excellencies which would be found in them, should they be taken away. And in conclusion, I saw clearly that there was a real valuableness in all the common things; in the scarce, a feigned.

III, 53

Our greatest pleasure

In giving us himself, in giving us the world, in giving us our souls and bodies, [God] hath done much, but all this had been nothing unless he had given us a power to have given him ourselves, in which is contained the greatest pleasure and honor that is.

IV, 45

Like a mirror

As a mirror returneth the very selfsame beams it receiveth from the sun, so the soul returneth those beams of love that shine upon it from God. For as a looking glass is nothing in comparison of the world, yet containeth all the world in it, and seems a real fountain of those beams which flow from it, so the soul is nothing in respect of God, yet all eternity is contained in it, and it is the real fountain of that love that proceedeth from it. They are the sunbeams which the glass returneth, yet they flow from the glass and from the sun within it. The mirror is the wellspring of them, because they shine from the sun within the mirror, which is as deep within the glass as it is high within the heavens. And this showeth the exceeding richness and preciousness of love. It is the love of God shining upon and dwelling in the soul, for the beams that shine upon it reflect upon others and shine from it.

IV, 84

The absence of God

All sorrows should appear but shadows beside that of [God's] absence. And all the greatness of riches and estates swallowed up in the light of his favor

IV, 91

FOR REFLECTION AND DISCUSSION

As a youngster, Traherne had asked, "How can I believe that [God] gave his Son to die for me who having power to do otherwise gave me nothing but rags?" How do you think the mature Traherne would have dealt with this question?

Define happiness and say something about how to find it.

What are the implications of Traherne's writings for Christian stewardship?

In your opinion, why does the world value most what Traherne valued least?

What do you feel Traherne meant in saying that the earth is the footstool of *our* throne?

What do you think of the statement that the glory of God is to make us happy? What does this statement imply about the nature of God?

Chapter 9

WILLIAM LAW

1686-1761

Commando in the Chapel of Ease

Pow! Bam! Whack! Like a superhero battling the archfiend, William Law flays the demon of superficial religion. No ambiguity, no middle ground, no compromising — just one clear choice, either right or wrong, love of God or love of this world, obedience or else.

Such at least has been the reputation of William Law for three centuries, based almost entirely on a single book, *A Serious Call to a Devout and Holy Life*. Published in 1729, it has never been out of print. Samuel Johnson found it "an overmatch for me," challenging him for the first time to take his faith seriously, and John Wesley said it would never be excelled "either for beauty of expression, or for justness and depth of thought." A century later, John Keble said that to label *A Serious Call* "a clever book" was like calling Judgment Day "a pretty sight," and C. S. Lewis said reading it made him feel "pierced" like a butterfly on a card.

Eighteenth-century England needed such a book. As the nation became more prosperous and powerful, the fractious religious passions of the past were largely set aside in favor of a sometimes bland, lethargic, and complacent tolerance. Church attendance remained high among the well-to-do, but any hint of enthusiasm was frowned upon. Ordination was seen as a suitable profession for the second son of a landed family, regardless of his sanctity. Preachers often assured worshipers that so long as they said their prayers, behaved decently, and gave something to the poor, all would be well and God would be pleased. The publication of *A Serious Call* was like a grenade hurled into this complacent scene. No reader of the book, then or now, is unfazed.

A Serious Call builds upon (but does not repeat) a book Law had published three years earlier entitled *Christian Perfection*. Both books are addressed to avowed Christians. Law assumes at least a perfunctory commitment to the church on the part of his reader; no attempt is made to explain Christian faith to doubters or unbelievers. The main thrust of both books is the same: Christian devotion concerns not merely religious exercises and good works, but the whole of life — our use of time and money, every relationship, every thought and deed. It is a life totally given to God and thereby transformed into the likeness of Jesus Christ. When Law looked out at the world around him, he saw little of such devotion. The reason, he said, was not that professing Christians didn't understand the will of God or were too weak to obey God, but that they never intended to. Law cuts straight through to the place where sin originates — the human will. He strips the soul bare of its self-justifying pretenses. The problem is not inadvertent oversights or slips of behavior, but a paralysis of intention.

Law writes to the Christian whose religion is an add-on to a life already full of other concerns. A devotion consisting only of Sunday worship, private prayers, and occasional charitable acts will not suffice. This does not mean that acts of piety were unimportant to Law. He himself was faithful in prayers and public worship, and he includes a helpful "how to" section on prayer in *A Serious Call*. The bottom line for Law is that a Christian is called to emulate Jesus Christ in *all* of life, and Law is certain that anyone who truly desires to emulate Christ can do so. He makes allowance for human frailty, but not as an excuse for laziness or lack of intention. We will be judged, he says, not on whether we have always lived up to our intentions, but on whether our intentions were the best they could possibly be.

The chief difference between *Christian Perfection* and *A Serious Call* is the series of vivid caricatures with which Law illustrates the latter work. These caricatures are like cartoons, slightly overstated, but realistic enough to nail home the point, and all the more telling for their exaggerated details. It is a brilliant literary device, drawing the reader into the book and stirring the imagination, even as Law drives home a message the reader would rather not hear. So entertaining are these caricatures that it is almost impossible to grow angry at Law, even as he fillets your soul. Law's caricatures can leap into the twenty-first century with all their powers intact. While Law offers portraits of both faithful and unfaithful Christians, the unfaithful ones pack the most punch. We meet distracted Calidus, perpetually doing business; stylish Flavia, often at church and always well dressed; prosperous Flatus, seeking happiness in gambling, drinking, hunting, building, and travel, but never finding it; worldly Cognatus, a clergyman who pays as much heed to his investments as to the gospel; and practical Mundanus, who passes by both devotional and spelling books "because he remembers that he learned to pray, so many years ago, under his mother, when he learned to spell." Characters such as these, sprinkled throughout *A Serious Call*, seem familiar to many a modern churchgoer, strangely suggesting the person in the next pew, or even the person in the mirror.

William Law lived what he wrote, never one to compromise a principle, even at great cost to himself. Ordained in 1711 and awarded his M.A. from Emmanuel College, Cambridge, the next year, he seemed on the fast track for a prominent ecclesiastical post. But in 1714 he refused to swear allegiance to King George I, knowing this would bar him from a career in the church. For the rest of his life, Law never served a parish, making his living as a tutor and writer. He wrote his brother at the time that although his prospects for a church career were "melancholy," yet his education would have been "miserably lost if I had not learnt to fear something more than misfortune."

Years later, now well known as the author of *A Serious Call*, Law was approached by a stranger while standing outside a London shop. "Are you, sir, the Reverend William Law?" the stranger asked. Law answered that he was. The stranger then handed Law an envelope containing 1,000 pounds sterling, a huge sum in those days (Samuel Johnson lived comfortably a few years later on a pension of 300 pounds a year). Law used the money to found, endow, and run a school for fourteen young indigent women in the Northampton village of King's Cliffe, where he had grown up.

Law later returned from London to King's Cliffe, where he spent the final twenty-two years of his life in a semi-monastic setting, with two devout women, for whom he served as spiritual director. The two women were wealthy — their combined income ran to 2,500 pounds per year — yet the three lived frugally, giving away ninety percent of their income to the indigent. So generous were they that King's Cliffe became a magnet for beggars. This displeased the townspeople, including the rector of the village church, who often rebuked Law from the pulpit. In 1753, the rector and other townspeople, tired of itinerant mendicants in the village square, approached the local magistrate to compel Law and his two companions to leave town, creating what must have been a curious if not bizarre scene — a priest of the church suing his parishioners to restrain them from acts of mercy. The controversy died down, apparently, for Law and the two women remained in King's Cliffe, continuing to give most of their money away.

William Law has never lacked for critics. He has been called stern, dour, coldly rational, and advocating a righteousness based on legalism and good works. But these accusations miss the mark. Although denied the career he sought and distrusted in his home town, Law was never bitter. It was only rebellion against God, he said in *A Serious Call*, that caused "imaginary wants and vain disquiets," while the life of devotion offered "the greatest peace and happiness."

It is William Law's later — and rarely read — works that prove beyond doubt that those who see him as legalistic and dour are mistaken. Sometime in the 1730s, Law read the works of the German peasant mystic Jakob

Boehme. Boehme provided the impetus for Law, already familiar with classical mystical writings, to explore a warmer, even rhapsodic region of his soul. Law never recanted anything he had written earlier, and the difference between his earlier and later writings is merely one of emphasis — but it is a marked difference. He continues to stress self-renunciation and the importance of emulating Christ, but the tone has changed. The later works are often lyrical, soaring, luxurious. Prayer continues to be a main theme, but there is now less on the technique of prayer and more on the spirit of prayer. Christ is discussed more as an indwelling presence in the believer's heart, imparting to the believer a real change of life. There is a new emphasis on the sacraments (which are not even mentioned in *A Serious Call*). The soul is seen not as created by God from nothing, but as an eternal spark of the divine. The love of God is celebrated again and again, even to the point of saying the "wrath of God" is found not in God, but in the unfaithful heart. Law has been accused of believing that everyone will be saved, and he comes close to saying this in his later works, but he always affirmed that the atonement, though a fact for everyone, must be embraced to take effect.

Of all his writings, two of Law's later works, *The Spirit of Prayer* (1749) and *The Spirit of Love* (1752), were his own favorites. The structure of both books is awkward, relying on the clumsy device of long conversations among fictitious characters. These conversations do not work. The reader of these works may heed only the speeches of Theophilus, whose voice represents Law. These speeches contain passages of extraordinary, numinous prose which have caused more than one commentator to judge *The Spirit of Love* as Law's greatest book.

IN HIS OWN WORDS

One standard for all

This is the perfection which this treatise endeavors to recommend — a perfection that does not consist in any singular state or condition of life, or in any particular set of duties, but in the holy and religious conduct of ourselves in every state of life. It calls no one to a cloister, but to a full performance of those duties which are necessary for all Christians and common to all states of life.

Christian Perfection (1726)

Pointless laboring

How many things in life do people labor after which, when gotten, are as much real use to them as a staff and shoes to a corpse underground?

Christian Perfection

Friendship and devotion

Friendship does not require us to be always waiting upon our friends in external services; these have their times and seasons of intermission. It is only the service of the heart, the friendship of the mind that is never to intermit. It is not to begin and end as external services do, but is to persevere in a constancy like the motion of the heart, or the beating of the pulse. It is just so in devotion. Prayers have their hours, their beginning and ending, but the disposition of the heart towards God, which is the life and spirit of prayer, is to be as constant and lasting as our own life and spirit.

Christian Perfection

True devotion

Devotion is neither private nor public prayer, but prayers, whether private or public, are particular parts or instances of devotion. Devotion signifies a life given, or devoted, to God. He, therefore, is the devout man, who lives no longer to his own will, or the way of the world, but to the sole will of God; who serves God in everything, who makes all the parts of his common life parts of piety, by doing everything in the name of God, and under such rules as are conformable to his glory.

A Serious Call (1729)

What are your intentions?

It may now be reasonably inquired, how it comes to pass, that the lives even of the better sort of people are thus strangely contrary to the principles of Christianity. It is because men have not so much as the intention to please God in all their actions. . . . And if you will here stop, and ask yourselves, why you are not as pious as the primitive Christians were, your own heart will tell you, that it is neither through ignorance nor inability, but purely because you never thoroughly intended it.

A Serious Call

Falling short

You perhaps will say that all people fall short of the perfection of the gospel, and therefore you are content with your failings. . . . The question is not whether gospel perfection can be fully attained, but whether you come as near it as a sincere intention and careful diligence can carry you.

A Serious Call

Calidus

Calidus has traded above thirty years in the greatest city of the kingdom. Every hour of the day is with him an hour of business, and though he eats and drinks very heartily, yet every meal seems to be in a hurry, and he would say grace if he had time. Calidus ends every day at the tavern, but has not leisure to be there till near nine o'clock. He is always forced to drink a good hearty glass, to drive thoughts of business out of his head, and make his spirits drowsy enough for sleep. He does business all the time that he is rising, and has settled several matters before he can get to his counting-room. His prayers are a short ejaculation or two, which he never misses in stormy, tempestuous weather, because he has always something or other at sea. Calidus will tell you, with great pleasure, that he has been in this hurry for so many years, and that it must have killed him long ago, but that it has been a rule with him to get out of the town every Saturday, and make the Sunday a day of quiet, and good refreshment in the country. . . .

Now this way of life is at such a distance from all the doctrine and discipline of Christianity, that no one can live in it through ignorance or frailty. Calidus can no more imagine that he is "born again of the Spirit," that he lives here as a stranger and a pilgrim, setting his affection on things above and laying up treasures in heaven — he can no more imagine this, than he can think that he has been all his life an apostle working miracles and preaching the gospel.

A Serious Call

Fiscal madness

If a man had eyes and hands and feet that he could give to those that needed them, if he should either lock them up in a chest or please himself with some needless or ridiculous use of them instead of giving them to his brethren that were blind and lame, should we not justly reckon him an inhuman wretch? If he should rather choose to amuse himself with furnishing his house with those things than to entitle himself to an eternal reward by giving them to those that needed eyes and hands, might we not justly reckon him mad? Now money has very much the nature of eyes and feet. If we either lock it up in chests or waste it in needless and ridiculous ornaments of apparel, while others are starving in nakedness, we are not far from the cruelty of him that chooses rather to adorn his house with the hands and eyes than to give them to those that need them.

A Serious Call

A hidden danger

The world, by professing Christianity, is so far from being a less dangerous enemy than it was before, that it has by its favors destroyed more Christians than ever it did by the most violent persecution. It is a greater enemy because it has greater power over Christians by its favors, riches, honors, rewards, and protection than it had by the fire and fury of its persecutions. It is a more dangerous enemy by having lost its appearance of enmity. Its outward profession of Christianity makes it no longer considered as an enemy, and therefore the generality of people are easily persuaded to resign themselves up to be governed and directed by it.

A Serious Call

The Incarnation

God became man, took upon him a birth from the fallen nature. But why was this done? . . . It is because nothing less than this mysterious Incarnation (which astonishes angels) could open a way, or begin a possibility, for fallen man to be born again from above, and made again a partaker of the divine nature.

The Spirit of Prayer (1749)

A similitude

A grain of wheat has the air and light of this world enclosed or incorporated in it. This is the mystery of its life, this is the power of growing, by this it has a strong continual tendency of uniting again with that ocean of light and air from whence it came forth, and so it helps to kindle its own vegetable life. On the other hand, that great ocean of light and air, having its own offspring hidden in the heart of the grain, has a perpetual strong tendency to unite and communicate with it again. From this desire of union on both sides, the vegetable life arises and all the virtues and powers contained in it. But here let it be well observed that this desire on both sides cannot have its effect till the husk and gross part of the grain falls into a state of corruption and death. Till this begins, the mystery of life hidden in it cannot come forth. The application here may be left to the reader.

The Spirit of Prayer

The nature of God

As certainly as [God] is the creator, so certainly is he the blesser of every created thing, and can give nothing but blessing, goodness, and happiness from himself because he has in himself nothing else to give. It is much more possible for the sun to give forth darkness than for God to do, or be, or give forth anything but blessing and goodness.

The Spirit of Love (1753)

The greatest blessing

Would you know the blessing of all blessings? It is this God of love dwelling in your soul and killing every root of bitterness which is the pain and torment of every earthly, selfish love. For all wants are satisfied, all disorders of nature are removed, no life is any longer a burden, every day is a day of peace, everything you meet becomes a help to you because everything you see or do is all done in the sweet, gentle element of love. For as love has no by-ends, wills nothing but its own increase, so everything is as oil to its flame. . . . And therefore it meets wrath and evil and hatred and opposition with the same one will as the light meets the darkness, only to overcome it with all its blessings.

The Spirit of Love

Nature

Look at all nature, through all its height and depth, in all its variety of working powers; it is what it is for this only end, that the hidden riches, the invisible powers, blessings, glory, and love of the unsearchable God may become visible, sensible, and manifest in it and by it.

The Spirit of Love

FOR REFLECTION AND DISCUSSION

What parallels do you see between eighteenth-century England and where you live? What elements of Law's message apply here and now?

Do you agree that the main reason more Christians are not truly devout is that they don't intend to be? If you agree, what do they intend, and why are they in church at all?

What would an impartial evaluation of your life reveal your intentions to be?

What reasons might the rector of King's Cliffe have given in 1753 for asking Law and his companions to leave town? Do you agree with him?

What might account for the difference between Law's early and his late writings?

List some things which might serve as an answer to this question: "How many things in life do people labor after which, when gotten, are as much real use to them as a staff and shoes to a corpse underground?"

What evidence might be cited to support Law's comments on "a hidden danger"?

Chapter 10

JOSEPH BUTLER

1692-1752

The Thinking Man's Bishop

O NE HUNDRED FIFTY years ago, Joseph Butler's *The Analogy of Religion* was read by (or at least assigned to) all aspiring clergymen, and summaries of the book — crib notes — can still be found in the stacks of seminary libraries. John Henry Newman, writing at the time, called Butler "the greatest name in the Anglican Church." But today, Butler's rigorously rational approach to theology and morals is no longer in vogue, and he is not so widely appreciated. Such are the whims of theological fashion.

The early eighteenth century was the height of the Age of Reason. Two centuries earlier, Protestant reformers had encouraged people to read their Bibles and think for themselves, and Richard Hooker had then pointed to reason as the interpreter of scripture. But the reformers and Hooker would have cringed at what later thinkers would say about reason. One of the theological expressions of the Age of Reason is called deism. The main outlines of deism can be seen as early as 1624 with the publication of *De veritate,* by Edward, Lord Herbert of Cherbury (the older brother of poet George Herbert). Herbert identified five "notions" which he said comprise true religion: (1) There is a supreme God. (2) This God should be worshiped. (3) Virtue should be cultivated. (4) Wickedness is abolished by repentance and faith in God. (5) There are rewards and punishments after this life. These five notions, Herbert said, are "derived from the evidence of immediate perception and admitted by the whole world" — that is to say, the human mind can figure them out on its own, without the aid of a Bible or special revelation.

Later thinkers, invigorated by the new Newtonian physics, with its orderly and understandable universe, went far beyond Herbert. John Toland published *Christianity Not Mysterious* in 1696. In his view, a mystery was not a truth beyond human understanding — there were no such truths — but merely a truth which not everyone yet recognized. Mysteries would be eliminated by the proper application of human reason (a viewpoint that would eventually lead to scientific secularism and its assumption that human beings can manipulate and control nature). Toland, although a clergyman in the Church of England, threw out much of historic Christian belief as contrary to reason — revealed truth, the Trinity, the Incarnation and Atonement, sacraments, the power of prayer. What, then, was left? — and did it bear any resemblance to historic Christianity? Had the deists, as they claimed, liberated Christianity from the oppressive weight of authority and superstition, or had they gutted the Christian faith? To some, the deist gospel tasted like a chowder without the clams and vegetables — why bother with it?

It was into this world that Joseph Butler was born. The son of Presbyterian parents, he converted to the Church of England as a young man and was ordained priest in 1718. He was preacher at London's Rolls Chapel from 1718 to 1726, where his sermons gained him a reputation as a moral philosopher. He later served as bishop of Bristol and, for the two years prior to his death, as bishop of Durham. Private and bookish by nature, Butler never married and lived a simple, austere life.

Butler was not a prolific writer, publishing only two works (he instructed that upon his death, everything else he had written be burned). In both of them, he sought to make sense of Christianity to sophisticated unbelievers by demonstrating that Christian faith was consistent with reason. His first work, *Fifteen Sermons,* published in 1726, has had a lasting influence in moral philosophy and is today more widely appreciated than the *Analogy.* Butler sought in his sermons to expound the ways of God in terms of human nature. The gloomy Thomas Hobbes, writing a century earlier, had argued that all human behavior was motivated by selfishness, but Butler believed people were motivated by a higher purpose. Human beings know right from wrong, he said. Love — of self, of neighbor, of the created universe, of God — brings fulfillment and happiness. In his sermons Butler developed a moral psychology by identifying five faculties of the human mind: appetites (physical desires), passions (mental or emotional desires), benevolence (concern for others), self-love (concern for self), and conscience (the ruling faculty which sorts through the other four and decides what is right). Self-love, Butler said, is a good and natural thing which, together with benevolence, provides a solid grounding for human behavior, with conscience both analyzing situations to determine the right action and exercising the authority to mandate that action. Vice, he said, is contrary to human nature. Butler was seeking to restore a sense of larger purpose to the eighteenth-century world of rational science and competitive commerce. This larger purpose was the mystery of divine love.

The last three of Butler's *Fifteen Sermons* disclose the personal dimension of his faith. Here Butler writes of the love of God and of humanity's response. It is natural, he says, that we love, revere, and fear God, and most importantly, resign ourselves to the divine will. We must not seek answers to questions beyond our understanding, but yield and submit to God, trusting that God is good. By accepting the limitations of our knowledge, we will never be surprised to encounter things incomprehensible to us and readily acknowledge realities unseen. Only in this way will we find peace and contentment, Butler says.

The Analogy of Religion, Natural and Revealed, to the Constitution and Course of Nature, published in 1736, remains Butler's most famous (if rarely read) work. The full title is important. It tells us precisely what Butler set out to do and how he did it: An analogy is a likeness. Butler examined the natural order, as something his contemporaries felt they knew and understood, and pointed to ways that religion, less easily known and understood, was like nature. He included both natural religion (the knowledge of God which unaided reason can discern), and revealed religion (knowledge of God known only through divine revelation). Butler's purpose in writing was, in fact, to demonstrate to intellectuals of the day who prized reason but scoffed at revelation that *revelation* was *reasonable.* Butler did not set out to *prove* the truth of Christian revelation, but to show that Christian revelation was compatible with reason, and therefore *likely* to be true.

The Analogy of Religion is in two parts. The first shows how the concepts of natural religion, accepted by the deists, are like the phenomena of nature; the second shows how the revealed truths of Christianity, rejected by the deists, are also like the phenomena of nature.

The opening chapter of the *Analogy,* entitled "Of a Future Life," provides an example of Butler's method. He says it is a general law of nature that living things, including human beings, undergo changes — worms change into flies; eggs hatch into birds. As they grow older, creatures also acquire knowledge and skills that would have been beyond their ability at a younger age. By analogy with nature, therefore, it is reasonable to believe that death is another such change, from one stage of existence to another. Moreover, the natural phenomena of sleep and swoons demonstrate that mental capacities continue in existence when the body is not exercising them. By analogy, therefore, it is reasonable to believe that our mental capacities will continue after the body dies. Most deists would not have quarreled with this, and by similar analogies, Butler argues for other truths of "natural religion" acknowledged by the deists.

In the second part of the *Analogy,* however, Butler takes on the deists with regard to revealed truth. He begins with a discussion of the importance of Christianity. First, it proclaims the truths of natural religion in an authoritative manner. This is important because although such truths are apparent to reason, most people do not exercise their rational powers to the fullest and therefore miss the truths of reason. But beyond confirming what reason already knows, Christianity also includes special, revealed truths which reason could never discern on its own. Revealed truths include the trinitarian nature of God, the incarnation of the Son of God in the person of Jesus, and the salvation of humankind. The character of revealed truth (though not its content) is also reasonable, based on the analogy to nature. For example, some deists pointed to the apparently foolish, inconsistent, and unconvincing features of the Bible and questioned why God, seeking to reveal truths to human beings, would choose such a faulty means of communicating them. This should surprise no one, Butler said, because something analogous is found in nature. Natural phenomena such as intuition, language, and the capacity of human beings to invent things would seem unlikely and are fraught with limitations and ambiguities. It is therefore reasonable to assume, Butler said, that were God to disclose himself by means of revelation, similar limitations and ambiguities would attend such revelation.

It is often pointed out that while Butler wrote against the deists, he had much in common with them. Like the deists, he often wrote about abstractions such as religion, truth, and deity rather than in more personal ways. The most famous incident in his life is reported by John Wesley in the latter's journal. Butler, bishop of Bristol at the time, encountered the young Wesley preaching to coal miners in an open field. Wesley claimed to have been inspired by the Holy Spirit. Butler said to him, "Sir, the pretending to extraordinary revelations and gifts of the Holy Spirit is a horrid thing, a very horrid thing!" Butler then pointed out to Wesley that he was not licensed to preach in the Diocese of Bristol and told him to move along. It is not difficult to imagine this scene. Butler was a logical and measured thinker. Wesley's spontaneous enthusiasm cannot but have alarmed him.

Joseph Butler is an example of a type found in every period of Anglican history — the thinker seeking to restate the Christian gospel in terms meaningful to the age in which he lives. Such efforts are often controversial at the time, and the writings of such thinkers are not always appreciated by readers of a later time, when attitudes and assumptions may have shifted. The confidence in human reason which Butler shared with others of his day may seem implausible today, after a century of world wars, genocides, and environmental destruction. But we all live within the thought forms of our time, and in every age an effort must be made to restate the gospel for a new generation. Butler is perhaps the most brilliant and scrupulous exemplar of this honorable tradition.

IN HIS OWN WORDS

Self-love

The thing to be lamented is not that men have so great regard to their own good or interest in the present world, for they have not enough; but that they have so little to the good of others. . . . Upon the whole, if the generality of mankind were to cultivate within themselves the principle of self-love, if they were to accustom themselves often to set down and consider what was the greatest happiness they were capable of attaining for themselves in this life, and if self-love were so strong and prevalent as that they would uniformly pursue this their supposed chief temporal good, without being diverted from it by any particular passion, it would manifestly prevent numberless follies and vices.

Fifteen Sermons, Preface (1726)

Benevolence and self-love

There is a natural principle of *benevolence* in man; which is in some degree to *society,* what *self-love* is to the *individual.* And if there be in mankind any disposition to friendship; if there be any such thing as compassion, for compassion is momentary love; if there be any such thing as the paternal or filial affections; if there be any affection in human nature the object and end of which is the good of another — this is itself benevolence or the love of another. . . . I must however remind you that though benevolence and self-love are different, though the former tends most directly to public good and the latter to private, yet they are so perfectly coincident that the greatest satisfactions to ourselves depend upon our having benevolence in a due degree, and that self-love is one chief security of our right behavior toward society.

Sermon No. 1

Conscience

But there is a superior principle of reflection or conscience in every man, which distinguishes between the internal principles of his heart, as well as his external actions: which passes judgment upon himself and them; pronounces determinately some actions to be in themselves just, right, good; others to be in themselves evil, wrong, unjust: which, without being consulted, without being advised with, magisterially exerts itself, and approves or condemns him the doer of them accordingly. . . . It is by this faculty, natural to man, that he is a moral agent, that he is a law to himself . . . considered as a faculty in kind and in nature supreme over all others, and which bears its own authority of being so.

Sermon No. 2

Conscience and self-love

Conscience does not only offer itself to show us the way we should walk in, but it likewise carries its own authority with it, that it is our natural guide; the guide assigned us by the Author of our nature: it therefore belongs to our condition of being, it is our duty to walk in that path, and follow this guide, without looking about to see whether we may not possibly forsake them with impunity. . . . Conscience and self-love, if we understand our true happiness, always lead us the same way.

Sermon No. 3

Christian religion

Christianity lays us under new obligations to a good life, as by it the will of God is more clearly revealed, and as it affords additional motives to the practice of it, over and above those which arise out of the nature of virtue and vice; I might add, as our Savior has set us a perfect example of goodness in our own nature. Now love and charity is plainly the thing in which he hath placed his religion; in which, therefore as we have any pretense to the name of Christians, we must place ours.

Sermon No. 11

Resignation

Resignation to the will of God is the whole of piety: It includes in it all that is good, and is a source of the most settled quiet and composure of mind. . . . Thus is human nature formed to compliance, yielding, submission of temper. . . . Nature teaches and inclines us to take up with our lot. The consideration that the course of things is unalterable hath a tendency to quiet the mind under it, to beget a submission of temper to it. But when we can add that this unalterable course is appointed and continued by infinite wisdom and goodness, how absolute should be our submission, how entire our trust and dependence! . . . Our resignation to the will of God may be said to be perfect when our will is lost and resolved up into his, when we rest in his will as our end, as being itself most just and right and good.

Sermon No. 14

True devotion

This is piety and religion in the strictest sense, considered as an habit of mind, an habitual sense of God's presence with us, being affected towards him, as present, in the manner his superior nature requires from such a creature as man: this is to *walk with God*. . . . Devotion is retirement from the world [God] has made, to him alone: it is to withdraw from the avocations of sense, to employ our attention wholly upon him as upon an object actually present, to yield ourselves up to the influence of the divine presence, and to give full scope to the affections of gratitude, love, reverence, trust, and dependence, of which infinite power, wisdom, and goodness is the natural and only adequate object.

Sermon No. 14

Clouds and darkness

The Almighty may cast clouds and darkness round about him, for reasons and purposes of which we have not the least glimpse or conception.

Sermon No. 15

Our province

Other orders of creatures may perhaps be let into the secret counsels of heaven and have the designs and methods of Providence in the creation and government of the world communicated to them, but this does not belong to our rank or condition. *The fear of the Lord and to depart from evil* is the only wisdom which man should aspire after, as his work and happiness. . . . Our province is virtue and religion, life and manners, the science of improving the temper and making the heart better. This is the field assigned to us to cultivate; how much it has lain neglected is indeed astonishing.

Sermon No. 15

The force of the *Analogy*

The force of analogy is this, that it refers what is doubtful to something like it, which is not in question, that it may prove things uncertain by things certain.

The Analogy of Religion, title page (1736)

Virtue and vice

Tranquility, satisfaction, and external advantages, being the natural consequences of prudent management of ourselves, and our affairs; and rashness, profligate negligence, and willful folly, bringing after them many inconveniences and sufferings; these afford instances of a right constitution of nature. . . . In the natural course of things virtue *as such* is actually rewarded, and vice *as such* punished; which seems to afford an instance or example, not only of government, but of moral government.

The Analogy

Visible and invisible things

And suppose the invisible world and the invisible dispensations of Providence to be in any sort analogous to what appears, or that both together make up one uniform scheme, the two parts of which, the part which we see, and that which is beyond our observation, are analogous to each other, then there must be a like natural tendency in the derived power throughout the universe, under the direction of virtue, to prevail in general over that which is not under its direction, as there is in reason, derived reason in the universe, to prevail over brute force.

The Analogy

Importance of Christianity

But the importance of Christianity will more distinctly appear by considering it more distinctly: *First,* as a republication and external institution of natural or essential religion, adapted to the present circumstances of mankind, and intended to promote natural piety and virtue; and *secondly,* as containing an account of a dispensation of things not discoverable by reason, in consequence of which several distinct precepts are enjoined us. For though natural religion is the foundation and principal part of Christianity, it is not in any sense the whole of it.

The Analogy

On reason

I express myself with caution, lest I should be mistaken to vilify reason, which is indeed the only faculty we have wherewith to judge concerning anything, even revelation itself.

The Analogy

Religion is practical

Religion is a practical thing, and consists in such a determinate course of life, as being what, there is reason to think, is commanded by the Author of nature, and will, upon the whole, be our happiness under his government.

The Analogy

Reason for the *Analogy*

[Some people] ridicule and vilify Christianity, and blaspheme the author of it. . . . To these persons, and to this state of opinion concerning religion, the foregoing treatise is adapted. For, all the general objections against the moral system of nature having been obviated, it is shown, that there is not any peculiar presumption at all against Christianity, either considered as not discoverable by reason, or as unlike to what is so discovered; nor any worth mentioning against it as miraculous, if any at all; none, certainly, which can render it in the least incredible.

The Analogy

FOR REFLECTION AND DISCUSSION

It has been said that the faith of the typical person in the pew even today is not far from the five notions of Lord Herbert of Cherbury. Do you agree?

What is a mystery and what is the place of mystery in Christian faith?

Do you feel Butler was right in his assessment of the usefulness of self-love as a component of Christian living?

What does the word reason mean to you and how does reason function in the life of faith?

What do you think of Butler's use of nature as an analogy to religion? How does it relate to modern ecological issues?

Think of someone of your own day who is seeking to restate the Christian gospel in contemporary thought forms. Assess that person's approach to the Christian gospel.

Chapter 11

JOHN WESLEY

1703-1791

Outside Agitator

"In the evening I went very unwillingly to a society in Aldersgate Street, where one was reading Luther's preface to the Epistle to the Romans. About a quarter before nine, while he was describing the change which God works in the heart through faith in Christ, I felt my heart strangely warmed. I felt I did trust in Christ, Christ alone, for salvation; and an assurance was given me that he had taken away my sins, even mine, and saved me from the law of sin and death."

So did John Wesley describe his experience of Wednesday, May 24, 1738, at a small meeting on a London back street. It is possible to make too much or too little of this experience. Wesley never wrote of it again and he didn't call it his "conversion." He had a few other moments of spiritual intensity before and after his Aldersgate experience and he was no stranger to religious work at the time, having been ordained for over a decade and having returned four months earlier from a (hugely unsuccessful) missionary journey to Savannah, Georgia. But without doubt, Aldersgate was a turning point for John Wesley. The tone and emphasis in his life shifted after Aldersgate. Nervous compulsiveness gave way to a trust in Christ's love. Where he had felt more like a servant of God before, now he felt like a son. Wesley never lost sight of right thinking and behavior, but an immediate experience of the heart now became the focus.

John Wesley's father, Samuel Wesley, rector of the parish in the Lincolnshire village of Epworth, was noted for his stubbornness (he once refused for over a year to live with his wife because of her liberal political views) and his mother for her piety and fertility (she seemed perpetually with child, giving birth to nineteen children, ten of whom survived to adulthood). Graduating from Oxford in 1724 and ordained the next year, Wesley served briefly as his father's curate in Epworth, then returned to Oxford, where he lectured in Greek and joined a small club which included his brother Charles, called the "Holy Club" and soon tagged with the derisive nickname "methodists" because of their rigorous discipline of study, devotion, and good works.

In many ways Wesley was a catholic churchman. He received Holy Communion regularly and to the end of his life urged his followers to do the same. He valued order and tradition. But after Aldersgate, Wesley found himself increasingly at odds with the established church. Lacking a parish of his own, he depended on invitations to preach, and these became fewer and fewer. The leaders of the Church of England in the eighteenth century feared religious "enthusiasm." Enthusiasts were viewed almost as insurrectionists, and John Wesley was, without question, enthusiastic.

Enter Wesley's friend and fellow preacher George Whitefield. Whitefield had begun preaching in the open air to anyone who would stop to listen, and he appealed to Wesley for assistance. Preaching out of doors was not an idea Wesley took to immediately. "I could scarcely reconcile myself at first to this strange way of preaching in the fields, of which he [Whitefield] set me an example this Sunday," Wesley wrote on March 29, 1739. "I had been all my life (till very lately) so tenacious of every point relating to decency and order that I should have thought the saving of souls almost a sin if it had not been done in a church." But Wesley, like Whitefield, had a passion to preach, so he preached his first outdoor sermon on April 2, 1739 — "I submitted to be more vile and proclaimed in the highways the glad tidings of salvation," he wrote. Thus began a half century of preaching, three and four times a day, never repeating a sermon, in fields, highways, streets, and village squares, in churches when invited, wherever he could gather a crowd. And gather them he did, often in the thousands. Wesley preached his last open air sermon on October 7, 1790. It is estimated he rode 250,000 miles throughout the British Isles, most of it on horseback, and preached upwards of 40,000 sermons. The constant travel was never easy, and Wesley's often strained marriage (he married in 1751) undoubtedly suffered from it. As late as 1773, he could write, "To this day field-preaching is a cross to me. But I know my commission and see no other way of 'preaching the gospel to every creature.'" He sometimes began preaching at 5:00 AM.

Wesley's problems with the Church of England did not diminish once he took to the open air. The country was organized into geographically defined parishes, with a priest in charge of each parish. The system functioned rather in the way that municipal governments function — the mayor of one town lacks jurisdiction and does not exercise his office in another town, and a fiery politician who comes in from outside can be seen as a troublemaker and rabble-rouser. Such was John Wesley. In a time of massive social upheaval, with factories opening, agriculture declining, and city populations rising rapidly, vast numbers of people among the poor and laboring classes had never heard the Christian gospel and were entirely untouched by the ministry of the established church. These were the people Wesley was reaching. The problem was not so much ill will on the part of church authorities as that the Church of England was set up to maintain an existing system rather than to adapt to a new social reality.

Wesley kept a daily journal from 1735 to 1790. Besides giving a picture of life in eighteenth-century England, Wesley's journal offers a colorful account of his experiences. Take, for example, his hometown of Epworth. Wesley's father had died in 1735. His successor as rector was one John Romley who, perhaps not surprisingly, did not take kindly to his predecessor's son riding into town, stirring up the parish, then moving on. Romley not only declined to invite Wesley to preach from the pulpit where his father had preached (whereupon, on several occasions, Wesley climbed atop his father's stone tomb in the churchyard and gathered a crowd there, choosing texts such as "Quench not the Spirit"), but denied Wesley the Holy Communion on grounds that he was "not fit" and railed against Wesley from his pulpit while drunk. Scenes elsewhere, though not always so dramatic, were of a kind.

What did John Wesley actually say when he preached? Wesley was not a simplistic thinker. A number of influences can be traced in his thinking, from his father's high church Anglicanism to the Moravians. He was widely read and thought deeply about what he read (the popular image of Wesley reading while riding his horse is an accurate one). There was a new emphasis on the conversion of the heart and assurance, but Wesley's thought was within the compass of British Protestant understandings. It was primarily his unorthodox evangelistic methods and the "enthusiasm" they engendered that aroused hostility.

Although he was not entirely consistent and his understanding evolved as he grew older, Wesley's message is most easily grasped if thought of as a series of stages in the life of a Christian. The grace of God, God's undeserved love and power in our lives active at each stage, is the key to his thought. Wesley gives names to the working of God's grace at each point.

Begin with the fact of human sin. All people, because we are fallen creatures, rebel against God. This binds us and hinders us from receiving the bounty of God. Intentional acts of willfulness add to this burden, leading to guilt and a sense of being lost. Often we try to set things right ourselves through compulsive, legalistic, driven behaviors. God, meanwhile, does not sit idly by, but, even before we turn to him, moves in our souls by means of what Wesley calls "prevenient" or "preceding grace." Though not a new idea, this is a distinctive emphasis in Wesley's thought. Prevenient grace stirs our consciences, moves us to do good, and creates a hunger for God, eventually driving us to our knees. Finally there comes a moment of breakthrough. We know we have been set right with God through Jesus Christ; we become conscious of God's "saving" or "justifying grace." It has been a fact all along, but now we know it. We say, "Aha!" (or possibly, "I felt my heart strangely warmed"), and then begin to *experience* the love of God. The emphasis on experience is another distinctive Wesley emphasis.

Wesley used several words for what comes next — sanctification, re-generation, holiness, and (a word that led to misunderstanding) perfection. By his "sanctifying grace," God not merely changes our status from guilty to acquitted, but changes our actual selves, does something not only *for* us, but *in* us. We begin to grow in Christlikeness. When Wesley calls this perfection, he means a process of growth in love, not a realized state. Finally comes as-surance, another distinctive Wesley note. Assured of union with God, we are filled with peace, joy, and love. Later in his life, Wesley modified his doc-trine of assurance, allowing that in some cases, moments of doubt and fear may still intrude, but the dominant note for him, throughout his long life, was that Christians enjoy a "blessed assurance."

John Wesley was not only a great evangelist, but also great organizer. The Christian life for him was not a matter between the individual believer and God, but a set of relationships. The Wesleyan movement prospered and spread around the world because Wesley organized small groups wherever he went and entrusted their leadership to lay persons who would remain behind. No English Christian has exerted so wide an influence upon the broader Christian church as John Wesley. Not only did he chal-lenge and revitalize his own Church of England, unwelcoming though it often was to him, but he helped reshape Protestant spirituality generally and prepare the way for the Methodist Church, and later the Salvation Army and the Pentecostal and Holiness churches, all of which bear the stamp of his influence.

IN HIS OWN WORDS

Regeneration

Men are generally lost in the hurry of life, in the business or pleasures of it, and seem to think that their regeneration, their new nature, will spring and grow up within them, with as little care and thought of their own as their bodies were conceived and have attained their full strength and stature;

whereas, there is nothing more certain than that the Holy Spirit will not purify our nature, unless we carefully attend to his motions.

Sermon "On Grieving the Holy Spirit (1732)

A blessed sermon

I believe it pleased God to bless the first sermon most, because it gave most offense.

Journal (1738)

Preaching and faith

Immediately it struck into my mind, "Leave off preaching. How can you preach to others who have not faith yourself?" I asked [Peter] Bohler whether he thought I should leave it off or not. He said, "Preach faith till you have it; and then, because you have it, you will preach faith."

Journal (1738)

Salvation

This then is the salvation which is through faith, even in the present world: a salvation from sin, and the consequences of sin, both often expressed in the word *justification;* which taken in the largest sense, implies a deliverance from guilt and punishment, by the atonement of Christ actually applied to the soul of the sinner now believing on him, and a deliverance from the whole body of sin, through Christ formed in his heart. So that he who is thus justified, or saved by faith, is *indeed* born again.

Sermon on "Salvation by Faith" (1738)

The Lord's Supper

I showed at large (1) That the Lord's supper was ordained by God to be a means of conveying to men either preventing, or justifying, or sanctifying grace, according to their several necessities. (2) That the persons for whom it was ordained are all those who know and feel that they want the grace of God, either to restrain them from sin, or to show their sins forgiven, or to renew their souls in the image of God. (3) That inasmuch as we come to his table not to give him anything but to receive whatsoever he sees best for us, there is no previous preparation indispensably necessary but a desire to receive whatsoever he pleases to give. (4) That no fitness is required at the time of communicating but a sense of our state of utter sinfulness and helplessness.

Journal (1740)

Perfection

Christian perfection, therefore, does not imply (as some men seem to have imagined) an exemption either from ignorance, or mistake, or infirmity, or temptations. Indeed, it is only another term for holiness. They are two names for the same thing. Thus everyone that is holy is, in the scripture sense, perfect. Yet we may, lastly, observe that neither in this respect is there any absolute perfection on earth. There is no *perfection of degrees*, as it is termed, none which does not admit of a continual increase.

Sermon "Christian Perfection" (1741)

The use of money

Gain all you can, without hurting either yourself or your neighbor, in soul or body, by applying hereto with unintermitted diligence and with all the understanding which God has given you. Save all you can, by cutting off every expense which serves only to indulge foolish desire; to gratify either the desire of the flesh, the desire of the eye, or the pride of life; waste nothing, living or dying, on sin or folly, whether for yourself or your children. And then give all you can, or in other words, give all you have to God. . . . Render to God not a tenth, not a third, not a half, but all that is God's, be it more or less, by employing all on yourself, your household, the household of faith, and all mankind, in such a manner that you may give a good account of your stewardship when ye can be no longer stewards. . . .

Sermon "On the Use of Money" (1760)

Just do it!

O begin! Fix some part of every day for private exercises. You may acquire the taste for which you have not: What is tedious at first will afterwards be pleasant. Whether you like it or not, read and pray daily. It is for your life: there is no other way. . . . Do justice to your own soul: give it time and means to grow. Do not starve yourself any longer. Take up your cross and be a Christian altogether. Then will the children of God rejoice.

Personal letter (1760)

Assurance

[The Spirit of God] so works upon the soul by his immediate influence and by a strong though inexplicable operation, that the stormy wind and troubled waves subside, and there is a sweet calm; the heart resting as in the arms of Jesus and the sinner being clearly satisfied that God is reconciled, that all his "iniquities are forgiven, and his sins covered."

Sermon "The Witness of the Spirit II" (1767)

The Witness of the Spirit

If the Spirit of God does really testify that we are children of God, the immediate consequence will be the fruit of the Spirit, even "love, joy, peace, long-suffering, gentleness, goodness, fidelity, meekness, temperance." And however this fruit may be clouded for a while during the time of strong temptation, so that it does not appear to the tempted person while "Satan is sifting him as wheat," yet the substantial part of it remains, even under the thickest cloud. . . . when we have once received this "Spirit of adoption," that "peace which passes all understanding" and which expels all painful doubt and fear will "keep our hearts and minds in Christ Jesus." And when this has brought forth its genuine fruit, all inward and outward holiness, it is undoubtedly the will of him that calleth us to give us always what he has once given. So that there is no need that we should ever more be deprived of either the testimony of God's Spirit or the testimony of our own, the consciousness of our walking in all righteousness and true holiness.

"The Witness of the Spirit II"

Real religion

Here then we see in the clearest, strongest light, what is real religion: A restoration of man by him that bruises the serpent's head to all that the old serpent deprived him of, a restoration not only to the favor but likewise to the image of God, implying not merely deliverance from sin, but being filled with the fulness of God . . . nothing short of this is Christian religion. . . . Not *anything* else: Do not imagine an outward form, a round of duties, both in public and private is religion! Do not suppose that honesty, justice, and whatever is called *morality* (though excellent in its place) is religion! And least of all dream that orthodoxy, right opinion (vulgarly called *faith*) is religion. Of all religious dreams, this is the vainest, which takes hay and stubble for gold tried in the fire!

Sermon "The End of Christ's Coming" (1781)

Sanctifying grace

There is likewise great variety in the manner and time of God's bestowing his sanctifying grace, whereby he enables his children to give him their whole heart, which we can in no wise account for. . . . God undoubtedly has reasons, but those reasons are generally hid from the children of men. Once more: Some of those who are enabled to love God with all their heart and with all their soul retain the same blessing, without any interruption, till they are carried to Abraham's bosom; others do not retain it, although they are not conscious of having grieved the Holy Spirit of God. This also we do not understand: We do not herein "know the mind of the Spirit."

Sermon "The Imperfection of Human Knowledge" (1784)

Preventing grace

No man living is entirely destitute of what is vulgarly called *natural conscience*. But it is not natural: It is more properly termed *preventing grace*. Every man has a greater or less measure of this, which waiteth not for the call of man. Everyone has, sooner or later, good desires, although the generality of men stifle them before they can strike deep root or produce any considerable fruit. Everyone has some measure of that light, some faint glimmering ray, which, sooner or later, more or less, enlightens every man that cometh into the world. . . . So that no man sins because he has not grace, but because he does not use the grace which he hath.

Sermon "On Working Out Our Own Salvation" (1785)

To the rich

O ye that have riches in possession, once more hear the word of the Lord! Ye that are rich in this world, that have food to eat, and raiment to put on, and something over, are you clear of the curse of loving the world? Are you sensible of your danger? . . . Is not your belly your god? Is not eating and drinking, or any other pleasure of sense, the greatest pleasure you enjoy? Do not you seek happiness in dress, furniture, pictures, gardens, or anything else that pleases the eye? Do not you grow soft and delicate, unable to bear cold, heat, the wind or the rain, as you did when you were poor? Are you not increasing in goods, laying up treasure on earth instead of restoring to God in the poor, not so much, or so much, but all that you can spare? Surely, "it is easier for a camel to go through the eye of a needle than for a rich man to enter into the kingdom of heaven!"

Sermon "On God's Vineyard" (1787)

FOR REFLECTION AND DISCUSSION

Have you had an experience like Wesley's at Aldersgate? If so, how is your life different because of it?

Make a list of ways that "institutional maintenance" obstructs the church's mission today.

Can "enthusiasm" be dangerous?

Wesley is sometimes said to have added experience as a fourth source of authority for the church, after scripture, tradition, and reason. How is experience related to the three traditional sources of authority?

How are Wesley's three kinds of grace related, and how have you experienced them in your life?

The three verbs *earn, save,* and *give* are central in Wesley's sermon on "The Use of Money." What do you think accounts for his omission of the verbs *spend* and *borrow*?

Jot down some elements in Wesley's theology that have entered modern popular religion. Then jot down some that have not.

Chapter 12

CHARLES WESLEY

1707-1788

Skylark

D ISAGREEMENT ABOUT what kind of songs to sing in worship is not unknown today, but modern worshipers will not easily believe that the singing of any hymn in the modern sense was suspect in Anglican churches until around 1800. The Puritan insistence that every detail of life be regulated by scripture had left a residue in the Church of England. If the congregation sang anything (and often it did not), the words were to be drawn directly from scripture. The only flexibility was for the use of two metrical translations (some would call them paraphrases) of the biblical Psalms, the often labored and wooden *Whole Book of Psalms* by Thomas Sternhold and John Hopkins, published at the time of the Reformation, and the more poetical "New Version" by Nahum Tate and Nicholas Brady, published in 1696. Not until 1707 did the first book containing non-biblical songs for worship appear, by the Congregationalist preacher Isaac Watts, often called the "father of English hymnody." But hymn singing remained suspect, especially when the text was not biblical. Songs "of mere human composure" were called "profane," "obscene," and "promiscuous," and their authors "fanatics," "quacks," and "instigators of enthusiastic ravings."

Whatever it was called, hymn singing flourished among the Methodist societies in the eighteenth century, due largely to the work of Charles Wesley and his brother John. When someone today refers to "Wesley," it is assumed that John is meant — the older Wesley was the more visible of the two brothers and the better organizer. But few people can quote anything John Wesley wrote or said, whereas millions of Christians, from all denominations, can recite (or more likely sing) from memory at least a few lines from Charles. Music readily roots itself in the memory, and with repetition, saturates the soul like water dripping onto a sponge. Worshipers at Methodist chapels sang and hummed the songs of Charles Wesley all week long. By the beginning of the nineteenth century, these songs were gaining acceptance even among Anglicans who had never set foot in a Methodist chapel. As a result, Charles Wesley's compositions, more than those of any other writer save Thomas Cranmer, have shaped the typical Anglican's devotion for the past two hundred years. Outside Anglicanism, their influence far exceeds that of Cranmer.

The relationship between the two Wesley brothers was very close. During their undergraduate days, both were members of the "Holy Club" at Oxford, which was given the derisive nickname "methodists." As young men, both went to Georgia as missionaries. Both were ordained in the Church of England. Both became successful itinerant preachers — Charles often opened his Bible and preached on the first verse his eye lit upon; it was said he could fashion a sermon on "Christ crucified" from any verse of scripture. Both could preach rousing sermons and attracted large crowds, and both produced hymns, Charles specializing in original compositions while John translated hymns from the German and served as editor for his brother's work. The two brothers published several hymnbooks together. The differences between the two are also significant. Whereas John relished the limelight, Charles was more retiring. John was at times heady and analytical; Charles was more intuitive. Charles married in 1749 and enjoyed thirty-nine happy years with his wife Sally, whereas the marriage John struck in 1751 was tense at best. John spent his entire life traveling across England preaching wherever he could gather a crowd, but after two decades of itinerant preaching, Charles gave it up in 1756 and settled into parish life in Bristol and London.

Perhaps the most important difference between the two brothers was that hymn writing was a small piece of what John Wesley did, but it was the lifelong passion of Charles. Charles wrote not only in his study, but everywhere, even while riding his horse. He was known to dismount after a ride, run into a friend's house, and shout, "Pen and paper! Pen and paper!" It is estimated that Charles wrote 9,000 hymns, of which some 400 are still in use among Christians in some part of the world. That is an average of three hymns a week for sixty years — and some of them contain over twenty stanzas.

Although Charles Wesley's hymns are not translations or paraphrases of biblical texts, they can hardly be called unbiblical. A few, such as the evocative "Come, O thou traveler unknown," which uses the story of Jacob's wrestling with God in Genesis 32 to probe the Christian's struggle for perfect love, are based on a single biblical passage. But most of Wesley's hymns weave together phrases and images from many parts of scripture. J. E. Rattenbury goes too far, however, in saying that "a skillful man, if the Bible were lost, might extract it from Wesley's hymns." Not quite, or at least, not any longer — because only someone already expert in the scriptures would recognize all these biblical allusions and be able to "extract" the Bible from them, and few people today possess such knowledge. Often each line of a Wesley hymn will contain a separate biblical allusion or quotation. Many of them are active, visual images — of burning, running, leaning, thirsting, rising, standing, melting, shouting. This gives Wesley's hymns an earthy, sinewy vigor.

Theologically, there were few differences between the Wesley brothers. Two are significant: first, John tended to stress instantaneous conversion, while Charles emphasized gradual growth in holiness, and, secondly, John approved, towards the end of his life, the formation of a separate Methodist denomination, but Charles was unwaveringly loyal to the Church of England, strongly opposing separatist suggestions. On the whole, however, the two brothers shared a warm, Spirit-filled, evangelical faith, and Charles's hymns express a piety common to both. For the Wesleys, theological ideas emerged not merely from a mind thinking of Christ, but from a soul in love with Christ. Several typically Wesleyan themes recur again and again in Charles's hymns: Through the death of Christ, God invites *all* persons to be reconciled to him (this emphasis distanced the Wesleys from the Calvinists who taught that only the "elect" are saved). Charles Wesley drew in his hymns on all the major biblical metaphors referring to human salvation or atonement — purchase/redemption, pardon/acquittal, cleansing/purification, and victory/liberation. To receive the gift of salvation, human beings are called to make a free response (another distancing of the Wesleys from the Calvinists). Christian faith leads to a joyful heart and an obedient life; growth in holiness follows conversion. The eucharist is a means of grace in the life of the believer.

Many of Charles Wesley's hymns have a specific liturgical or seasonal orientation. He published two volumes of hymns in 1745, one for Christmas (including "Come, thou long-expected Jesus") and one of eucharistic hymns, and two in 1746, one for Easter (including "Rejoice, the Lord is King!") and one for Ascension Day and Pentecost.

Another feature of Charles Wesley's hymns is their warm, personal tone. They do more than teach right beliefs. They celebrate a person's *relationship* to God, and cover the whole range of emotions which a deep relationship entails, from penance to praise, from judgment to joy, from the shadows to the sunshine. These emotions are made all the more real through the frequent use of the first person singular pronoun. Isaac Watts' "When I survey the wondrous cross" was the first English hymn written in the first person. Many at the time considered it vain because it called attention to the author rather than focusing entirely on God. It was Wesley, however, who popularized the use of the first person pronoun. His hymns are seasoned with phrases like "enable *me* to stand," "keep *me* ever thine," "*I* seek to touch *my* Lord," "the joy prepared for *me*." The result is that Wesley's own experiences of the grace and love of God connect with worshipers and give his hymns uncommon intimacy and power. They invite the singer not only to praise the Lord, but to *experience* the Lord.

A look at three of Charles Wesley's best-known texts will illustrate these features:

"**O for a thousand tongues to sing.**" Methodists regard this as Wesley's signature hymn. In Methodist hymnals throughout the world, it is hymn number 1. All 18 stanzas of the original appear below. Modern hymnals usually begin with the original stanza 7, followed by all or most of stanzas 8 through 12, sometimes concluding with the original stanza 1.

The hymn abounds with vibrant images and lively rhythms. Wesley celebrates his discovery of God's grace at his conversion, when he "ceased to grieve" and "began to live." He twice refers to the heart as the place where conversion occurs. The references to Christ's blood in stanzas 5 and 10 are vintage Wesley — the blood shed on the cross is for him a symbol of Christ's victorious love. Also typical of Wesley is the repetition of the pronoun *me* in stanza 5 to emphasize that God's love is not some generalized divine quality, but a specific act for specific persons. A transition occurs after stanza 11, from personal testimony to an invitation to the sinner to open his heart to the healing power of Jesus. Wesley writes not merely for the devout, but for "every soul of man," even seemingly hopeless reprobates, mentioned specifically in stanzas 15 and 16. When I underwent life-threatening surgery as a young man, I sang stanza 12 over and over to myself as I was wheeled to the operating room and put to sleep. It banished my fears, and to this day, I thank God and Charles Wesley for those words.

"**Jesus, Lover of my soul.**" Autobiographical references occur in many of Wesley's hymns, though they are not always apparent. The story is told of how a songbird, pursued by a hawk, flew exhausted through Wesley's open window and into his arms, where it found safe refuge. That incident suggested to Wesley the opening image of this hymn. He was probably also influenced by his voyage across the Atlantic just two years earlier. The text is intensely personal, probing the sinner's guilt and need for God, his fear and doubt, the "plenteous grace" found in the arms of Jesus, and the need to be both made pure and kept pure within. One scholar has counted sixty-seven biblical allusions in these five stanzas.

"**Love divine, all loves excelling.**" This is Wesley's strongest plea for the gift of holiness. The fifth line of the second stanza has raised some eyebrows (many hymnals delete the stanza) because it seems to ask that human free will be canceled. That was not Wesley's intent. God cannot sin, yet God is free — this is a prayer for holiness like that of God, for prayers as pure as those of the saints above, for a will so devoted to God that sin is inconceivable. That such holiness is beyond our reach in this life is no reason to lose sight of it, or to cease to pray for it. The hymn glows with confidence in the power of God to "finish then thy new creation," to complete what God began in us at our baptism. It contains a reference to heaven or eternity in every stanza. When the teenage son of a friend died suddenly several years ago, I used the final stanza of this hymn as my prayer for him, changing "us" to "him."

IN HIS OWN WORDS

Free Grace

1 And can it be, that I should gain
    An interest in the Savior's blood?
    Died he for me? — who caused his pain!
    For me? — who him to death pursued.
    Amazing love! how can it be
    That thou, my God, shouldst die for me?

2 'Tis mystery all! th' Immortal dies!
    Who can explore his strange design?
    In vain the first-born seraph tries
    To sound the depths of Love divine.
    'Tis mercy all! Let earth adore;
    Let angel minds inquire no more.

3 He left his Father's throne above,
    (So free, so infinite his grace!)
    Emptied himself of all but love,
    And bled for Adam's helpless race:
    'Tis mercy all, immense and free!
    For, O my God! it found out me!

4 Long my imprisoned spirit lay,
   Fast bound in sin and nature's night:
   Thine eye diffused a quickening ray;
   I woke, the dungeon flamed with light;
   My chains fell off, my heart was free,
   I rose, went forth, and followed thee.

5 Still the small inward voice I hear,
   That whispers all my sins forgiven;
   Still the atoning blood is near,
   That quenched the wrath of hostile heaven:
   I feel the life his wounds impart;
   I feel my Savior in my heart.

6 No condemnation now I dread,
   Jesus, and all in him, is mine:
   Alive in him, my living Head,
   And clothed in righteousness divine,
   But I approach th' eternal throne,
   And claim the crown, through Christ, my own.

(1739)

For the anniversary of one's conversion

1 Glory to God, and praise and love
   Be ever, ever given;
   By saints below, and saints above,
   The church in earth and heaven.

2 On this glad day the glorious Sun
   Of righteousness arose;
   On my benighted soul he shone,
   And filled it with repose.

3 Sudden expired the legal strife;
   'Twas then I ceased to grieve;
   My second, real, living life
   I then began to live.

4 Then with my heart I first believed,
   Believed with faith divine;
   Power with the Holy Ghost received
   To call the Savior mine.

5 I felt my Lord's atoning blood
   Close to my soul applied;
   Me, me he loved — the Son of God
   For me, for me, he died!

6 I found, and owned his promise true,
   Ascertained of my part;
   My pardon passed in heaven I knew,
   When written on my heart.

7 O for a thousand tongues to sing
   My dear Redeemer's praise!
   The glories of my God and King,
   The triumphs of his grace.

8 My gracious Master, and my God,
   Assist me to proclaim,
   To spread through all the earth abroad
   The honors of thy name.

9 Jesus, the name that charms our fears,
   That bids our sorrows cease;
   'Tis music in the sinner's ears,
   'Tis life, and health, and peace.

10 He breaks the power of canceled sin,
   He sets the prisoner free;
   His blood can make the foulest clean,
   His blood availed for me.

11 He speaks; and, listening to his voice,
   New life the dead receive,
   The mournful, broken hearts rejoice,
   The humble poor believe.

12 Hear him, ye deaf; his praise, ye dumb,
   Your loosened tongues employ;
   Ye blind, behold your Savior come;
   And leap, ye lame, for joy.

13 Look unto him, ye nations; own
   Your God, ye fallen race!
   Look, and be saved through faith alone;
   Be justified by grace!

14 See all your sins on Jesus laid;
   The Lamb of God was slain,
   His soul was once an offering made
   For every soul of man.

15 Harlots, and publicans, and thieves
   In holy triumph join;
   Saved is the sinner that believes
   From crimes as great as mine.

16 Murderers, and all ye hellish crew,
   Ye sons of lust and pride,
   Believe the Savior died for you;
   For me the Savior died.

17 Awake from guilty nature's sleep,
   And Christ shall give you light,
   Cast all your sins into the deep,
   And wash the Ethiop white.

18 With me, your chief, you then shall know,
   Shall feel your sins forgiven;
   Anticipate your heaven below,
   And own that love is heaven.   (1739)

Jesus, Lover of my soul

1 Jesus, Lover of my soul,
   Let me to thy bosom fly,
   While the nearer waters roll,
   While the tempest still is high:
   Hide me, O my Savior hide,
   Till the storm of life be past:
   Safe into the haven guide;
   O receive my soul at last.

2 Other refuge have I none,
   Hangs my helpless soul on thee:
   Leave, ah! Leave me not alone,
   Still support and comfort me.
   All my trust on thee is stayed;
   All my help from thee I bring:
   Cover my defenseless head
   With the shadow of thy wing.

3 Wilt thou not regard my call?
   Wilt thou not accept my prayer?
   Lo! I sink, I faint, I fall,
   Lo! on thee I cast my care:
   Reach me out thy gracious hand!
   While I of thy strength receive,
   Hoping against hope I stand,
   Dying, and behold I live!

4 Thou, O Christ, art all I want,
   More than all in thee I find:
   Raise the fallen, cheer the faint,
   Heal the sick, and lead the blind.
   Just and holy is thy name,
   I am all unrighteousness,
   False and full of sin I am,
   Thou art full of truth and grace.

5 Plenteous grace with thee is found,
  Grace to cover all my sin:
  Let the healing streams abound,
  Make and keep me pure within:
  Thou of life the fountain art:
  Freely let me take of thee,
  Spring thou up within my heart,
  Rise to all eternity!

(1740)

Eucharistic Hymn No. 8

1 Come, to the supper, come,
  Sinners, there still is room;
  Every soul may be his guest,
  Jesus gives the general word;
  Share the monumental feast,
  Eat the supper of your Lord.

2 In this authentic sign
  Behold the stamp divine:
  Christ revives his sufferings here,
  Still exposes them to view;
  See the crucified appear,
  Now believe he died for you.

(1745)

Eucharistic Hymn No. 86

1 And shall I let him go?
  If now I do not *feel*
  The streams of living water flow,
  Shall I forsake the well?

2 Because he hides his face,
  Shall I no longer stay,

But leave the channels of his grace,
And cast the means away?

3 Get thee behind me, fiend,
   On others try thy skill,
   Here let thy hellish whispers end,
   To thee I say, *Be still!*

4 Jesus hath spoke the word,
   His will my reason is;
   Do this in memory of thy Lord,
   Jesus hath said, *Do this!*

5 He bids me eat the bread,
   He bids me drink the wine;
   No other motive, Lord, I need,
   No other word than thine.

6 I cheerfully comply
   With what my Lord doth say;
   Let others ask a reason why,
   My glory is t' obey.

7 His will is good and just:
   Shall I his will withstand?
   If Jesus bids me lick the dust,
   I bow at his command.

8 Because he said, *Do this,*
   This I will always do;
   Till Jesus come in glorious bliss,
   I *thus* his death will *show.*

(1745)

Redemption Hymn No. 9

1 Love divine, all loves excelling,
   Joy of heaven, to earth come down,

Fix in us thy humble dwelling,
All thy faithful mercies crown:
Jesu, thou art all compassion,
Pure, unbounded love thou art,
Visit us with thy salvation,
Enter every trembling heart.

2 Breathe, O breathe thy loving Spirit,
Into every troubled breast,
Let us all in thee inherit,
Let us find that second rest:
Take away our power of sinning,
Alpha and Omega be,
End of faith as its beginning,
Set our hearts at liberty.

3 Come, almighty to deliver,
Let us all thy life receive;
Suddenly return, and never,
Nevermore thy temples leave.
Thee we would be always blessing,
Serve thee as thy hosts above,
Pray, and praise thee without ceasing,
Glory in thy perfect love.

4 Finish then thy new creation,
Pure and spotless let us be,
Let us see thy great salvation,
Perfectly restored in thee:
Changed from glory into glory,
Till in heaven we take our place,
Till we cast our crowns before thee,
Lost in wonder, love and praise!

(1747)

FOR REFLECTION AND DISCUSSION

Look in the index of your hymnal for the hymns by Charles Wesley. Look
    them up and read them, then choose one not discussed above and
    write a few sentences on what it means to you.
Think of a time when a hymn or spiritual song helped you.
What dangers or excesses are possible from singing hymns written in the
    first person singular? Can you think of particular texts which seem to
    encourage such dangers and excesses?
Why do we sing hymns?
Make a list of criteria to evaluate a hymn text.

Chapter 13

SAMUEL JOHNSON

1709-1784

Spiritual Gladiator

S AMUEL JOHNSON is the subject of the world's most famous biography. In his majestic work, James Boswell quotes hundreds of conversations in which Johnson not only airs his views on issues of the day but discloses his inner life as well. Johnson's own prolific writings, when added to Boswell, give us a fuller picture of Samuel Johnson than we have of any other figure in history. We laugh at his quips, raise our eyebrows at his prejudices, wrestle with his doubts and fears, grieve over the death of his wife, pray the prayers in which he bares his soul. As essayist, poet, novelist, literary critic, and author of the first English language dictionary, Johnson was also the foremost English man of letters of his generation, perhaps of any generation.

Samuel Johnson's father was a Lichfield bookseller, but it was his mother who most influenced the young boy. Years later, Johnson recalled the moment, near his fourth birthday, when his mother, lying in her bed with young Sam at her side, told him of heaven, "a place to which good people went," and hell, "a place to which bad people went." All his life, Johnson was gripped by eternity, and by this life as a prelude to it. His faith was restless, brooding, and unflinching. Every word he wrote was undergirded by that faith, although it was often more implied than stated. Even when selecting quotations from literature to illustrate word usage in his dictionary, Johnson cited only authors who provided what he deemed a healthy moral influence.

The decade of the 1750s was Johnson's most productive. Not only did he publish his celebrated dictionary in 1755, but he turned out a series of outstanding works on the moral life. The decade began with the publication of a 368-line poem entitled "The Vanity of Human Wishes" and ended with a short novel, *The History of Rasselas, Prince of Abyssinia*. Between these two works came hundreds of reviews and periodical essays. Johnson also wrote as many as fifty sermons throughout his life (all for other people — he never mounted the pulpit himself), about half of which have survived. In these works Johnson explored not only human behavior, but the thinking that motivated it. Morality for him included desires, values, and the imagination as well as actions.

Johnson was a keen observer of others, but a particularly keen observer of himself. "Every man," said the character Imlac in *The History of Rasselas*, "may, by examining himself, guess what passes in the minds of others." That was Johnson's method. He probed his own hopes and fears, his desires and motivations, and these insights informed his analysis of what he saw in others. Johnson produced no personal exposés, no "true confessions," nor was he interested in the new and novel. He drew from personal observation (and from the Bible and Christian teaching) to discern the moral laws and principles established by God and applicable to all persons. People already knew these truths deep within them, Johnson felt. "Men more often require to be reminded than informed," he said.

Although Johnson wrote many of his essays under pressure of deadline (procrastination was a major feature of his character), the literary quality of his writing is remarkably consistent. His prose is precise, graceful, and economic; every word is chosen for a reason, and every word is the right one. Several themes recur in Johnson's great moral writings: the brevity and unpredictability of life, the urgency of making the most of the present moment, the danger of idleness, the vanity of human desires, the tendency to rationalize selfish behaviors, the importance of intellectual and moral honesty, purity of motive, and compassion for others.

Johnson was keenly aware of human misery and was known for his compassion and acts of charity. He treated servants generously and kindly. Until granted a pension in 1762, Johnson had struggled to make ends meet, yet he often shared what he had. When questioned why he gave money to beggars who might use it for gin and tobacco, Johnson said he saw no reason to strip life still barer for those who suffered the most and to deny them "such sweeteners of their existence." Uncompromising in the standards he set for himself, he readily tolerated the failings and moral lapses of others, often taking the part of debtors and prisoners. Finding a poor woman late one night lying helpless and exhausted in the street, Johnson carried her to his own house, and upon discovering she was sick and a prostitute, cared for her "for a long time, at a considerable expense, till she was restored to health, and endeavored to put her into a virtuous way of living," Boswell reports. Johnson was a brilliant satirist, but rarely wrote satire because he felt it encouraged uncharitable feelings. In one essay which does border on the satirical, he excoriates the British settlers of America for their inhumanity to the innocent natives.

Beneath his measured, devout exterior, however, violent emotional whirlpools swirled in Johnson's soul. Like most English intellectuals of his day, Johnson trusted reason as a source of truth and the regulator of the human mind. But reason did not take him where he sought to go. Johnson longed for rational proof of his faith but did not find it. Fears and doubts dogged him all his life. These were fed from several sources and Johnson was ever striving to stay their flow.

One of these sources was Johnson's naturally despondent temperament. He occasionally experienced periods of what was then called melancholy and would today probably be called psychological depression. For extended times — once for a period of years in his early fifties — Johnson rarely worked, confining himself to his quarters, able to do little more than shuffle papers when he tried to write. A sense of oblivion threatened to swallow him up. The specter of lunacy terrified him during these periods.

Another source of these swirling emotions was Johnson's perfectionism regarding his own thoughts and behavior. He blamed himself for his lapses into melancholy and feared he would be held responsible for failing to use fully the talents God had given him. Several of his essays concern the danger to the soul of indolence or idleness. Johnson prayed "that I may not lavish away the life which thou hast given me on useless trifles." He often composed a prayer for New Year's Day, and many of these contain pleas for divine aid that he not squander the next year as he had the year just ended. In one such prayer he refers to himself as "the wretched misspender of another year which thy mercy has allowed me."

Johnson was also troubled by thoughts he believed unworthy of a Christian soul. He had been devoted to his wife Tetty, and her death in 1752, when Johnson was forty-two years old, brought on a period of searing loneliness. Some of Johnson's most moving prayers were written just after Tetty's death, but he was uncertain how to pray for her and whether Christian doctrine permitted him to ask her to pray for him in heaven. Moreover, Johnson's sexual drive was apparently strong, and following Tetty's death, he had no morally acceptable means to satisfy it. He was assaulted by unwanted fantasies, and Boswell hints that Johnson may have succumbed to sexual temptation after his wife's death. A lacerating sense of guilt haunted him. These are perhaps among the "inordinate desires," "corrupt passions," "vain terrors," and "perturbations of my mind" from which he repeatedly prayed to be delivered.

Another source of Johnson's violent emotions, made all the stronger by his perfectionism, was his fear of hell. One question preoccupied him — *Shall I be saved?* — and for most of his life he did not feel confident of the answer. Johnson saw himself as suspended over the abyss of eternal perdition, held only by the thread of life, which would soon end — and then what? He believed Christ had died to open the way of salvation, but that each individual must step through that door, by means of obedience and repentance. Was his Christian conviction sufficient? His written prayers typically conclude with a plea to God to "receive me to everlasting happiness."

Boswell summarizes Johnson's emotional life in these words: "His mind resembled the vast amphitheatre, the Colisaeum at Rome. In the center stood his judgment, which, like a mighty gladiator, combated those apprehensions that, like the wild beasts of the arena, were all around in cells, ready to be let out upon him. After a conflict, he drove them back into their dens; but not killing them, they were still assailing him."

What, then, shall we make of the witness of Samuel Johnson? He derived little comfort or joy from his faith. His understanding of Christian living seems to have centered largely on well-regulated thoughts and deeds. He was preoccupied with his own salvation, and his conception of God was more that of a stern judge than of a forgiving father or mother. But his courage, generosity, integrity, and piety inspired all who knew him, and his faith provided him a beacon in the often dark and turbulent sea that was his mind. Moreover, during the final years of his life, Johnson seems to have found something of the peace that had so long eluded him. He experienced a healing a few months before his death which he described to his friend John Hawkins as "wonderful, very wonderful" and which was apparently spiritual as well as physical. He told Hawkins on November 28, 1784, just two weeks before his death, that he had "rays of hope shot into my soul." Johnson wrote his last prayer on December 5. Though not inconsistent with his earlier devotional writing, it shows a new emphasis as Johnson speaks of hope, confidence, and his own redemption. Boswell reports that in his final days, as his strength ebbed, Johnson "became quite composed, and continued so till his death." Samuel Johnson died on December 13, peacefully and unattended, at his home in London.

IN HIS OWN WORDS

Prayer for his work

Almighty God, the giver of all good things, without whose help all labor is ineffectual and without whose grace all wisdom is folly, grant, I beseech thee, that in this my undertaking, thy Holy Spirit may not be withheld from me, but that I may promote thy glory and the salvation both of myself and others; grant this, O Lord, for the sake of Jesus Christ. Amen.

on writing for *The Rambler* (1750)

The excellency of art

It is justly considered as the greatest excellency of art to imitate nature; but it is necessary to distinguish those parts of nature which are most proper for imitation: greater care is still required in representing life which is so often discolored by passion or deformed by wickedness. If the world be promiscuously described, I cannot see of what use it can be to read the account; or why it may not be as safe to turn the eye immediately upon mankind, as upon a mirror which shows all that presents itself without discrimination. It is therefore not a sufficient vindication of a character that it is drawn as it appears, for many characters ought never to be drawn.

Rambler essay #4 (1750)

An act of providence?

It was, perhaps, ordained by providence, to hinder us from tyrannizing over one another, that no individual should be of such importance as to cause, by his retirement or death, any chasm in the world.

Rambler essay #6 (1750)

Self-deceit

We are easily shocked by crimes which appear at once in their full magnitude, but the gradual growth of our own wickedness, endeared by interest and palliated by all the artifices of self-deceit, gives us time to form distinctions in our own favor, and reason by degrees submits to absurdity, as the eye is in time accommodated to darkness.

Rambler essay #8 (1750)

Words and actions

It is not difficult to conceive, however, that for many reasons a man writes much better than he lives. For, without entering into refined speculations, it may be shown much easier to design than to perform. A man proposes his schemes of life in a state of abstraction and disengagement, exempt from the enticements of hope, the solicitations of affection, the importunities of appetite, or the depressions of fear, and is in the same state with him that teaches upon land the art of navigation, to whom the sea is always smooth, and the wind always prosperous. . . . We are, therefore, not to wonder that most fail, amidst tumult and snares and danger, in the observance of those precepts, which they laid down in solitude, safety, and tranquillity, with a mind unbiased, and with liberty unobstructed. . . . Nothing is more unjust, however common, than to charge with hypocrisy him that expresses zeal for those virtues which he neglects to practice; since he may be sincerely convinced of the advantages of conquering his passions, without having yet obtained the victory.

Rambler essay #14 (1750)

The shortness and uncertainty of life

As he that lives longest lives but a little while, every man may be certain that he has no time to waste. The duties of life are commensurate to its duration, and every day brings its task, which if neglected, is doubled on the morrow. But he that has already trifled away those months and years in which he should have labored, must remember that he has now only a part of that of which the whole is little, and that since the few moments remaining are to be considered as the last trust of heaven, not one is to be lost.

Rambler essay #71 (1750)

Envy

Almost every other crime is practiced by the help of some quality which might have produced esteem or love, if it had been well employed; but envy is mere unmixed and genuine evil; it pursues a hateful end by despicable means, and desires not so much its own happiness as another's misery.

Rambler essay #183 (1751)

Prayer after the death of his wife

O Lord, Governor of heaven and earth, in whose hands are embodied and departed spirits, if thou hast ordained the souls of the dead to minister to the living, and appointed my departed wife to have care of me, grant that I may enjoy the good effects of her attention and ministrations, whether exercised by appearance, impulses, dreams or in any other manner agreeable to thy government. Forgive my presumption, enlighten my ignorance, and however meaner agents are employed, grant me the blessed influences of thy Holy Spirit, through Jesus Christ our Lord. Amen. (1752)

Departed souls

We know little of the state of departed souls, because such knowledge is not necessary to a good life. Reason deserts us at the brink of the grave and can give no further intelligence. Revelation is not wholly silent: "There is joy in the angels of heaven over one sinner that repenteth"; and surely this joy is not incommunicable to souls disentangled from the body, and made like angels. Let hope therefore dictate what revelation does not confute, that the union of souls may still remain; and that we who are struggling with sin, sorrow, and infirmities may have our part in the attention and kindness of those who have finished their course and are now receiving their reward. These are the great occasions which force the mind to take refuge in religion: when we have no help in ourselves, what can remain but that we look up to a higher and a greater power; and to what hope may we not raise our eyes and hearts, when we consider that the greatest power is the best.

Idler essay #41 (1759)

Prayer and madness

Madness frequently discovers itself merely by unnecessary deviation from the usual modes of the world. My poor friend [Christopher] Smart showed the disturbance of his mind by falling upon his knees and saying his prayers in the street, or in any other unusual place. Now although, rationally speaking, it is greater madness not to pray at all than to pray as Smart did, I am afraid there are so many who do not pray that their understanding is not called in question. . . . I did not think he ought to be shut up. His infirmities were not noxious to society. He insisted on people praying with him; and I'd as lief pray with Kit Smart as anyone else. Another charge was that he did not love clean linen; and I have no passion for it.

> from Boswell's *Life of Johnson,* in defense of the poet Christopher Smart, who had been confined to an insane asylum (1763)

Resolution

I have now spent fifty-five years in resolving; having, from the earliest time almost that I can remember, been forming schemes of a better life. I have done nothing. The need of doing, therefore, is pressing, since the time of doing is short. O God, grant me to resolve aright, and to keep my resolutions, for Jesus Christ's sake. Amen.

> Good Friday resolution (1764)

Spreading the gospel

To omit for a year, or for a day, the most efficacious method of advancing Christianity, in compliance with any purposes that terminate on this side of the grave, is a crime of which I know not that the world has yet had an example, except in the practice of the planters of America, a race of mortals whom, I suppose, no other man wishes to resemble.

> Personal letter (1766)

Charity to the undeserving

Some readily find out, that where there is distress there is vice, and easily discover the crime of feeding the lazy, or encouraging the dissolute. To promote vice is certainly unlawful, but we do not always encourage vice when we relieve the vicious. It is sufficient that our brother is in want; by which way he brought his want upon him let us not too curiously inquire. We likewise are sinners.

Sermon on I Peter 3:8

The religious life

To live religiously is to walk, not by sight, but by faith; to act in confidence of things unseen, in hope of future recompense, and in fear of future punishment.

Sermon on Galatians 6:7

Church attendance

To be of no church is dangerous. Religion, of which the rewards are distant and which is animated only by faith and hope, will glide by degrees out of the mind unless it be invigorated and reimpressed by external ordinances, by stated calls to worship, and the salutary influence of example.

Life of Milton (1781)

Last prayer

Almighty and most merciful Father, I am now, as to human eyes it seems, about to commemorate, for the last time, the death of thy Son Jesus Christ our Savior and Redeemer. Grant, O Lord, that my whole hope and confidence may be in his merits, and his mercy; enforce and accept my imperfect repentance; make this commemoration available to the confirmation of my faith, the establishment of my hope, and the enlargement of my charity; and make the death of thy Son Jesus Christ effectual to my redemption. Have mercy upon me, and pardon the multitude of my offenses. Bless my friends; have mercy upon all men. Support me, by the grace of thy Holy Spirit, in the days of weakness, and at the hour of death; and receive me, at my death, to everlasting happiness, for the sake of Jesus Christ. Amen.

before receiving Holy Communion,
December 5, 1784, eight days before his death

FOR REFLECTION AND DISCUSSION

Do you agree that faithful living pertains as much to thoughts and motivations as to outward behavior? What does Jesus say about this in the Sermon on the Mount (Matthew 5-7)?

Is the chief significance of this life that it is a prelude to eternity?

How would modern publishing, film, broadcasting, and art be changed if Johnson's view of the excellency of art were universally implemented? Would this be a good thing?

What does the modern world need to learn from the life and writings of Johnson?

If you were able to write a letter to Samuel Johnson to be read by him while he was still alive, what would you say?

Write a prayer for someone you love who has died.

Chapter 14

HANNAH MORE

1745-1833

More than Lady Bountiful

F OR MUCH of her life, Hannah More was a socialite in London's fashionable salons and the darling of the city's literary, dramatic, and artistic set. Her light verse and drama were much in vogue; she was accustomed to fawning adoration. She flirted with prominent people — Samuel Johnson once referred to her "vehemence of praise" — and one of the city's matrons told her, "My dear, you are the fashion!" Like many English people, More looked upon class divisions as part of the natural order, the way God had set up the world. Her view of society was static — people were born into one rank or another, and they were to carry out the duties of persons born to that rank. To the poor, More counseled diligence, patience, and submission. Unhappy conditions among the poor might be alleviated, but the basic social structure was not to be challenged. The French had done that in their revolution of 1789, and bloody chaos had come of it — why should England take such chances? Stability, order, structure — that was the English way (or at least the upper-class way), and Hannah More was happy to serve beneath that banner.

A person holding these views might be called a reactionary today. But by eighteenth-century standards, Hannah More was in the forefront of social change — and as a leading author and professional woman, she might even be seen as a forerunner of modern feminism.

Hannah More was the second youngest of five daughters born to a Bristol schoolmaster. Family life was comfortable and devout. As a child, Hannah was regarded as the brightest of the sisters, but all were intelligent and accomplished. When they reached maturity, the five sisters founded and ran a school in Bristol which became known for the excellence of its academic and moral education. All five sisters remained unmarried, although Hannah came within an eyelash of marriage three times. She accepted three proposals from one William Turner of Bristol, only to have him break off each engagement as the wedding day approached. Hannah More had given up her interest in the sisters' school to marry Turner. After standing her up the third time, Turner offered her 200 pounds a year, a large sum, as compensation, which she initially refused but later accepted. She swore she would decline any further proposals of marriage, and in subsequent years was given several opportunities to show she meant it.

In 1774 More went to London, where she began spending several months each year. Her unassuming, uncritical good humor opened many doors for her into London society, but in one respect More stood out among her London friends — she went to church. Their Christian faith had been important to the More sisters in Bristol, but among London's high society, Christianity was often espoused but seldom taken seriously. It was a largely intellectual faith, rarely applied to daily living. A turning point for More came when she met William Wilberforce, the abolitionist member of Parliament, in 1787. He enlisted her support in the movement to abolish the slave trade, and More quickly turned out several short works condemning slavery and challenging the upper classes to live the faith to which they gave nodding assent, both for their own sakes and as an example to the lower classes. It was careless Christians, not the openly profane, she said, who posed the greatest danger to church and society. In words reminiscent of William Law sixty years earlier, she wrote, "Religion is a disposition, a habit, a temper. It is not a name but a nature . . . a turning of the whole mind to God." Most of More's friends accepted these literary efforts, and her books were widely read throughout the country, but some began to detect a hint of the dreaded "enthusiasm" in More's writings. What was happening to the charming, sociable, witty Hannah More?

The second half of More's life was about to begin, and it would differ markedly from the first. Her involvement with the campaign to end the slave trade had brought her into a new circle of acquaintances, people who cared as much about their Christian faith as she did and were eager to live out its social implications. She began to put her spiritual house in order. During the 1790s, she published a series of tracts for the moral and religious instruction of the poor. It is hard to know what impact they had among the poor, but the middle class bought and read them, in England and abroad. The best known of the tracts, *The Shepherd of Salisbury Plain,* is a study of poverty and spiritual isolation in a west country village. It was not designed to alleviate poverty, but to provide solace and inspiration to the poor.

But Hannah More was not one to sit in her parlor writing tracts while others suffered. Since 1785, More and her sisters had summered at Cowslip Green, a cottage they had built near Bristol. In 1789, Wilberforce visited the sisters there, and they took him to see the famous caves in nearby Cheddar. What impressed Wilberforce about Cheddar, however, was not the scenic caves, but the grinding poverty of the people of the village. With the arrival of the industrial age, the old system of education through guilds and apprenticeships had broken down, and Wilberforce rightly perceived lack of education as part of the problem. He asked More "to do something for Cheddar," and within days, she was establishing schools for the poor, both for education and for moral rejuvenation. The problem, as More saw it, was not primarily economic, but spiritual, and she designed a curriculum to teach the Christian faith through Bible study and prayer and to instill virtue, industry, temperance, and thrift. She trudged miles through muddy fields in all seasons of the year, recruiting students and confronting angry farmers (one landowner's wife told her the poor were intended to be slaves), indifferent clergy, inept teachers, and skeptical parents. More was invariably polite and kind — and the children came, five hundred of them in Cheddar alone, and similar numbers in two other schools in neighboring villages. There were several smaller schools as well.

More was loudly criticized for acting autocratically (she was called "the She-Bishop") and for her "methodist" or "enthusiast" religious leanings. The criticisms were groundless — More was a convinced Anglican and she sought (usually unsuccessfully) to work closely with the local clergy — but the criticism took its toll. In 1801, she joined her four sisters to build a home at Barley Wood where they might spend the remainder of their years caring for the poor and in reading and reflection. The schools closed, and More's diary reveals that she blamed it on her own lack of humility. "I hoped that I had learned to value praise and reputation only as an instrument of usefulness," she wrote. She saw herself as a failure.

Much of Hannah More's best writing was yet to come, however. She wrote her only novel in 1808, *Coelebs in Search of a Wife*, and it was an immediate best seller. The novel concerns a young man of genteel background traveling around to find a suitable wife. In evangelical homes, serious discourse about religion and morals was much encouraged, and there is a lot of this in *Coelebs*. Consisting mostly of conversations in parlor rooms about domestic duties and sermons heard at church, it is hardly an "action novel." Its purpose, clearly, is to make an appeal for evangelical Christianity, and despite the somewhat labored conversations, it succeeds remarkably well. Often one of the characters in *Coelebs*, articulating the views of More, will offer psychological and spiritual wisdom in crisp, compelling prose.

More's crowning literary achievement was a trilogy of books on the spiritual life, *Practical Piety* (1811), *Christian Morals* (1812), and *The Character and Practical Writings of St. Paul* (1815). The first two of these books show Hannah More at her most mature and insightful. She seeks to avoid controversial questions, focusing on the dynamics of day-to-day Christian living. More often rises to great heights, offering practical suggestions as to conduct along with insights into motivation and the will. *Practical Piety* discusses the joy Christian faith brings to the human heart when we make God truly the center of our lives. It sold even more copies than *Coelebs*. The second volume, *Christian Morals*, is addressed, like many of More's works, to persons of social rank, emphasizing the need to cultivate noble habits of mind and action. She asserts that the world is ordered according to a moral purpose by God's providential rulership. The third book, on the apostle Paul, is not up to the quality of the other two, due to More's lack of familiarity with biblical scholarship.

Hannah More outlived all her four sisters by fourteen years. Her final years were spent at Barley Wood, where guests from around the world, including Buddhists and Muslims, went to call on her. (I first heard her name in a student barroom song at my *alma mater,* Kenyon College. The school was founded by Philander Chase, first bishop of Ohio, who called upon More at Barley Wood in 1824, a visit mentioned in the song.)

Assessing Hannah More's witness today is not easy. She accepted the stratified class structure of English society, seeking to relieve the consequences of poverty, but not questioning the economic and political system that contributed to it. Her theology was limited (her books hardly mention the Trinity or the Incarnation) and she tended to separate devotion from the intellect. She can appear self-satisfied in places. More's vision of Christian faith was incomplete — but of whom can that not be said? Within that vision, she acted with extraordinary courage, integrity, and nobility. Her work in education helped diminish the division between social classes. She tirelessly labored to alleviate the suffering that resulted from the industrial revolution, mass migration to the cities, and the widespread abuse of alcohol among the poor. She showed compassion to everyone she met, of whatever rank or station. And from the best of Hannah More's writing, an authentic, radiant devotion still shines.

IN HER OWN WORDS

Assisting the poor

"Shepherd," continued he [the character Mr. Johnson], "if I were a king and had it in my power to make you a rich and great man with a word speaking, I would not do it. Those who are raised by some sudden stroke much above the station in which divine Providence had placed them seldom turn out very good or very happy. I have never had any great things in my power, but as far as I have been able, I have been always glad to assist the worthy. I have, however, never attempted or desired to set any poor man much above his natural condition, but it is a pleasure to me to lend him such assistance as may make that condition more easy to himself and to put him in a way which shall call him to the performance of more duties than perhaps he could have performed without my help, and of performing them in a better manner."

The Shepherd of Salisbury Plain (1795)

Our undoing

It is no new remark that more men are undone by an excessive indulgence in things permitted than by the commission of avowed sins.

Coelebs in Search of a Wife (1808)

The mind of Christ

"Let the same *mind* be in you which was also in Christ Jesus" [Philippians 2:5]. If, therefore, we happen to possess that wealth and grandeur which he disdained, we should *possess them as though we possessed them not*. We have a fair and liberal permission to use them as his gift, and to his glory, but not to erect them into the supreme objects of our attachment. In the same manner, in every other point, it is still the spirit of the act, the temper of the mind, to which we are to look.

Coelebs

Listening to sermons

As we walked from church one Sunday, Miss Stanley told me that her father does not approve the habit of criticizing the sermon. He says that the custom of pointing out the faults cannot be maintained without the custom of watching for them.

Coelebs

The promises of God

[God] is a consolation only to the heavy laden, a refuge to those alone who forsake sin. The rest he promises is not a rest from labor, but from evil. It is a rest from the drudgery of the world, but not from the service of God. It is not inactivity, but quietness of spirit; not sloth, but peace. He draws men indeed from slavery to freedom, but not a freedom to do evil, or to do nothing. He makes his service easy, but not by lowering the rule of duty, not by adapting his commands to the corrupt inclinations of our nature. He communicates his grace, gives fresh and higher motives to obedience, and imparts peace and comfort, not by any abatement in his demands, but by this infusion of his own grace, and this communication of his own Spirit.

Coelebs

Religious ardor

The truth is, Sir John, *your* society considers ardor in religion as the fever of a distempered understanding, while in inferior concerns they admire it as the indication of a powerful mind. Is zeal in politics accounted the mark of a vulgar intellect? . . . Ardor in religion is as much more noble than ardor in politics as the prize for which it contends is more exalted.

Coelebs

Dangerous religion

I was buoyed up with an unfounded confidence. I adopted a religion which promised pardon without repentance, happiness without obedience, and heaven without holiness. I had found a short road to peace. I never inquired if it were a safe one.

Coelebs

The evangelistic temper

The combination of integrity with discretion is the precise point at which a serious Christian must aim in his intercourse, and especially in his debates on religion with men of the opposite description. He must consider himself as not only having his own reputation but the honor of religion in his keeping. While he must on the one hand "set his face as a flint" against anything that may be construed into compromise or evasion, into denying or concealing any Christian truth, or shrinking from any commanded duty, in order to conciliate favor, he must, on the other hand, be scrupulously careful never to maintain a Christian doctrine with an unchristian temper. In endeavoring to convince he must be cautious not needlessly to irritate. He must distinguish between the honor of God and the pride of his own character, and never be pertinaciously supporting the one under the pretense that he is only maintaining the other.

Practical Piety (1811)

The Christian life

The essential spirit of the Christian life may be said to be included in this one brief petition of the Christian's prayer, *"Thy will be done."*

Christian Morals (1812)

Resignation

True resignation is the hardest lesson in the whole school of Christ. It is the oftenest taught and the latest learned. It is not a task which, when once got over in some particular instance, leaves us master of the subject. The necessity of following up the lesson we have begun presents itself almost every day in some new shape, occurs under some fresh modification. The submission of yesterday does not exonerate us from the resignation of today.

Christian Morals

Church disputes

We cannot dispute ourselves into heaven, but we may lose our way thither while we are litigating unimportant topics — things which a man may not be much the better if he hold and which, if he hold them unrighteously, he might be better if he held them not. The enemies of religion cannot injure it so much as its own divisions about itself.

Christian Morals

Humility

Humility may be said to operate on the human character like the sculptor who, in chiseling out the statue, accomplishes his object not by laying on, but by paring off, not by making extraneous additions, but by retrenching superfluities, till every part of the redundant material is cleared away. The reduction which true religion effects, of swelling passions, irregular thoughts, and encumbering desires, produces at length on the human mind some assimilation to the divine image.

Christian Morals

Low standard of religion

A low standard of religion flatters our vanity, is easily acted up to, does not wound our self-love, is practicable without sacrifices, and respectable without self-denial. It allows the implantation of virtues without irradicating vices, recommends right actions without expelling wrong principles, and grafts fair appearances upon unresisted corruptions.

Christian Morals

The design of the gospel

It is not the design of the gospel merely to announce to us a state of future blessedness, but to fit us for it. It is but half of the work of infinite love to provide a heaven for man; it is its completion to make man a suitable recipient of the bliss prepared for him. Without this gracious provision, Christianity had been a scheme to tantalize, and not to save us.

Christian Morals

Hints of God

Whatever good there is even in the renewed man is but a faint adumbration of the perfections of God. The best created things, light itself, lose all their brightness when compared with the uncreated glory from which all they have is borrowed. . . . Hence in the highest qualities of the best Christian we have a hint, a rudiment which serves to recall to our mind the divine excellence of which they are an emanation.

Reflections on Prayer (1819)

Prayer

Prayer is the application of want to him who alone can relieve it, the voice of sin to him who alone can pardon it. It is the urgency of poverty, the prostration of humility, the fervency of penitence, the confidence of trust. It is not eloquence, but earnestness; not figures of speech, but compunction of soul.

The Spirit of Prayer (1825)

Perseverance

Thus to persevere when we have not the encouragement of visible success is an evidence of tried faith.

The Spirit of Prayer

Loving God

All desire the gifts of God, but they do not desire God. If we profess to love him, it is for our own sake; when shall we begin to love him for himself?

The Spirit of Prayer

God's government

We are more disposed to lay down rules for the regulation of God's government than to submit our will to it as he has settled it. If we do not now see the efficacy of the prayer which he has enjoined us to present to him, it may yet be producing its effect in another way. Infinite wisdom is not obliged to inform us of the manner or the time of his operations; what he expects of us is to persevere in the duty.

The Spirit of Prayer

FOR REFLECTION AND DISCUSSION

Assess Hannah More's view of poverty. Is that view still widely held? Compare her view to your view.

What do you find most edifying about More's life? What do you find least edifying?

Meeting Wilberforce was a turning point in More's life. When in your life have you experienced a similar turning point?

What does it mean to be resigned to the will of God? How does it differ from fatalism?

If you were to state "the essential spirit of the Christian life" in a sentence or phrase, what would it be?

Chapter 15

CHARLES SIMEON

1759-1836

Pulpit Revolutionary

THE WARDENS of Holy Trinity Church, Cambridge, were not pleased when young Charles Simeon stepped into their pulpit for the first time on January 4, 1783. Simeon was but twenty-three years old and not yet even ordained to the priesthood. Why the Bishop of Ely had named Simeon vicar of Holy Trinity, they could not imagine (Simeon's father, a friend of the bishop, had asked him to). Life at Holy Trinity in the 1780s must have been riveting, as the new young vicar, burning with a desire to preach, tried to do so, while the equally hot church wardens tried to prevent him. The wardens refused to attend services conducted by Simeon and locked the doors of their old-fashioned box pews (which were rented by families in something like the way box seats are rented at modern athletic stadiums) so no one else could sit in them, either. At his own expense, Simeon bought benches to set up in the aisles, but the wardens dragged them into the churchyard. For several years, Simeon preached to a "standing room only" congregation in a church full of empty seats. Simeon proposed a Sunday evening service at which worshipers might be allowed to sit, but the wardens made certain the building was locked on Sunday evenings. The wardens had favored one John Hammond, who had served as curate under the previous vicar, and they invited Hammond to deliver a lecture at Holy Trinity every Sunday afternoon, for which they paid him twice what Simeon earned as vicar of the parish. Simeon finally took to riding his horse into the neighboring countryside on Sunday afternoons, where he preached in small churches which could not afford to pay a preacher — to increasingly large and appreciative crowds. What no one could have imagined in 1783 was that Charles Simeon would occupy the pulpit at Holy Trinity Church for fifty-four years, become the most influential preacher in the land, and single-handedly redefine what a sermon was supposed to be.

Simeon lived to preach. This was unusual at a time when most sermons were dry, learned discourses, memorized word-for-word or read from a manuscript. Many preachers used sermons written by other people, taken from books. Listeners were expected to think about the ideas expressed, but rarely were they challenged to change their lives. This was not for Charles Simeon, who saw such preaching as an invitation to a self-satisfied, lukewarm piety. Simeon not only wrote his own sermons, but spent twelve hours preparing each one, sometimes longer. And he sought to engage not only the minds, but the hearts and wills of his listeners. Although he shared the distrust of "enthusiasm" typical of the day, he did not hesitate to appeal to the emotions as well as to the intellect. His sermons were dramatic and fervent. Cambridge was not ready for Simeon, and congregations were small at first (due in part, no doubt, to the creative efforts of the wardens to keep them small). But within a decade, people began to fill the pews of Holy Trinity (new, more sympathetic wardens opened the pews in 1790), and by the early 1800s, a Sunday congregation of a thousand worshipers was not unusual.

During his theological studies, Simeon had looked for guidance in preaching. There was none to be found — no books, no classes, no mentors. It was assumed (often wrongly) that preaching and other pastoral skills would be acquired on the job, after ordination. Lest others enter the field as poorly trained as he was, Simeon began to invite divinity students from Cambridge University to discuss preaching with him, and his preaching seminars, though not part of any formal curriculum, became immensely popular. One estimate is that over 1,100 aspiring clergymen learned to preach under Charles Simeon during his fifty-four years at Holy Trinity.

Simeon did not write books — he wrote sermons. But he began to collect and publish his sermons, finally producing in 1833 a 21-volume set, containing 2,536 sermons, covering the entire Bible. Called *Horae Homileticae*, it went through several editions. The volumes do not contain actual sermon texts, but what Simeon called "skeletons," or outlines of sermons, designed to spur the reader to fill in the details from his or her own life. But these "skeletons" are so detailed, containing in many cases several paragraphs on a single point, that they could pass for full-blown sermons. More than the skeletons themselves, Simeon's preface discussing his theories on preaching is of most interest today. Revolutionary at the time, those theories have since become standard fare in seminary homiletics classes: Scope out the biblical text and analyze it. Look at the context of the passage. Consider the literal meaning, but don't be bound by it. Discuss each part of the text in turn. Develop a unified theme, with an introduction, development, and conclusion. Don't read your own favorite ideas into the text. Avoid overly ornamental language and obscure references. Devise a style of delivery that suits your individual personality. Simeon believed a sermon should do three things — explain the Bible and church teaching, comfort listeners with the marvelous ways of God, and inflame their hearts to a life of holiness.

The most distinctive feature of Simeon's preaching was his faithfulness to scripture. He rose daily at 4:00 am and spent four hours a day in Bible study and prayer. Simeon knew the scriptures — he read the Bible far more than anything else — and believed the preacher's task was to allow the scripture to speak. "My goal," he said in the preface to *Horae Homileticae,* "is to bring out of the scripture what is there, and not to thrust in what I think might be there."

Simeon was wary of "theological systems" and kept his distance from the chief theological controversy of the day among evangelicals, a version of the sovereignty of God versus free will debate that had been simmering since the Reformation. All agreed that divine grace was essential to human salvation. In Simeon's day, those insisting that salvation was entirely the act of a sovereign God were called Calvinists (after the sixteenth-century French reformer John Calvin), while those allowing for a measure of human free will in the response to divine grace were called Arminians (after the early-seventeenth-century Dutch theologian Jacobus Arminius). Simeon said both groups were right, because scripture contained material supporting both positions. That this seemed a self-contradiction did not bother him in the least. "The truth is not in the middle, and not in one extreme, but in both extremes," he said. If not entirely convincing to the partisans involved, it was at least a novel view. The important thing for Simeon was to let the Bible speak. He once wrote to a friend, "If I were asked, 'Are you a Calvinist?' I should answer, No. 'Are you an Arminian?' No. 'What then are you?' I should answer, a Bible Christian. All that God says in his word, I say, without embarrassment and without fear, and on whichever side of the post the inspired writers run, I run after them, and if any tell me, 'You are wrong,' I reply, Tell Paul so, and Peter so, for I am misled by them." Every single sermon in *Horae Homileticae* is an exposition of scripture.

What did Simeon find when he probed the scriptures? His theological position is usually called "evangelical," and it is an apt label. Simeon preached for conversion. His own conversion had come to him as a surprise. He was not thinking religious thoughts as a new arrival on the Cambridge campus in 1779, but when he discovered that students were required to receive Holy Communion several times a year, he experienced a crisis of faith. He began reading religious literature and soon came to a profound conversion experience. As a new and excited Christian convert, Simeon had no one with whom to share his faith — what Christians there were on campus seemed to him lukewarm — but Simeon knew God had acted in his life. He had a strong conviction of human sin, beginning with his own, and he knew his need to be reconciled to a holy God. Christ's act of love, dying on the cross for human sin and bringing about the Atonement, was the driving force in Simeon's faith and preaching. Because of Christ's death on the cross, human repentance brings reconciliation to God. Then comes a life of holiness, in response to God's action in Christ. These are the themes that emerge in sermon after sermon in *Horae Homileticae,* and these are the themes that drew many thousands of searching souls to Holy Trinity Church for over half a century.

Some have faulted Simeon because not once in his sermons did he address slavery, the greatest moral issue of his time. He was, however, active in other causes, including the founding of the Church Missionary Society, the recruitment of chaplains for the East India Company, and efforts to convert the Jews. But perhaps his most controversial legacy was his founding of the Patronage Trust. The right to appoint the priest in many parishes was held by a lay person descended from the local medieval landlord, who had been responsible for the spiritual as well as the temporal affairs of his domain. These appointments, or "advowsons," as they were called, guaranteed a decent income for life, often with little expectation of work. In time, the right to appoint came to be bought and sold, and the purchaser often appointed a son or nephew to the position, regardless of the appointee's spiritual qualifications. The result was that many of the eager young ordinands trained by Simeon found themselves frozen out of positions filled by better connected but less devout men. Simeon used his considerable income, partly inherited, partly from the sales of *Horae Homileticae,* to buy up these advowsons. His goal was to provide challenging ministries for committed clergy. He shrewdly concentrated on growing urban areas, with the result that strong evangelical preaching began to revitalize the church in many cities.

Simeon met John Wesley once but was not a disciple of Wesley. By Simeon's day, many of those influenced by the eighteenth-century Wesleyan revival had left the Church of England to worship in the new Methodist chapels. Simeon was an evangelical Christian, but a loyal Anglican. Perhaps his greatest contribution was to show how evangelical Christianity can flourish within established church order. After Simeon, evangelical believers would not only be assured of a home within the Anglican tent, but have in the great Cambridge preacher a luminary of their own to show the way.

IN HIS OWN WORDS

His conversion

On my coming to college, Jan. 29, 1779, the gracious designs of God towards me were soon manifest. It was but the third day after my arrival that I understood I should be expected in the space of about three weeks to attend the Lord's Supper. What! said I, must I attend? On being informed that I *must*, the thought rushed into my mind that Satan himself was as fit to attend as I. . . . Within the three weeks I made myself quite ill with reading, fasting, and prayer. . . . I knew that on Easter Sunday I must receive it again. . . . I set myself immediately to undo all my former sins, as far as I could, and did it in some instances which required great self-denial, though I do not think it quite expedient to record them. . . . My distress of mind continued for about three months, and well it might have continued for years. . . . But in Easter week, as I was reading Bishop Wilson on the Lord's Supper, I met with an expression to this effect, "that the Jews knew what they did when they transferred their sin to the head of their offering." The thought rushed into my mind — What! May I transfer all my guilt to another? Has God provided an offering for me that I may lay all my sins on his head? Then, God willing, I will not bear them on my own soul one moment longer. Accordingly, I sought to lay my sins upon the sacred head of Jesus . . . [and on Easter Day, April 4,] I awoke early with those words upon my heart and lips, "Jesus Christ is risen today! Hallelujah!"

Memoir (1813)

Note: Simeon normally referred to himself in the third person, as "the author." In the quotations below, this has been changed to the first person for the sake of clarity.

Speak as the Bible speaks

On every point I have spoken freely and without reserve. As for names and parties in religion, I equally disclaim them all: I take my religion from the

Bible and endeavor, as much as possible, as in the scriptures themselves, to speak as that speaks.

"Preface" to *Horae Homileticae* (1833)

When Bible passages seem to conflict

While too many set these passages at variance, and espouse the one in opposition to the other, I dwell with equal pleasure on them both and think it, on the whole, better to state these apparently opposite truths in the plain and unsophisticated manner of the scriptures than to enter into scholastic subtleties that have been invented for the upholding of human systems. . . . I have no desire to be wise above what is written, nor any conceit that I can teach the apostles to speak with more propriety and correctness than they have spoken.

"Preface"

The preacher's test

I would wish this work to be brought to this test: Does it uniformly tend *to humble the sinner? to exalt the Savior? to promote holiness?* If in one single instance it lose sight of any of these points, let it be condemned without mercy.

"Preface"

"No friend to systematizers"

I am no friend to systematizers in theology. . . . I am disposed to think that the scripture system, be it what it may, is of a broader and more comprehensive character than some very exact and dogmatical theologians are inclined to allow, and that, as wheels in a complicated machine may move in opposite directions and yet subserve one common end, so may truths *apparently opposite* be perfectly reconcilable with each other, and equally subserve the purposes of God in the accomplishment of man's salvation.

"Preface"

When all are on their knees

I bitterly regret that men will range themselves under human banners and leaders and employ themselves in converting the inspired writers into friends and partisans of their peculiar principles. Into this fault I trust I have never fallen. One thing I know, namely, that pious men, both of the Calvinistic and Arminian persuasion, approximate very nearly when they are upon their knees before God in prayer, the devout Arminian then acknowledging his total dependence upon God as strongly as the most confirmed Calvinist, and the Calvinist acknowledging his responsibility to God and his obligation to exertion in terms as decisive as the most determined Arminian. And what both these individuals are upon their knees, it is my wish to become in my writings.

"Preface"

Genuine edification

Many, if their imaginations are pleased and their spirits elevated, are ready to think that they have been greatly edified, and this error is at the root of that preference which they give to extempore prayer, and the indifference which they manifest towards the prayers of the established church. But real edification consists in humility of mind, and in being led to a more holy and consistent walk with God, and one atom of such a spirit is more valuable than all the animal fervor that ever was excited. It is with *solid truths,* and not with *fluent words,* that we are to be impressed, and if we can desire from our hearts the things which we pray for in our public forms, we need never regret that our fancy was not gratified or our animal spirits raised by the delusive charms of novelty.

Sermon No. 192

Revelation

In different ages of the world it has pleased God to reveal himself to men in different ways, sometimes by visions, sometimes by voices, sometimes by suggestions of his Spirit to their minds: but since the completion of the sacred canon, he has principally made use of his written word, explained and enforced by men whom he has called and qualified to preach his gospel, and though he has not precluded himself from conveying again the knowledge of his will in any of the former ways, it is through the written word only that we are now authorized to expect his gracious instructions.

Sermon No. 1933

The content of preaching

What is that truth which ministers are bound to preach and which their people should be anxious to hear? . . . [St. Paul] studiously avoided all that gratified the pride of human wisdom and determined to adhere simply to one subject, *the crucifixion of Christ for the sins of men.*

Sermon No. 1933

What is an evangelical?

As though men needed not to be evangelized now, the term *evangelical* is used as a term of reproach. . . . It is not our design to enter into any dispute about the use of a *term,* or to vindicate any particular party, but merely to state, with all the clearness we can, a subject about which everyone ought to have the most accurate and precise ideas. . . . We have already seen what was the great subject of the apostle's [Paul's] preaching, and which he emphatically and exclusively called *the gospel,* and if only we attend to what he has spoken in the text, we shall see what really constitutes evangelical preaching. *The subject* of it must be "Christ crucified," that is, Christ must be set forth as the only foundation of a sinner's hope, and holiness in all its branches must be enforced, but a sense of Christ's love in dying for us must be inculcated as the main spring and motive of all our obedience. *The manner* of setting forth this doctrine must also accord with that of the apostle. . . . in proportion as any persons, in their spirit and in their preaching, accord with the example in the text, they are properly denominated *evangelical.*

Sermon No. 1933

To the land of oblivion

We do indeed . . . urge the necessity of repentance; but no man must rest in his repentance, however deep it may be. The offender, under the [Jewish] law, not only confessed his sins over his sacrifice, but laid them upon the head of the victim. So must we do. We must transfer all our sins to the head of our Great Sacrifice, and he, like the scapegoat, will carry them all away to the land of oblivion.

Sermon No. 1974

Authorized expositions

The scriptures alone are the proper standard of truth, but the Articles, Homilies, and liturgy of the Church of England are an authorized exposition of the sense in which all her members profess to understand the scriptures. To these therefore we appeal as well as to the sacred records.

Sermon No. 2000

Three essentials

There are three things which, as it is our duty, so also it is our continual labor, to make known, namely, *our lost estate, the means of our recovery,* and *the path of duty.*

Sermon No. 2000

Repentance

By repentance we do not mean that superficial work which consists in saying, "I am sorry for what I have done," but such a deep sense of our guilt and danger as leads us with all humility of mind to God and stirs us up to a most earnest application to him for mercy. We must feel sin to be a burden to our souls; we must be made to tremble at the wrath of God which we have merited; we must cry to him for deliverance from it.

Sermon No. 2000

Atonement

It is the blood of Christ, and that alone, that can atone for our guilt.

Sermon No. 2000

The path of duty

We are not satisfied with that standard of holiness which is current in the world. We require a higher tone of morals. In addition to sobriety and honesty, we insist upon a life entirely devoted to God. We affirm that it is every man's duty to delight himself in God, to have such a lively sense of Christ's love to him as shall constrain him to an unreserved surrender of all his faculties and powers to the service of his Lord. We must live for God.

Sermon No. 2000

FOR REFLECTION AND DISCUSSION

Do you agree with Simeon's advice to preachers? What would you add or delete?

What do you think of the statement, "The truth is not in the middle, and not in one extreme, but in both extremes"? Apply it to a debate going on today.

What are the values and the drawbacks of Simeon's belief that the scriptures should be allowed to speak for themselves?

What is the difference between a "systematizer" and a person with clear, definite beliefs?

Do you agree that since the Bible was completed, God "has principally made use of his written word" as the means of revelation?

What is an evangelical?

Chapter 16

JOHN KEBLE

1792-1866

Herald of Revival

Herald of Revival

F EW SERMONS have rattled more ecclesiastical cages than the one preached on Sunday, July 14, 1833, in St. Mary's Church, Oxford, before the king's Judges of Assize. The sermon made no great stir that day. One judge who heard it called it "an appropriate discourse." But ten days later, four young men met to discuss the sermon, and within a year, presses were pouring out petitions, tracts, and letters to the editor in a steady stream which did not abate for several decades. When it was all over, much of the Church of England — and Anglicans around the world — had a very different understanding of who they were and what they were about.

The preacher that day was no firebrand. John Keble, forty-one years old at the time, was a priest and professor of poetry at Oxford, known chiefly for his sanctity and quiet demeanor and for a volume of verses on the liturgical year published six years earlier. But something was churning in Keble's soul, and it erupted that Sunday morning. To most people, the occasion giving rise to the sermon would hardly have seemed worth turning an entire church upside down over. Parliament had just voted to consolidate the thirty-two dioceses of the (Anglican) Church of Ireland (then part of the United Kingdom) into twenty-two dioceses. A census had revealed there were only 852,000 Anglicans in Ireland, just eleven percent of the population, but their thirty-two bishops were supported, often in high style, by the enforced tithes of the Roman Catholic majority. The problem Keble (pronounced KEE-ble) saw was not that the Irish church needed no reform, but that the agency undertaking the reform was Parliament. By what authority did Parliament, a secular body whose members were often not even active Christians, undertake to reform the church of God? If Parliament could close down church offices in Ireland, what would come next? Was the church a mere department of state, like the army or the courts? If not, then what was it?

The Irish bill was but a small piece of what alarmed Keble. There was no sense of mission in the church. The eucharist was rarely celebrated, and confirmation was often treated as an occasion to dress up and go on an outing. The conduct of worship was generally shoddy. Christian life was seen as little more than a kind of bland gentility. Many bishops lived in luxury off endowment income while clergy in the smaller congregations were virtual paupers. Candidates for ordination often sought merely to "derive a living" that required little of them, sometimes not even residence in the community where their parish was located. And the church leadership seemed to see nothing awry in any of this.

Keble entitled his sermon "National Apostasy" (it is also known as his "Assize Sermon"). Choosing for his text I Samuel 12:23, the prophet Samuel's response to Israel's rejection of the Lord and asking to be like other nations, Keble addressed two questions: How can one tell when a Christian nation has alienated itself from God, and what should faithful Christians do when that happens? Look for several things, he said: indifference to the religious life of others, failure to instruct children, casual tolerance of unbelief, disregard of voluntary oaths, and "disrespect to the successors of the apostles." In the case of ancient Israel, the first step was the usurping of "the sacrificial office" by the state, Keble said — and Britain had followed a similar path. What did Samuel do? He prayed for the nation. He relied on God and did not give up. And he taught the truth. A faithful British Christian in 1833 was called to do the same, Keble concluded, and "is calmly, soberly, demonstrably sure that, sooner or later, his will be the winning side and that the victory will be complete, universal, eternal."

Keble's sermon was the opening shot of the Oxford Movement, so called because its leaders were associated with Oxford University. It is also called the Tractarian Movement because it spread, initially, through the publication and distribution of tracts. A religious tract, even then, was not seen as the most eminent form of theological discourse, but a tract could be printed cheaply and distributed widely. These "Tracts for the Times" took the debate out of Oxford's ivory towers and into the parishes.

At the heart of the debate was the nature of the church. The Tractarians said the church was created and commissioned by God, and is accountable to God — not to the state or even to church members. Bishops were successors to the apostles, standing in a direct line reaching back through the centuries to them; they represented Christ, not the government, and their authority came from Christ. As successors to the apostles, bishops were to guard "the deposit of the faith." This doctrine of "apostolic succession" was an element of the "one holy catholic and apostolic church" as understood by medieval theologians and by the sixteenth- and seventeenth-century Anglican reformers. By the nineteenth century, however, this understanding of the church had been forgotten, and the result, said the Tractarians, was a dull, demoralized church.

The tracts, ninety in all, appeared from 1833 to 1841. The early ones were short, forceful statements, published anonymously; the later ones were signed and often of book length. Fourteen authors contributed to the series; John Keble wrote eight. Many of the tracts were controversial. Take, for example, Keble's tract No. 40. Marriage in the church had come to be seen as the right of every British citizen. Keble recounts an incident when a parishioner asked his advice as to whether he should stand as best man at the wedding of his nephew when the bride had not been baptized. "I put it to him this way," Keble wrote. "If marriage is a different thing to a Christian from what it would be to anyone else, if it is not only one of the greatest earthly blessings, but also a special and holy token, appointed by God to signify unto us the mystical union that is betwixt Christ and his church, then to enter on it without prayer, or in any other but a religious way, must be almost as affronting to the Almighty as if one profaned the sacrament of his Son's body and blood." Heeding Keble's words, the parishioner declined to take part in the ceremony, earning cold stares from his peeved family. Keble was not, however, trying to be difficult, exclusive, or sanctimonious. His point was that the sacraments of the church are not casual ceremonies for anyone who may desire them, for any reason, but solemn rites through which the church conveys the blessings of God to those who have committed themselves to God.

The Oxford Movement's acknowledged leader quickly became the ascetic vicar of St. Mary's, Oxford, John Henry Newman, whose brilliant sermons were widely read and quoted. Newman wrote many of the most effective tracts. Keble, always happier in the parish than in the classroom, accepted the position of curate of Hursley, five miles west of Winchester, in 1836. He married soon thereafter and spent the rest of his life as a pastor and writer in Hursley, far from the hurly-burly of Oxford.

Keble's role in the Oxford Movement was far from ended, however. Newman saw little change and grew impatient. When he finally gave up on the Church of England and joined the Roman Catholic Church in 1845, Keble was devastated — Newman had been his intimate friend and colleague. Many felt Newman's departure discredited the Oxford Movement, revealing it as nothing more than papist teaching beneath an Anglican veneer. With Newman gone, however, Keble came into his own. He held fast, calling for loyalty to the Church of England as one would stand by one's mother. Together with Oxford don Edward Bouverie Pusey, Keble continued to push for the recovery of ancient tradition. Keble's church at Hursley became one of the earliest parishes to implement Tractarian principles, and by the time of Keble's death in 1866, the Oxford Movement had effected great changes in thousands of dioceses and parishes.

Perhaps the key difference in outlook between Keble and Newman was their understanding of Christian tradition. Tradition was crucial to both of them, as seen in their production of new editions of the works of Richard Hooker, Lancelot Andrewes, and other classical Anglican authors. But Newman saw tradition as constantly evolving, making possible the addition of new elements, such as the infallibility of the pope and the assumption of the Blessed Virgin Mary. For Keble, however, tradition was primarily faithfulness to the past, especially (as for Hooker and Andrewes) the first five centuries of the Christian era. The Bible and ancient tradition are in harmony, Keble said. "Tradition teaches the sufficiency of the written Word, and the Bible confirms and illustrates what tradition teaches."

A word should be said about Keble's extraordinarily popular little book of poems, *The Christian Year*. It went through 140 editions between 1827 and 1873, with 305,500 copies printed. The book includes a poem for every Sunday and major holy day of the church year. It was especially popular with Oxford Movement enthusiasts (although others loved it as well), even though it hardly mentions the major themes of the Oxford Movement. It is concerned with personal religion and most of the poems have a somber, soothing tone, often including descriptions of natural scenes. A few of the poems stand out (the best known is the evening hymn "Sun of my soul! Thou Savior dear") but most of *The Christian Year* sounds forced and sentimental to the modern ear. Keble's biographer Georgina Battiscombe comments that "no book was ever more to the liking of its own age or less to the taste of the present one."

The Oxford Movement was not without its excesses. F. D. Maurice commented that it occasionally erred "in opposing to the spirit of this present age the spirit of a former age, instead of the everliving and active Spirit of God, of which the spirit of each age is at once the adversary and the parody." These occasional excesses do not, however, erase the blessings which the Oxford Movement brought to the church, some of them beyond anything envisioned by the original Tractarians. Parliament had its way with the Irish bishoprics, but a tacit understanding emerged that the government would no longer determine church policy. Beyond this, the Oxford Movement also generated a new dignity in worship, higher standards among the clergy, a revival of Anglican monastic orders, new mission work among the poor, missionary expansion outside England, the restoration of old churches and construction of new ones, and a burst of new hymns and devotional writing.

IN HIS OWN WORDS

In the waste howling wilderness
   The Church is wandering still,
Because we would not onward press
   When close to Sion's hill.
Back to the world we faithless turned
   And far along the wild,
With labor lost and sorrow earned
   Our steps have been beguiled.

The Christian Year (1827)

Legislature has usurped church

The legislature (the members of which are not even bound to express belief in the Atonement) has virtually usurped the commission of those whom our Savior entrusted with at least one voice in making ecclesiastical law in matters wholly or partly spiritual. The same legislature has also ratified this principle, that the apostolic church is only to stand, in the eyes of the state, as one sect among many, depending for any pre-eminence she may still appear to retain merely upon the accident of her having a strong party in the country.

Advertisement to Sermon
on "National Apostasy" (1833)

Apostasy

The point really to be considered is whether, according to the coolest estimate, the fashionable liberality of this generation be not ascribable, in a great measure, to the same temper which led the Jews voluntarily to set about degrading themselves to a level with the idolatrous Gentiles. And if it be true anywhere that such enactments are forced on the legislature by public opinion, is *apostasy* too hard a word to describe the temper of that nation?

"National Apostasy"

A nation like Saul?

God forbid that any Christian land should ever, by her prevailing temper and policy, revive the memory and likeness of Saul, or incur a sentence of reprobation like his. But if such a thing should be, the crimes of that nation will probably begin in infringement on apostolical rights; she will end in persecuting the true church; and in the several stages of her melancholy career, she will continually be led on from bad to worse by vain endeavors at accommodation and compromise with evil. Sometimes toleration may be the word, as with Saul when he spared the Amalekites [I Sam. 15]; sometimes state security, as when he sought the life of David [I Sam. 19]; sometimes sympathy with popular feeling, as appears to have been the case, when violating solemn treaties, he attempted to exterminate the remnant of the Gibeonites, in his zeal for the children of Israel and Judah [II Sam. 21:2]. Such are the sad but obvious results of separating religious resignation altogether from men's notions of civil duty.

"National Apostasy"

To restore the church

The surest way to uphold or restore our endangered church will be for each of her anxious children, in his own place and station, to resign himself more thoroughly to his God and Savior in those duties, public and private, which are not immediately affected by the emergencies of the moment: the daily and hourly duties, I mean, of piety, purity, charity, justice.

"National Apostasy"

Apostolic succession

Why then should any man here in Britain fear or hesitate boldly to assert the authority of the bishops and pastors of the church, on grounds strictly evangelical and spiritual, as bringing men nearest to Christ our Savior and conforming them most exactly to his mind, indicated both by his own conduct and by the words of his Spirit in the apostolic writings? Why should we talk so much of an *establishment* [of the national church] and so little of an *apostolical succession?* Why should we not seriously endeavor to impress our people with this plain truth — that by separating themselves from our communion they separate themselves not only from a decent, orderly, useful society, but from *the only church in this realm which has a right to be quite sure that she has the Lord's body to give to his people?* Nor need any man be perplexed by the question, sure to be . . . asked, "Do you then unchurch all the Presbyterians, all Christians who have no bishops? Are they to be shut out of the covenant, for all the fruits of Christian piety, which seem to have sprung up not scantily among them?" Nay, we are not judging others, but deciding on our own conduct.

Tract No. 4 (1833)

Authority of the clergy

Look on your pastor as acting by man's commission, and you may respect the authority by which he acts, you may venerate and love his personal character, but it can hardly be called a *religious* veneration; there is nothing, properly, *sacred* about him. But once learn to regard him as "the deputy of Christ, for reducing man to the obedience of God," and everything about him becomes changed, everything stands in a new light.

Tract No. 4

Preserve the faith

The one thing needful is to "*retain* the mystery of the faith;" to "*abide* in the good instruction whereto we have already attained;" to "teach no *other* doctrine;" to be on our guard against those who resist the truth under pretense of "proceeding further," assured that such, although they seem to be "ever learning," shall never be able to "come to the knowledge of the truth"; they will "*proceed*" indeed, but it will be from bad to worse!

Sermon on "Primitive Tradition Recognized
in Holy Scripture" (1836)

And with no faint nor erring voice
   May to the wanderer whisper, "Stay;
God chooses for thee; seal his choice,
   Nor from thy Mother's shadow stray;
For sure thy Holy Mother's shade
   Rests yet upon thine ancient home:
No voice from heaven has clearly said,
   'Let us depart'; then fear to roam."

Lyra Innocentium (1846)

BY JOHN HENRY NEWMAN

To the clergy

Christ has not left his church without claim of its own upon the attention of men. Surely not. Hard Master he cannot be, to bid us oppose the world, yet give us no credentials for so doing. There are some who rest their divine mission on their own unsupported assertion; others, who rest it upon their popularity; others, on their success; and others, who rest it upon their temporal distinctions. This last case has, perhaps, been too much our own; I fear we have neglected the real ground on which our authority is built — *our apostolical descent.* We have been born, not of blood, nor of the will of the flesh, nor of the will of man, but of God. The Lord Jesus Christ gave his spirit to his apostles; they in turn laid their hands on those who should succeed them; and these again on others; and so the sacred gift has been handed down to our present bishops, who have appointed us as their assistants, and in some sense representatives.

Tract No. 1 (1833)

The power of ordination

Thus we have confessed before God our belief, that through the bishop who ordained us, we received the Holy Ghost, the power to bind and to loose, to administer the sacraments, and to preach. Now how is he able to give these great gifts? . . . Whence, I ask, his right to do so? Has he any right, except as having received the power from those who consecrated him to be a bishop? He could not give what he had never received. It is plain then that he but *transmits;* and that the Christian ministry is a *succession.* And if we trace back the power of ordination from hand to hand, of course we shall come to the apostles at last. We know we do, as a plain historical fact; and therefore all we, who have been ordained clergy, in the very form of our ordination acknowledged the doctrine of the *apostolical succession.* And for the same reason, we must necessarily consider none to be *really* ordained who have not *thus* been ordained.

Tract No. 1

A creation of the state?

Are we content to be accounted the mere creation of the state, as schoolmasters and teachers may be, or soldiers, or magistrates, or other public officers? Did the state make us? Can it unmake us? Can it send out missionaries? Can it arrange dioceses? Surely all these are spiritual functions, and laymen may as well set about preaching and consecrating the Lord's Supper as assume these.

Tract No. 2 (1833)

FOR REFLECTION AND DISCUSSION

Keble described the church he knew as listless and demoralized. Compare the church Keble knew with the church you know.

From what foundational beliefs did the Tractarians begin when they defined the church? From what foundational beliefs would you begin?

Write a few sentences defending Keble's position on marriage in Tract No. 40, then write a few sentences opposing his position. What are the values underlying each position?

Assess and compare Keble's and Newman's understandings of tradition.

Are there other ways of understanding the succession of bishops than the way the Tractarians understood it?

The Oxford Movement held ordination in high esteem. What would have been the role of lay people in the church as understood by the Oxford Movement?

State why you agree or disagree with F. D. Maurice that the Spirit of every age is "the adversary and the parody" of the Spirit of God.

Keble believed the government should keep "hands off" the church. Would his understanding also require the church to keep "hands off" the government? What is your understanding of the relationship between church and government?

Chapter 17

FREDERICK DENISON MAURICE

1805-1872

Citizen of the Kingdom

L ET US ADMIT at the outset that Frederick Denison Maurice was a muddy writer. He piled rhetorical questions one upon another and concocted long artificial dialogues between himself and his opponents. Reading this convoluted prose is like hacking one's way through a swampy thicket of overgrown sentences and tangled paragraphs.

Literary style aside, Maurice was also one of the nineteenth century's most original, complex, and far-ranging thinkers. Among Anglicans, he was without peer. Maurice (he pronounced it Morris) defies pigeonholing: He has been viewed at different times as a radical and a reactionary, a high churchman and a low churchman, an intellectual and an activist, an ecumenist and an Anglican polemicist — and a case can be made for each of these labels. Always, however, he wrote his books as he lived his life — as a devoted citizen of the kingdom of Jesus Christ.

The Kingdom of Christ was, in fact, both the organizing principle of Maurice's life and thought and the title of his most important book. Maurice believed not that Christ should be king or would be king someday, but that Christ *is* king, not merely of the church but of the entire human race. There is a divine order, established by God in creation with Christ as its head, in which all human beings take part, whether or not they acknowledge it. That conviction underlay everything Maurice thought and did.

Take baptism, for example. Two rival parties disputed the nature of baptism in the mid-nineteenth century. The Evangelicals taught that the conversion of the heart, denoted by baptism, brought salvation, while the Anglo-Catholics taught that incorporation into the Body of Christ, effected by baptism, brought salvation. Both understandings left out the great majority of people, and Maurice had no use for either. He called baptism "the sacrament of constant union." It did not bring a person under the rule of Christ, Maurice wrote, but testified that the person was already under the rule of Christ. Baptism did not signify a change in status, but unveiled a status that had been there from the beginning.

Or take heaven and hell. Most people in that day thought the reality of eternal rewards and punishments was not only central to the Christian gospel, but necessary to restrain sinful human nature and maintain social order. Maurice took what was then the novel view that heaven and hell are experiences not in the next life, but right here and right now. Eternity, Maurice wrote, is not merely time without beginning or end, but a reality outside time altogether. Moreover, he said, it's not punishment for sin, eternal or otherwise, that people need delivering from, but sin itself — and

Christ has accomplished this by his sacrifice on the cross. He saw fellowship with God through Christ as a present fact for all people, available for the claiming. If this sounded suspiciously like universalism, the belief that believers and unbelievers alike are saved, Maurice did not deny it, although he stopped just short of saying it explicitly. The doctrinal statements of the Church of England, he said, allow for universalist belief, though they do not require it. In any case, no one can know who or how many are saved, Maurice said. He developed this controversial idea in the final chapter of his book *Theological Essays,* published in 1853, which resulted in his dismissal from his teaching position at King's College in London. A year later he founded the Working Men's College in London.

The founding of the college and Maurice's controversial involvement in other social reforms also arose from his conviction that Christ is king. If Christ is truly king of the human race under a divinely constituted order, Maurice thought, then those who claim his name should act like it. Capitalism, he wrote, was based on an appeal to selfishness, hardly a suitable foundation for a kingdom of love. Maurice was one of the founders of the Christian Socialist movement in England. As promoted by Maurice, Christian socialism, unlike Marxist socialism, did not resort to violence or push for government ownership of the means of production, but rallied around the conviction that all workers were brothers and sisters under Christ and that cooperation, not competition, should guide the nation's economy. Maurice not only preached these words, but lived them. In addition to the Working Men's College, he was among the founders in 1848 of Queen's College for women, where he advocated a curriculum for women identical to that offered elsewhere to men, a revolutionary idea at the time.

This is not to say that Maurice was a social liberal in every respect. Not at all — he believed that a strong monarchy and aristocracy were part of the order God had laid out for humanity, that the king was God's agent under Christ, and that church and state should work closely together under the king. Maurice thought democracy was silly and blasphemous. Rather than a new constitution based on the sovereignty of the people, he called for the old constitution, based on kings reigning by the grace of God, to exhibit its true functions and energies.

Maurice loathed the disunity among Christians which he saw all around him because it denied the universal kingship of Christ. He often railed against sects, philosophical schools, and "systems" which divided people from one another, and felt called to "metaphysical and theological grubbing" for the purpose of uncovering the truth underlying each such group's experience and upon which unity might be achieved. In the opening section of *The Kingdom of Christ,* Maurice sets out to identify these truths. He addresses in turn an imaginary Quaker, Protestants of different affiliations, a Unitarian, and representatives of several philosophical and political parties of the day. In each case, he states the point of view of his opponent, focusing on the truth, or "positive principle," which his opponent affirms. Each group was formed around an experience of reality, its "positive principle," but then constructed a "system" which included detailed explanations and requirements that kept people out. Membership came to be defined not on the basis of the positive principle, but on the basis of negative principles. The message ceased to be "We affirm our truth" and became "We deplore your errors." A divisive party spirit was the result.

Throughout history, Maurice said, people have hungered for something more. The beliefs of ancient religions point to such a hunger. Is there anywhere a society, a constitution manifesting God's glory? Is there a spiritual order ordained by God on the basis of which the kingdom of Christ rests and the unhappy divisions among people may be resolved? In short, is there a catholic (or universal) church? These are the questions Maurice seeks to answer in *The Kingdom of Christ.* There is, he acknowledges, a church claiming to manifest God's order, but the assertions of the "Romanists" do not hold. To identify such a spiritual society, Maurice looks for "signs" which will have been observed across many centuries, nations, and cultures — and he finds six of them: baptism, creeds, forms of worship, eucharist, the ordained ministry, and the scriptures.

Maurice believed these "signs" both pointed to a spiritual society ordained by God and provided that society's context. At its most basic level, this context is seen in the family unit. Then comes the nation, built on loyalty to family. Maurice spoke of the "sanctity, the grandeur, the divinity of national life." That God places human beings in such social relationships, Maurice felt, is a reflection of the nature of God himself, for it is the interaction of Father, Son, and Holy Ghost within the Godhead that sets the norm for human relationships.

Where, then, might one find these six signs in their purest expression? At this point, Maurice begins to sound like a Church of England propagandist, for it is precisely in the Church of England that Maurice finds that expression. He is aware of the shortcomings in the Church of England over the years, but feels that the six signs of a universal spiritual society are most fully manifest there. This does not mean everyone should rush to sign on with the Church of England. Far from it — each nation should foster within its own people a church manifesting these signs, but differing in ways appropriate to that nation.

Maurice's six "signs" have had an interesting history. In 1888, the Lambeth Conference, consisting of Anglican bishops from around the world, adopted the "Lambeth Quadrilateral," a statement on the basis of which Anglicans invited other Christians to enter into discussions of unity. The Lambeth Quadrilateral appears in several modern Anglican prayer books. It consists of a modified version of Maurice's six signs of a universal spiritual society. Set forms of worship was dropped, and baptism and eucharist were combined into one sign — resulting in the document which remains to this day the foundational document for all Anglican ecumenical discussions.

Assessing the life and thought of F. D. Maurice is as difficult now as it was in his own day. He was never afraid to pose the hard question or to follow his understanding of the Christian faith to its logical conclusion, controversial though that often was. Nor did he hesitate to live the faith of which he wrote and spoke. He was a man who died a century before some of his key ideas gained wide acceptance, and even now, many who slog their way through his dense prose find themselves challenged and rewarded. Above all, F. D. Maurice sought to advance the kingdom of Jesus Christ on earth and to live his life in obedience to his King.

IN HIS OWN WORDS

Quarrelsome age

Persecution provoked the spirit which it strove to extinguish. Have compromise and liberality succeeded in repressing it? Is this age, in which all opinions are so commonly believed to be indifferently true, less fruitful of party notions and animosities than any previous age? Do men find fewer excuses than formerly, for quarreling with each other, and hating each other? Would it not be more correct to say, that our modern liberalism means permission to men to quarrel with and hate each other as much as they please?

The Kingdom of Christ (1838)

Need for a divine scheme

If there be no great scheme through which God is manifesting forth his own glory; if we are to invent the schemes for promoting that glory, we soon become the objects of our own worship. If it be merely in nature that God hath made a manifestation of himself, we may see power and order; goodness and truth we cannot see.

The Kingdom of Christ

Divisive spirit

At present, most of our books are written against some past or prevailing notion; Papists write against Protestants, Protestants against Popery; the supporters of the *via media* [middle way] against both. It is impossible for men holding one view to read the words written on the opposite hypothesis, except for the purpose of finding fault with them. It is impossible for those who adopt none of the views to gain quiet and comfortable instruction from the writers who have defended them. Thus three-fourths of our time for reading is spent in finding out what we may abuse.

The Kingdom of Christ

Forget self

I do not tell a man that he is to ask himself, how much faith he has, and if he have so much, to call himself justified. What I tell him is precisely that he is not to do this. . . . He is not to think or speculate about his faith at all. He is to believe, and by believing, to lose sight of himself and to forget himself.

The Kingdom of Christ

Human relationships

Human relationships are not artificial types of something divine, but are
actually the means and the only means, through which man ascends to any
knowledge of the divine; . . . every breach of a human relation, as it implies
a violation of the higher law, so also is a hindrance and barrier to the perception of that higher law — the drawing of a veil between the spirit of a
man and his God.

The Kingdom of Christ

Christianity and socialism

I seriously believe that Christianity is the only foundation of socialism and
that a true socialism is the necessary result of a sound Christianity.

Tracts on Christian Socialism (1838)

Systems

When once a man begins to build a system, the very gifts and qualities
which might serve in the investigation of truth become the greatest hin-
drances to it. He must make the different parts of the scheme fit into each
other; his dexterity is shown, not in detecting facts, but in cutting them
square.

Ecclesiastical History (1853)

Dogmatism

This age is impatient of distinctions — of the distinction between right
and wrong, as well as of that between truth and falsehood. Of all its perils,
this seems to me the greatest. . . . I should always denounce the glorification of private judgment, as fatal to the belief in truth, and to the pursuit
of it. We are always *tending* towards the notion that we may think what we
like to think; that there is no standard to which our thoughts should be
conformed. . . . But dogmatism is not the antagonist of private judgment.

The most violent assertor of his private judgment is the greatest dogmatist. And, conversely, the loudest assertor of the dogmatical authority of the church, is very apt to be the most vehement and fanatical stickler for his own private judgments.

Theological Essays (1853)

Sin

When once [a person] arrives at the conviction, "I am the tormenter — evil lies not in some accidents, but in me" — he is no more in the circle of outward acts, outward rules, outward punishments. . . . He has come unawares into a more inward circle — a very close, narrow, dismal one, in which he cannot rest. . . . he can only emerge out of it when he begins to say, "I have sinned against some Being — not against society merely, not against my own nature merely, but against another to whom I was bound." And the emancipation will not be complete till he is able to say . . . "*Father, I have sinned against thee.*"

Theological Essays

Christ in all persons

Christ is with those who seem to speak most slightingly of him, testifying to them that he is risen indeed, and that they have a life in him which no speculations or denials of theirs have been able to rob them of, even as we have a life in him, which our sins often hinder us from acknowledging, but cannot quench.

Theological Essays

The church and the world

The church is, therefore, human society in its normal state; the world, that same society irregular and abnormal. The world is the church without God; the church is the world restored to its relation with God, taken back by him into the state for which he created it. Deprive the church of its center, and you make it into a world. If you give it a false center, as the Romanists have done, still preserving the sacraments, forms, creeds, which speak of the true center, there necessarily comes out that grotesque hybrid which we witness, a world assuming all the dignity and authority of a church — a church practicing all the worst fictions of a world; the world assuming to be heavenly — a church confessing itself to be of the earth, earthly.

Theological Essays

The Trinity

When the gospel was preached, when the name of the Father, the Son, and the Holy Ghost, was uttered, when men had been baptized into it, idols fell down; the worship of the visible became intolerable; the sense of Unity profound. . . . We have sometimes fancied we could dwell simply on the thought of a Father; all others should be discarded as unnecessary. But soon it has not been a Father we have contemplated, it has been a mere substratum of the things we saw, a name under which we collected them. How rejoiced is the heart to pass from such a cold void to the thought of a Son filled with all human sympathies! But how soon does the sin-sick soul frame a thousand images and pictures of its own as a substitute for the perfect image; dream of mediators closer and more gracious than the One who died for all! What a relief to fly from these fancies to a divine Spirit! How we wonder that we should ever have thought that God could be anywhere but in the contrite heart and pure!

Theological Essays

Eternal life

Instead of picturing to ourselves some future bliss, calling that eternal life, and determining the worth of it by a number of years, or centuries, or millenniums, we are bound to say once for all: "This is the eternal life, that which Christ has brought with him, that which we have in him, the knowledge of God; the entering into his mind and character, the knowing him as we only can know any person, by sympathy, fellowship, and love."

Theological Essays

Leave all to God

I ask no one to pronounce, for I dare not pronounce myself, what are the possibilities of resistance in the human will to the loving will of God. There are times when they seem to me — thinking of myself more than of others — almost infinite. But I know that there is something which must be infinite. I am obliged to believe in an abyss of love which is deeper than the abyss of death: I dare not lose faith in that love. I sink into death, eternal death, if I do. I must feel that this love is compassing the universe. More about it I cannot know. But God knows. I leave myself and all to him.

Theological Essays

The deepest hell

Spiritual pride is the essential nature of the Devil. To be in that, is to be in the deepest hell.

Theological Essays

Every man in Christ

The truth is that every man is in Christ; the condemnation of every man is that he will not own the truth; he will not act as if this were true, he will not believe that . . . except he were joined to Christ, he could not think, breathe, live a single hour. This is the monstrous lie which the devil palms upon poor sinners; "You are something apart from Christ."

quoted in *The Life of Frederick Denison Maurice,*
written by his son in 1885

Do not praise the liturgy

I hope you will never hear from me such phrases as "our incomparable liturgy": I do not think we are to praise the liturgy but to use it. When we do not want it for our life, we may begin to talk of it as a beautiful composition. Thanks be to God, it does not remind us of its own merits when it is bidding us draw near to him.

Life of F.D.M.

Longing for God

Source of all life and goodness, where art thou? It is thyself and not any of thy treasures that I need. Take them away if thou wilt not reveal thyself while I possess them. Take them away if they hinder me from the revelation of thyself.

Life of F.D.M.

FOR REFLECTION AND DISCUSSION

Which of the theological labels mentioned in the second paragraph of this essay would you apply to Maurice, and why?

Would you say that Christ is king of the human race? What evidence is there for and against this claim? What effect does your answer have on how you live your life?

Do you believe in eternal rewards and punishments? On what grounds do you base your belief?

What do you make of the hints of universalism found in Maurice?

What do you feel Maurice would say about "systems" and quarreling among Christians today?

Does Christian faith lead to socialist politics? Can a Christian be a capitalist?

Chapter 18

WILLIAM PORCHER DUBOSE
1836-1918

Rebel with a Cause

A s a son of the landed Southern aristocracy, William Porcher DuBose had believed slavery was part of the divine order — he'd been reared with it, it seemed natural, it was in the Bible — and as a top graduate in 1855 of the Citadel, the Military College of South Carolina, he was soon given the opportunity to fight for his beliefs. DuBose was wounded three times in the American Civil War, had his horse shot out from under him at the Second Battle of Bull Run, and was kept for two months in a lice-infested prisoner-of-war camp. One night, lying awake under the stars after the Confederate troops had been routed at Cedar Creek, he suddenly realized the Confederacy would lose the war, a possibility that had never occurred to him until that moment and which "came over me like a shock of death." He felt that night "the utter extinction of the world."

When DuBose returned to South Carolina following the war, he found that both his parents had died and that General Sherman had burned his family's home to the ground. The scene, he said, was "unendurable and hopeless." Later in life, he buried two wives and a son. DuBose would spend his life searching for answers: How could he have been so wrong? Where is God in a world full of error, hardship, and grief? How does God bring unity out of division, renewal out of devastation, good out of evil, life out of death?

DuBose had studied for ordination in South Carolina prior to the war. He was ordained priest in 1866, a year after the end of the war, and then served parishes in Winnsboro and Abbeville, South Carolina. But the call that was to set his life's course came in 1871, when the trustees of the University of the South, then hardly more than a large tract of land on a mountaintop in Tennessee and an idea of a school, called DuBose as chaplain. From that time until his retirement in 1908, he served as chaplain, professor, promoter, dean of the School of Theology (which he helped establish in 1878), and mentor to two generations of clergy from all over the South. Even today, a visitor to Sewanee (as the university is usually called) cannot fail to see or hear the name DuBose.

Some historians regard DuBose as the most significant theological voice to emerge from the American Episcopal Church. He published six books of theology between 1892 and 1911, most of them based on his study of the New Testament, and a personal memoir in 1912. A few key ideas pop up in one book after another. One commentator has compared reading DuBose to watching a merry-go-round on which the rotating figures come around again and again. DuBose was a creative, original thinker, and many of his ideas, even when they have become familiar, can provoke the reader by challenging traditional views of the Incarnation, what it means to be "saved," and the nature of Christian dogma.

DuBose would never have held up his ideas, or even those of the classical creeds, as the final statements of Christian truth. Doctrinal statements must change, he said, because we and our conceptions of truth are always changing. Unlike some Christian thinkers, he embraced the new and controversial notion of evolution, seeing in it possibilities for fresh understandings of the Christian story. Christian doctrine, he said, is always evolving, and "no truth ought to be considered final and irreformable." He saw all human statements as imperfect and felt church teachings should be taken "out of their napkins" and allowed to take part in the give and take of ideas. Truth needs no fortress to protect it.

What, then, of the possibility that error might creep into church teaching? It's not a possibility, DuBose believed — it's a certainty, and there is no reason to be intimidated by it. The church should hear, test, and try every new idea, trusting that experience will separate truth from falsehood. DuBose's high regard for experience came from his own experiences of defeat during and following the war. Reflecting on those experiences had led him, after a time of disillusionment, back to God. In his Sewanee classrooms, DuBose encouraged challenging questions and viewpoints, even those with which he disagreed. Ultimately, DuBose felt, no individual believer can know or believe the whole truth. It is the church as a whole, with its many minds and lives, that discerns the whole truth, and even that is always evolving as new elements of the truth come to light.

The best place to begin looking at DuBose's own theology is probably with his understanding of the Incarnation, perhaps his most controversial teaching. DuBose accepted the traditional creedal statements about the person of Christ, but emphasized Christ's human nature, to the point that some critics accused him (wrongly) of denying the divinity of Christ. He felt Jesus' humanity had been neglected over the centuries, with costly consequences. Christ, DuBose stressed, was like us in *every* respect, save that he was without sin. That meant Christ shared all our weaknesses, including doubts, fears, ignorance of the future, and temptation with the real possibility of choosing evil over good. DuBose did not deny that Christ performed miracles, but he downplayed their significance. Anything short of this would have meant Christ did not share human experience and therefore could not have been our Savior. God could have disclosed himself to human beings and saved us only by becoming one of us, in *every* way, DuBose felt.

Then there is the other side of the Incarnation — humanity giving itself to God. Jesus was not only "God's absolute gift to the world," but, through his willing obedience, he was also "the world's supreme gift of itself to God." This gift is not yet fully completed or realized in every creature, DuBose admitted, but Christ represents all, and in Christ the world's gift of itself to God *is* completed and realized, and the estrangement between Creator and creature healed. DuBose was adamant in rejecting the idea that Christ died as a *substitute for* humanity. He insisted instead that Christ was the *representative of* humanity. Had Christ died as a substitute, he would have done something *for* us, whereas DuBose believed that as a representative, he did something *in* us, changing not merely our status, from guilty to acquitted, but our very nature.

This salvation (or at-one-ment with God, as DuBose liked to call it) is a process, not a completed state — sin remains to be dealt with — but that does not mean salvation is a mere hope or dream. It is a fact. Faith, DuBose says, "does not create a fact, it only accepts one." The Incarnation, seen fully in Christ, is also what God does in us. We are gradually transformed, as we live in Christ and he in us. What Christ did, we are learning to do — to give ourselves freely and lovingly to God. It is a process of becoming (evolution again), and our identity is defined not by what we are, but by what we are growing into. This is a paradox — our salvation, our transformation, is "already" but also "not yet."

The Holy Spirit is a key element in DuBose's thinking. The Spirit is divine assistance in our lives. Through the Spirit, the human Christ was enabled to obey perfectly the will of the Father, and through the Spirit we too shall be enabled to obey perfectly. No one is given the Holy Spirit against his or her will, but when we ask for and receive the Spirit, we are enabled to grow into the persons God has always envisioned us to be.

More than anywhere else, DuBose saw the Holy Spirit moving in the life of the Christian church. He had a "high" understanding of the church, taking St. Paul's metaphor of church as the Body of Christ almost literally — the church is the extension of the Incarnation. Incarnation is not merely something God did in Jesus, but is also something God *does* "in that mystical Body which is humanity realized and glorified in and through him." As the Lord assumed his fleshly human body, so has he assumed his mystical body, the church, which becomes "the humanity of his larger incarnation." The church doesn't merely proclaim Christ — it *is* Christ present in the world today, just as the body of the human Jesus was Christ present in ancient Judea. Christ does not guide the church from outside, but fills it with himself. Here, too, DuBose found the idea of evolution helpful. Wracked with divisions and infighting, the church is obviously not completely Christlike — not *yet*, but the process is underway; and DuBose defined the church not by what it is, but by what it is becoming.

DuBose's intellectual humility and sense of union with a loving God, through a still unfolding Incarnation, gave him an unyielding hope, despite the devastating losses he endured. This is perhaps the most compelling feature in his thought.

IN HIS OWN WORDS

Knowledge and virtue

The noble but merely rational idea that we may by knowledge and virtue attain unto God must be reversed into the truth that God in Christ incarnates himself in, and becomes, our knowledge and virtue. Our knowledge and virtue are not means to him; he is the means and cause of them.

The Soteriology of the New Testament (1892)

The Incarnation

If [Christ] is the Incarnation, he is it on both its sides. . . . He is not only God incarnating himself in man, but man incarnating God in himself. . . . He is not only the grace that imparts itself, but the faith which receives.

Soteriology

What proof?

God never meant to finally and forever prove or demonstrate himself by, and our Lord never meant to rest the proof of himself to the world upon external declarations and miraculous signs. The fact is, the ultimate proof of *all* truth is its truth, and not its proofs. What is true is going to live in the faith of men and to prove itself ever more and more to them; no other proof is essential, or can retain its force unimpaired by time or change. *How* do we know Christ to be the truth and the life? . . . Of whether he be the truth and the life, the criterion is within us.

Soteriology

Becoming Christ

[Christ] is not only our life-giver, but our life. He is the true personality and personal life of every person; the true selfhood of every self; the true manhood of every man. Every man only truly becomes himself in becoming Christ, and every man who becomes Christ does so by a personal act of Christ as well as of himself.

Soteriology

Baptism

All I claim is that Jesus Christ wholly and really *gives* himself in every baptism, not that he is wholly *received* in any, nor at all in many. But in any, the failure or limitation of the reception is in the human conditions, and not in the divine gift.

Soteriology

The coming of Christ

The truth of the Incarnation would be to me only an historical fact, an event of 1,800 years ago, without the truth of baptism, if he who became incarnate for me stopped, as it were, short of me, and did not become so in me.

Soteriology

The humanity of Jesus

The actual Jesus was indeed the most human of men; and we get farther and farther away from him, as well as from any real and saving hold upon the divine realized in him, the farther we get in any direction from the reality of his humanity.

The Ecumenical Councils (1896)

The cross

The principle of the cross itself was not a novelty. It had its truth for [Jesus] only as it has, and has always had, its truth for all. If he has made it the necessary and universal and everlasting symbol of all highest human motive and action, it is only because in itself and everywhere self-sacrificing love is the sole highest motive and action, not only for human but for all possible spiritual and free beings, including God himself.

The Ecumenical Councils

Transformed humanity

Humanity as our Lord received it was not what it is as he has made it.

The Ecumenical Councils

Double truth

What is of most consequence in what is revealed in [Christ] is not how God may be human but how man may become divine. . . . The Incarnation . . . must necessarily be equally God graciously fulfilling himself in humanity and humanity through faith, obedience, and self-sacrificing love, fulfilling God in itself and itself in God.

The Ecumenical Councils

Slavery and guilt

The world is constantly outgrowing and making sinful institutions which, however they are so now, were not so to it in the age or at the stage in which they prevailed. Polygamy was no sin to Abraham. Slavery was no sin to the consciousness or conscience of the New Testament. Feudalism was no sin in its day, but would be so now. Puritanism in forms which were once admirable would now be condemned. The time will come when war will be a sin. The South received and exercised slavery in good faith and without doubt or question, and, whatever we pronounce it now, it was not sin at that time to those people. Liable to many abuses and evils, it could also be the nurse of many great and beautiful virtues. There are none of us now who do not sympathize with its extinction as a necessary step in the moral progress of the world. It was natural that we who were in it and of it should be the last to see that, and be even made to see it against our will. Knowing as others could not, and loving the good that was in it, it was not strange that we should be more and longer than others blind to its evils, and unconscious of the judgment which the world was preparing, finally and forever, to pass upon it. Now that the judgment is passed, we join in it. Slavery we say, is a sin, and a sin of which we could not possibly be guilty.

"Wade Hampton" in the *Sewanee Review* (1902)

The kingdom of God

The kingdom of God, then, is not a kingdom of goodness as too many of us understand goodness. It is a kingdom not of absolute and unconditioned mercy shown to us, but of divine and therefore unconditioned mercy and goodness exercised by us.

The Gospel in the Gospels (1906)

God's self-fulfillment

When man through the perfect love and grace and fellowship of God in Christ has at last become himself in all the fulness of his divine predestination, has not also God in the consummated act of his own love and grace and self-fulfillment in man realized that in which in the highest his self-hood consists, and by the fact become his own highest self in the world and in us?

The Gospel in the Gospels

Christ present

He *is* here: The church is as much the sacrament of his presence as his human body was of the presence, the Incarnation, of God in himself. He is in us, *as* God was in him: there is no difference in the act and fact of his oneness with us from that of God's oneness with him — *other* than that which we place there by our want of faith in it.

The Reason for Life (1911)

Christ to me

Jesus Christ is to me, not a name, nor a memory or tradition, nor an idea or sentiment, nor a personification, but a living and personal reality, presence, and power. He is God for me, to me, in me, and myself in God. Wherein else do we see God, know God, possess God than as we are in him, and he in us? And wherein else are we so in him and he in us, as in Jesus Christ?

The Reason for Life

Attitude of suspense

I cannot think any real conflict between true religion, true history, true science, or true anything else. And each of these has its truth — to which I want to stand in the right relation — or if not that, at least in the right attitude. This puts me necessarily in a position of uncertainty upon points or details about which I was certain before. My attitude is in many respects one of suspense.

The Reason for Life

Truth will prevail

We say that truth is mighty and will prevail: well, how will it prevail? Not by being attested by anything outside itself, but by self-verification within itself. There is a great deal more in being true than in being proved.

The Reason for Life

The glory of God

The truest glory of the Highest is not merely that he can humble himself to behold the lowest, but that he can make himself one with the vilest sinner in his return. That the humiliation of Jesus was his glorification, that his deepest passion was his highest action, his bitterest suffering his highest perfection, his death for the world the life of the world — in a word, that eternal life is through mortal death, who could have invented or discovered that depth or summit of human truth and destiny, but that God himself had shown the way!

The Reason for Life

All the truth

My heart is very disposed to faith, to recognition of truth, to trust, and consent, and agreement. But my mind is naturally analytic and skeptical. I have all my life been coming to what of truth I hold, and there is truth to which I have all my life been coming, to which I have not yet come. All the truth of the church is not yet mine. There are points of it that I know to be true, because I have been all the time approximating to them, but I am still waiting, and shall probably die waiting, for them to become true to me. Truth is not an individual thing; no one of us has all of it — even all of it that is known. Truth is a corporate possession, and the knowledge of it is a corporate process.

Turning Points in My Life (1912)

Truth is plastic

Truth is not truth when it ceases to be plastic, and faith is faith only in the making. We cannot simply receive it, for then it is not yet ours; and we can never finish making it, for it ends only in all truth and all knowledge of the truth.

Turning Points

Skepticism

I believe that I always felt that skepticism and criticism were inevitable instruments of truth and righteousness and life, and that nothing in this world was proved, tested, or verified that had not passed through them to the uttermost end and limit.

Turning Points

Saints

Only the saint knows sin; only he who thus knows sin knows the cross; only he who knows the cross knows redemption and resurrection and eternal life.

Turning Points

Truth and liberty

Extremes always work themselves off best by freedom to work themselves out. The best expulsion of error is through the freedom permitted to it of self-exposure. Our end in view is not the licensing of error, but the ultimate best, if not only, method of eliminating error by suffering it to meet and be overcome by truth. By all means let the church guard and preserve her faith, order, and discipline, her creeds, her ministry, and her worship. But let her neither indulge the weak fear that these are really endangered or compromised by the fullest freedom conceded to and exercised by her members, nor imagine that danger or harm can be averted by the suppression or by the expulsion of that freedom. If our desire is to propagate error, there is no surer way than to persecute, suppress, and exclude liberty.

Turning Points

FOR REFLECTION AND DISCUSSION

What answers to you believe DuBose would give to the questions posed in the second paragraph of this essay?

What in DuBose's understanding of the Incarnation is new for you, and do you find it helpful?

Why did DuBose say that "no truth ought to be considered final or irreformable"? Do you agree?

Why does it matter whether Christ died as our substitute or as our representative?

Evaluate DuBose's statement on "Slavery and guilt."

Chapter 19

CHARLES GORE

1853-1932

Liberal or Conservative?

THE CONVENTIONAL wisdom of the Christian church was under attack as the nineteenth century drew to a close. Charles Darwin's *On the Origin of Species,* published in 1859, had challenged the literal understanding of the biblical Creation story, and a group of German scholars had begun using new literary and historical tools to question the accuracy and authorship of biblical texts. New ideas in psychology and physics would soon threaten received understandings of the mind and the natural world as well. Christian "Modernists" sought to rethink the faith to incorporate these ideas. The Roman Catholic hierarchy condemned Modernism in a papal encyclical in 1907 and a mandatory anti-Modernist oath in 1910, and among Protestants, a series of books called *The Fundamentals* (from which the Fundamentalist movement took its name) appeared in the United States between 1910 and 1915, defending the verbal inerrancy of the Bible. The name most associated with the controversy among Anglicans is that of Charles Gore — and some people still aren't sure which side he was on.

Gore was the grandson of two earls; his childhood home was on Wimbledon Common. Gore's parents were "low church" Anglicans for whom "popery" was another word for "catholicism." Sometime before his tenth birthday, young Charles was given a book about a Roman Catholic priest who converted to Protestantism. It didn't have the desired effect. Through this book Gore was introduced to confession, fasting, incense, and other "catholic" practices, and he said years later that he knew then that "this sort of sacramental religion was the religion for me." He was ordained priest in 1878. After the death in 1882 of Edward Bouverie Pusey, the last of the founders of the Oxford (or Tractarian) Movement, Gore's keen intellect and devotional temperament brought him quickly to a position of leadership in the Anglo-Catholic wing of the Church of England. He was appointed in 1883 the first principal of Pusey House, the library established as a memorial to Pusey at Oxford University, where he remained until 1893, influencing young ordinands at the university and writing several influential books defending apostolic succession and traditional understandings of the creeds.

The older Tractarians had seen Modernism as a threat to revealed truth and church authority. It was apparently assumed that Gore shared this view. But in 1889 a book of essays called *Lux Mundi* appeared, defending freedom of thought, evolution, and the new biblical criticism. The editor and the author of the book's most controversial essay was none other than Charles Gore. *Lux Mundi* would seem moderate by today's standards, but the book, and Gore's essay in particular, struck many Anglo-Catholics as an act of betrayal. Gore began his essay, entitled "The Holy Spirit and Inspiration," harmlessly enough, with a concise — and still helpful — discussion of the Holy Spirit in the church, identifying four characteristics of the Spirit's work: It is social rather than individualistic; it nourishes the unique individuality of each person; it consecrates every faculty of human nature, including the physical, spiritual, and intellectual; and it works gradually rather than suddenly. It was only towards the end of his essay that Gore ventured into disputed territory. The inspiration of scripture, he said, is not one of the "bases" of Christian faith, but part of the "superstructure." The church does not require its members to believe any particular theory as to how the Bible is inspired. There are degrees of inspiration, and the Bible contains various kinds of literature, inspired in different ways, Gore said. Inspiration does not lie in the words of the text themselves, but pertains to "the illumination of the judgment of the recorder," that is, to the authors. There is no reason to believe these inspired authors were given "miraculous communications of facts not otherwise to be known." The biblical records themselves are historical documents, not necessarily without error in matters of science and historical detail, and the new methods of biblical criticism, Gore said, can help the student uncover the spiritual truth which the inspired authors committed to the page.

Lux Mundi made possible a truce between Anglo-Catholics and Modernists. After the dust had settled, Modernist ideas were no longer automatically scorned among Anglo-Catholics, and some of the twentieth century's best biblical scholars had Anglo-Catholic roots. The book also made the name of Charles Gore famous — as a hero to some, a turncoat to others. But there was more to Gore than a devotion to intellectual freedom. Free thinker that he was, Gore's thoughts often brought him to orthodox conclusions. As an Anglo-Catholic, he treasured the church's apostolic roots. Even *Lux Mundi* had contained hints of Gore's traditionalist core. He had spoken in his essay of the need for the church "to keep her fundamental principles intact" and of Christ as having "secured" his revelation to be "without material alloy, communicated to the church which was to enshrine and perpetuate it." These are not the words of a biblical iconoclast. In subsequent years, it was this traditionalist side of Gore that came most often to the surface in his writings. Some have thought that the free-thinking young radical, when he became a bishop, was suddenly transformed into a champion of authority, discipline, and traditional doctrine — but that is entirely to misread Gore. His thought was consistent throughout his life. Gore held steady; it was the times that changed. Some would say they passed him by.

Gore was named bishop of Worcester in 1901. He engineered an overdue division of that large diocese, becoming the first bishop of the new diocese of Birmingham in 1905, and was made bishop of Oxford in 1911. He retired in 1919. All this time and following his retirement, Gore continued to write. He never disavowed anything he had written earlier and defended to the end the freedom to seek the truth, wherever it might be found. But the issues he was called upon to address in his later life were often matters (unlike biblical inspiration) which he regarded as the "bases" of Christian faith. The result was that Gore's reputation gradually changed from radical to reactionary — but the main threads of his thinking can be seen consistently throughout his work.

As bishop, Gore insisted his clergy not only recite the creeds, but believe literally creedal statements that refer to events in history. He could accept that statements about events outside history, such as Christ's sitting at the right hand of the Father, might be symbolic, but the heart of the Christian faith was the conviction that certain events, summarized in the creeds, had actually happened in history. It would not do, he said, to regard the virgin birth and the empty tomb of Easter morning as mere symbolic statements. The clergy were free to believe whatever they wished, but if they could not accept the church's foundational statements, in the way they were intended to be believed, they should resign their cures.

The issue for Gore ran deeper than acceptance of traditional dogmas. It had to do with the reality of the supernatural realm. This is seen most clearly in his discussion of miracles. Many intellectuals of the day, including many professing Christians, denied even the possibility of miracles. Like the eighteenth-century deists, they saw nature as a closed system. Events occurred within the natural order, but nothing from outside — that is, nothing *super*natural — entered in. Biblical miracles were explained away as the result of primitive understandings on the part of the biblical writers. For Gore, however, this abolished the distinction between Creator and creature. To deny even the possibility of a supernatural act within the natural order was, he felt, simply naive. That someone had not experienced a miracle and didn't expect one said more about that person's limited outlook than about what God might or might not do. Miracle was central to Gore's whole understanding of the Christian gospel, for the Incarnation of Jesus Christ was, in fact, *the* miracle, the moment above all others, when

God had invaded the created order from outside. This was a literal, historical fact, Gore insisted. It was in the Bible and the creeds — and he wasn't about to let it be rationalized away.

Gore's central concern was always that the essentials of the historic faith — as he understood them after free and careful investigation — remain "firm and unimpaired," that he himself and the Church of England be "of one mind across the ages with the ancient Christian church." Throughout his life, he was a passionate advocate of social justice, a concern derived from his understanding of the historic Christian faith. That understanding also led to his insistence on creedal orthodoxy and his uncompromising defense of apostolic succession, and it is the reason the accuracy of New Testament narratives (which he felt was demonstrable by the methods of the new biblical criticism) was so important to him.

It is not easy today, reading Charles Gore, to feel the excitement and anger his writing elicited a hundred years ago. Except among extreme conservatives, many of his "new" ideas have become commonplace, and his traditional positions, though not embraced by all, are within the range of Anglican norms. Gore was the foremost theological voice among Anglicans in the early twentieth century, and he remains today, as then, an enigmatic and paradoxical figure.

IN HIS OWN WORDS

Authority

True authority does not issue edicts to suppress men's personal judgment or render its action unnecessary, but it is like the authority of a parent, which invigorates and encourages, even while it restrains and guides the growth of our own individuality.

Roman Catholic Claims (1884)

Old and New Testaments

It is of the essence of the New Testament, as the religion of the Incarnation, to be final and catholic. On the other hand, it is of the essence of the Old

Testament to be imperfect, because it represents a gradual process of education by which man was lifted out of depths of sin and ignorance.

Lux Mundi (1889)

Tolerant church

The church must have her terms of communion, moral and intellectual; this is essential to keep her fundamental principles intact, and to prevent her betraying her secret springs of strength and recovery. But short of this necessity she is tolerant. It is her note to be tolerant, morally and theologically. She is the mother, not the magistrate.

Lux Mundi

Book or person?

[There is] a mode of reasoning which one had hoped had vanished from "educated circles" forever — that, namely, which regards Christianity as a "religion of a book" in such sense that it is supposed to propose for men's acceptance a volume to be received in all its parts as on the same level, and in the same sense, divine. On the contrary, Christianity is a religion of a Person. It propounds for our acceptance Jesus Christ, as the revealer of the Father. The test question of the church . . . has never been, "Dost thou believe the Bible?" but, "Dost thou believe that Jesus Christ is the Son of God?" . . . The Bible thus "ought to be viewed as not a revelation itself, but a record of the proclaiming and receiving of a revelation, by a body which is still existent, and which propounds the revelation to us; namely, the body of Christians commonly called the church."

Preface to *Lux Mundi*, tenth edition (1890)

"The crown of nature"

Something of God is manifest in the mechanical laws of inorganic structures: something more in the growth and flexibility of vital forms of plant

213

and animal; something more still in the reason, conscience, love, personality of man. Now from the Christian point of view, this revelation of God, this unfolding of divine qualities, reaches a climax in Christ. . . . Christ then, I say, is the crown of nature: He is thus profoundly natural, and to interpret the Christ we postulate only those spiritual realities, which . . . do in part find expression and in part lie hid behind the veil of nature.

The Incarnation of the Son of God (1891)

Miracle

What is a miracle? It is an event in physical nature which makes unmistakably plain the presence and direct action of God working for a moral end. God is always present and working in nature, and men were meant to recognize him in the ordinary course of events, and to praise him as they recognized him. But in fact man's sin has blinded his spiritual eye, he has lost the power of seeing behind the physical order; the very prevalence of law in nature, which is its perfection, has led to God being forgotten, his power depreciated, his presence denied. In a miracle, then, or what scripture calls a "sign," God so works that man cannot but notice a presence which is not blind force, but personal will.

The Incarnation of the Son of God

God in all things

To believe in God is to move about the world . . . [recognizing that] God is in all things. There is no creature so small, but represents something of his goodness. He is disclosed in all the grades and kinds of life: under the divers modes of beauty, and truth, and goodness, each with its own intrinsic value: through the ministries of artist and thinker, laborer, craftsman, statesman, reformer, priest. He is living in the life of nature and of man. One and unchanged he is revealed in all varieties of loveliness, all fragments and elements of knowledge, all traits of worthy character. Thus the Christian touches all things with a loving reverence, for within them God is hidden.

The Incarnation of the Son of God

The church

The church embodies the same principle as the "Word made flesh," that is, the expression and communication of the spiritual and the divine through what is material and human.

The Incarnation of the Son of God

Origin of the church

The more we study the gospels, the more clearly we shall recognize that Christ did not cast his gospel loose upon the world ... but he directed all his efforts to making a home for it, and that by organizing a band of men called "out of the world" and consecrated into a holy unity, who were destined to draw others in time after them out of all ages and nations. On this "little flock" he fixed all his hopes. . . . Christ then by his whole method declared his intention to found a church, a visible society of men — which should be distinct from the world and independent of it, even while it should present before the eyes of all men the spectacle of what their common life might become.

The Church and the Ministry (1888)

Valid ministry

That ministerial act alone is valid which is covered by a ministerial commission received from above by succession from the apostles.

The Church and the Ministry

"Natural sacraments"

So inextricably, in fact, is the human spirit implicated in the flesh, that it is only through the perceptions of the senses that it is able originally to act at all; and in the relations of men to one another their life is carried on ... upon a basis of what one may call natural sacraments. Thus handshaking is the sacrament of friendship, and kissing the sacrament of love. And each in expressing also intensifies the emotion which it expresses. The spirit in us feeds upon the material of its own symbols. . . . Thus there can be no doubt that, on all human analogy, a religion which, like the Christian religion, exists to realize communion with God under conditions of ordinary human life . . . must have developed, apart from any question of authority, sacramental ceremonies.

The Body of Christ (1901)

Two persons to resist

There are two classes of persons who have to be resisted — the one conservative and the other revolutionary. There are those who seem to think that in dangerous days such as these our only course is to hold fast, with an even blind adhesion, to our religion as it was handed down to us, unrevised and uncriticized. . . . On the other hand, you have the people who seem to think that every clever new criticism is destined to triumph over an established position. They forget that the revolutionists of history are always disappointed, that counter reformations follow reformations.

The New Theology and the Old Religion (1907)

Update the creeds?

Scholars sometimes contemplate the revision of the ancient catholic creeds and fundamental dogmas. They say — are we not endowed with all that our fathers were endowed with? Can we not, now that philosophy has changed its terms and methods, revise the ancient formulas, or do over again, for our age, what they did so well for theirs? There is much to say with regard to a proposition which sounds so reasonable. But at least this may be said: Can you suggest any other or better terms to express the same things, or is it the case that it is not the terms but the fundamental mind that you want altered?

The New Theology and the Old Religion

Biblical criticism

I say that it is impossible in any way to withdraw the historical basis of Christianity from the freest and frankest criticism. If there exist persons who say, Let the Old Testament be frankly criticized, for it is not so important, but not the New Testament, for it is vital; the claim must be utterly repudiated. In proportion to the important issues which hang upon the New Testament records, must be the frankness of the criticism to which they are subjected.

The New Theology and the Old Religion

The episcopate

The episcopate was intended then to be the bond of continuity and catholicity.

Orders and Unity (1909)

Anglicanism's role

The Anglican church in God's providence . . . preserved the whole of the ancient catholic structure, both creed and Bible, sacraments and order, beyond the reach of legitimate objection, and it coupled this conservatism with a repudiation of the supreme authority of the Pope, and a wholehearted acceptance of the principle of the doctrinal supremacy of scripture. This gives it, with all its faults, sins, and deficiencies, a unique opportunity for developing and presenting a really liberal catholicism.

Orders and Unity

Symbolic language

With regard, therefore, to what lies outside present human experience, we can only be taught, or formulate our beliefs, in *symbolical* language — language which is in a measure diverted from its original purpose. . . . But the central glory of the religion of the Incarnation is that God has revealed himself, distinctly, within human experience, in words and acts, some of them miraculous. Thus we have "seen with our eyes, and looked upon, and our hands have handled" divine things incarnate actually in human experience. Thus to apply the theory of symbolism to explain away the record of those events . . . is precisely to misapply the theory and to evacuate the Incarnation of its special and unique glory, which is the glory of literal fact.

The Basis of Anglican Fellowship (1914)

Religion and science

The church is put in trust of a treasury of spiritual knowledge and experience which it must jealously protect. But in regard to the secrets and processes of nature it has no authority at all.

Can We Then Believe? (1926)

Science and miracle

We can make no terms with a historical science — so called — which cannot find room for the supernatural Christ and is bound to explain him away. This sort of "science," physical or historical, we must regard as extravagant — as exceeding its legitimate boundaries; because it claims to have so complete a knowledge of the forces at work in the universe and in history as to be able to exclude certain evidence, however strong, in virtue of a dogma that such and such a kind of event cannot happen or cannot have happened.

Can We Then Believe?

Free thinker

I could never endure to be otherwise than a free-thinker. I mean by that that whatever obligation I may have inherited or contracted to any traditional system of belief or thought, I could never allow it to blind me to anything which might seem to be truth, whatever its origin, or to shackle me so that I could not follow the light of reason whithersoever it should lead.

The Philosophy of the Good Life (1930)

FOR REFLECTION AND DISCUSSION

Do you think Gore's thought is consistent throughout? Does it matter?

What is meant when a congregation responds after a scripture reading by saying, "The Word of the Lord"?

What limits, if any, do you feel should be placed on the spirit of free inquiry and investigation?

Why was it important to Gore that clergy believe the events mentioned in the historic creeds to be literal, historic facts? Do you agree with Gore?

Do you believe in miracles? If you do, what constitutes a miracle, what is its purpose, and how is it recognized?

Is it important that Christians today be "of one mind across the ages with the ancient Christian church"? Why, or why not?

Do you favor periodically updating or revising doctrinal statements?

Chapter 20

VIDA DUTTON SCUDDER

1861-1954

She Dreamt of a New World

V IDA SCUDDER pursued three callings, often simultaneously, throughout most of her long life: She was a professor of English at Wellesley
College for forty-one years. She was also a hands-on social reformer. And
she was a prolific author who produced literary criticism, social and economic commentary, fiction, biography, autobiography, and religious devotion. All this was stimulated and informed by a passionate Christian faith.

Vida (pronounced VEE-da) Scudder was born to privilege. Both her
parents were from prominent old Boston families. She graduated from
fashionable Smith College in 1884 and sailed to Europe with her mother a
year later (her father, a missionary in India, had been killed in a flood
shortly after Vida's birth). She joined the English faculty at Wellesley in
1887, continuing to live with her mother in nearby Boston (she moved with
her mother to Wellesley in 1912). Her course on "Social Ideals in English
Letters" quickly established her as a campus favorite.

Despite her comfortable life and professional success, however, Vida
Scudder was troubled. Looking back on those early years, she later wrote
(in her 1937 autobiography *On Journey*), "I had been beating my wings
against the bars — the customs, the assumptions, of my own class. I moved
in a garden enclosed, if not in a hothouse, an enclosure of gracious manners, regular meals, comfort, security, good taste. I liked the balmy air. Yet
sometimes it suffocated me." Privilege unshared, she wrote, was "a fret that
would not heal."

But Scudder did more than fret; she quickly moved from fretting to
action. During her first months at Wellesley, she organized a college settlement house in New York, and then two others, in Boston and Philadelphia.
These were part of a larger movement (of which the most famous example
became Hull House in Chicago) inviting young college women to live
among the poor between school terms to share what they were learning
with the poor and to learn from them. Scudder devoted many vacations
and sabbaticals to this work. Denison House in Boston became the center
of her social life.

Knowing the poor led Scudder to reconsider her Christian values. She
had been reared to believe that paying one's debts was the primary social
obligation, after which, if funds were available, charity was commendable.
But she found among the poor a patience, amiability, and hospitality that
amazed and humbled her, and she began to ask new questions: Is voluntary charity to relieve the consequences of social inequality a sufficient expression of Christian social conscience? Could the way money is made be

as much a matter of Christian concern as what the possessor does with it? Scudder would devote much of her life to questions such as these.

In 1894, Wellesley College was raising funds for construction and endowments. The Rockefeller family offered Wellesley a large gift, but Scudder led a group of faculty members who opposed accepting "tainted money" that had been amassed through unjust competition and labor practices. The college, to no one's surprise, accepted the money. Scudder's relations with the school's administration grew strained, and critics called for her to resign her teaching position. Scudder was also among the first to view labor relations as a moral issue. Speaking to a women's rally during the tense textile strike in Lawrence, Massachusetts, in 1912, she said, "I would rather never again wear a thread of woolen than know my garments had been woven at the cost of such misery." Her remarks were reprinted throughout the country, and again some called for her resignation from Wellesley. But by this time, Scudder had grown more secure in her views and commitments. She refused even to consider resigning.

Scudder had participated in socialist societies since the 1880s, but in 1911 she officially joined the Socialist Party and helped found the Church Socialist League, an organization within the Episcopal Church seeking to address social wrongs. A year later, she published *Socialism and Character*, setting out her views on social justice and Christian faith. It was her most influential book.

In *Socialism and Character*, Scudder discusses three responses to poverty: philanthropy (giving money directly to the poor), social reform (organized programs to meet the needs of the poor), and social transformation (changing the structures of society that cause poverty). Rejecting the first two approaches because history showed they had little effect, she began working for social transformation.

Scudder focuses in *Socialism and Character* on two key principles, economic determinism and class consciousness. Her experience in the settlement houses informed her understanding of economic determinism. She saw there that her efforts had less impact on poor women than their low wages, long hours, and demeaning working conditions. It was these unhappy facts, she felt, that determined the lives of working women and made impossible their full spiritual and intellectual development. Inevitably, this led to a stratified society with strong class consciousness, an "us versus them" mentality which soured human relationships. A fundamental change in the social order was needed. In the new order which Scudder envisioned, labor would be assigned on the basis of ability, pay would be based on workers' needs, and charity and compassion would enhance the personal growth of both giver and recipient.

But Scudder was no naïve idealist. Merely changing the social order would achieve little, she felt. Without an "inward transformation," a socialist society would soon degenerate into something as bad as or worse than what it had replaced. This is why she felt it imperative that Christian leaders join the socialist movement. Most socialists were not Christians and most Christians were not socialists, but Scudder believed that Jesus had taught socialist ideals and that Christianity led to socialism. Of all the world's religions, Scudder felt Christianity was best positioned to help bring about the new social order, because of its two key teachings, the Incarnation (God has in Jesus Christ personally entered human life and institutions and works within them) and the Atonement (God demonstrated on the cross that selflessness, not self-gratification, defines the good life). "The ultimate source of my socialist convictions was and is Christianity," Scudder wrote twenty-five years later, in her autobiography. "Unless I were a socialist, I could not honestly be a Christian."

Marxism is the best-known form of socialism, and economic determinism and class consciousness are two of its central tenets. For a time after World War I, Scudder had high hopes for the Marxist experiment in Russia, even hanging a red flag beside the crucifix where she said her private prayers. Marxism's rejection of Christianity she explained away on historic grounds, because an unfaithful church had often served the purposes of the wealthy classes. Scudder's writings from this time, especially her provocative *Social Teachings of the Christian Year*, combine Christian devotion with Marxist ideas, including the use of violence to achieve desired ends. But when brutality became a defining feature of Soviet Communism, she backed off from it. The Soviet system failed to realize its worthy goals, she felt, precisely because it lacked a Christian foundation; it sought social reform without inward transformation. Scudder became a pacifist in her later years.

Although Vida Scudder was reared in a Christian home and participated in church life from childhood, her faith deepened as an adult through her association with the monastic life. She joined the Companions of the Holy Cross in 1889, an order of Episcopal women who lived active lives outside the cloister but observed a monastic rule of life, made regular silent retreats, and ministered to the suffering. She maintained her association with this fellowship to the end of her life. When exhaustion brought about a severe illness in 1901, leading to a two-year leave of absence from Wellesley, Scudder traveled with her mother and a friend to Italy. She not only recuperated there, but also came to know two Italian saints, "spiritual guides," who, as she wrote in her 1937 autobiography, "have controlled the rest of my life" — Francis of Assisi and Catherine of Siena. She wrote several books about the two, including both historical novels and studies of their lives and works.

Scudder traveled to Assisi several times to study the life of Francis and the history of the Franciscan order. The simplicity of the thirteenth-century saint stirred her heart. Francis found joy by giving away his inherited fortune and embracing a life of poverty. What did this say about the ethics and effects of private ownership? Moreover, Francis had died frustrated and helpless, yet joyfully, with a vision of Christ before him. What did this say about faithfulness, about defeat and victory? And what of the subsequent history of the Franciscans, with its many tales of the tension between simple idealism and practical, "this is the way it is" realism?

Catherine of Siena's vision for fourteenth-century Europe, like Vida Scudder's for twentieth-century America, had included a more just, humane social order. But civil war broke out in Europe instead, and crass materialism and power politics engulfed the papacy. Catherine's mission failed. Yet she remained faithful and loyal to the institutional church. "No one," Scudder wrote of Catherine, "more perfectly presents the perpetual paradox, natural life fostered and triumphantly revealed through a church which too often crucifies the holy ones to whom it gives birth." Like Francis, Catherine posed for Scudder the questions of faithfulness, of defeat and victory.

Some of Vida Scudder's most winsome words were written after she had laid aside most of her responsibilities. Her autobiography, published nine years after she taught her last class at Wellesley, is lively and sunny. And the last paragraph of her last book, written at the remarkable age of 91, contains these words: "I draw a deep breath. . . . I pass into silence. Am I ready for that waiting eternity, that heaven, where love reigns, triumphant and serene? Not yet. But I must heed the relentless summons." Vida Scudder died two years later, on October 9, 1954, in her home in Wellesley, Massachusetts.

IN HER OWN WORDS

The poor are morally safer

The poor are in a much safer moral condition today than the rich. Their obvious defects, such as dirt, irresponsibility, thriftlessness, extravagance . . . none of them are incompatible with the traits of the True Citizen, as enumerated by Jesus — poverty of spirit, meekness, purity of heart, aspiration toward justice, and the rest. . . . Yet that the conditions of our proletariat as a whole are spiritually desirable can be maintained only at a distance from them and from reality. And when one finds persons who live softly adducing the words of Jesus as a reason for leaving these conditions untouched, one recoils with a shudder.

Socialism and Character (1912)

The Incarnation

The Christian who is also a socialist can say that . . . it has really been the belief in the Incarnation, working in the depths, misunderstood by its most ardent adherents, that has led the western nations on to their present strong and clear demand for the rehabilitation of the natural order . . . the Christian who reproaches the socialist with materialism, because he wants to begin the process of social redemption with the establishment of right physical conditions, is disloyal. Belief that the spirit must and can be revealed only through the instrument of flesh is natural to one who has knelt at Bethlehem.

Socialism and Character

A comfortable church

What accredited type of piety did the United States inherit from the last century? Suave-mannered, pleasant-voiced; endangering nothing in particular, an ornament to the Sunday pews; devoted to good causes in proportion to their remoteness, intent on promoting safe philanthropies and foreign missions, but, so far as home affairs are concerned, ignorant alike of the ardors of the mystic and the heroisms of the reformer. A queer type of Christianity if one thinks of it — cheerfully assuming that what is innocently agreeable is religious. Agonies of the social conscience deprecated in the name of spirituality, agonies of the inward life yet more deprecated in the name of sanity. No agonies at all, if you please: careless dependence rather on an affectionate God, confusedly mixed with a sentimental love of scenery. Parents more concerned with hygiene than with salvation for their offspring; sacrifice relegated to the foreign field, or to underpaid social workers. A domestic religion, mid-Victorian in effect, calculated to make life pleasant in the family circle — but curiously at ease in Zion.

"The Alleged Failure of the Church" (1916)

Prayer

Let us examine our prayers. How languid they are, how perfunctory, and alas! How often selfish! Sometimes one feels that men's prayers must sadden God even more than their sins. Prayer is the deepest and surest measure of personality. As men pray, so they really are. . . . A force more penetrating and powerful than gravitation or electricity is entrusted to us, and we are responsible for the steady use of it and its direction to the noblest ends.

"A Plea for Social Intercession" (1917)

"A permanent disgrace"

We are not allowed to forget that our industrial system virtually says, Cursed are the poor, Cursed are the meek. . . . Christian manufacturers, instead of giving unto the last as unto the first, are likely to buy their labor as cheap as they can get it, and are often disposed to fight a living wage to the finish. . . . The permanent contradiction between Christian morals and world morals is a puzzle, and a permanent disgrace.

Social Teachings of the Christian Year (1921)

The necessity of catastrophe

Jesus regarded catastrophe, no less than growth, as a normal and necessary element in human advance. He knew that violent disturbances were the condition and the preliminary of his coming. We cannot keep one factor in his teaching and reject another, dwell on the parable of the seed growing secretly, and forget the lightning flash.

Social Teachings of the Christian Year

Sacramental philosophy

But it is dangerous to avoid applying Christian principles to social and industrial life, by relegating them to a purely "spiritual" sphere. That time-honored evasion contradicts the whole sacramental philosophy. The very point of the great truths radiating from the Incarnation is that one harmonious law runs through all spheres of being, wherever the grace of God controls the world; and since our business is to regulate earthly dealings by this divine law, we have no right to deny economic significance to this parable [Matthew 20:1-16].

Social Teachings of the Christian Year

Beyond stewardship

[The doctrine of stewardship is the] belief that the Christian holds all his worldly possessions in trust for God and for his brothers. . . . The doctrine of stewardship is unsatisfactory on two counts. First . . . it implies no responsibility toward the *source* of wealth but only toward the *use* of it . . . [Christians must] consider the connotation of their incomes in human values at the source. . . . stewardship taken by itself has nothing to say to us about property as an instrument of power. But . . . the concentration of power is the chief evil which progress toward social justice has to dread . . . the main reason why possessions are valued is less the luxury they offer than the power they confer. . . . It behooves us to search our hearts, whether we escape the horrid dangers involved in ability to give money away.

The Christian Attitude Toward Private Property (1934)

Living brings certitude

Many thinking moderns who would like to be Christians spend their lives in a state of religious incertitude; we fall into two groups. Some, remaining poised in hesitation, including well-known minds I will not name, pause with imaginative and perhaps intellectual sympathy toward Christianity; others, passing beyond theory, make a definite venture of faith, and seek less to know the doctrine than to live the life. Through the years of which I am now writing, I came, deliberately and with finality, to range myself on their side of the barrier. After all, many initiates of reality assured me that it was by living not by thinking that certitude could be achieved.

On Journey (1937)

Always on the move

For to remain a member of an historic church is not to achieve finality. A creed is not an imprisoning wall, it is a gate, opening on a limitless country which can be entered in no other way. I am in that country, praise God, but I have only begun to explore it; I am finding it, now glorious in beauty, now arid and forbidding. Again and again the explorer hesitates in a maze of paths pointing in sundry directions. But he cannot stop; the religious life never suffers one to stand still.

On Journey

Immortality

Immortality does not interest me. Stress on duration seems to me the note of an imprisoned mind. Now, this fleeting instant, I experience the Eternal and it suffices me. . . . Survival? It is to me an unreal conception. Moreover, by what right do I demand from Deity a privilege which I have no reason to expect my cats to share? Or the roses in the garden? Though looking at the matter from another angle, I should not be surprised to find that all the roses which have ever bloomed on earth, blossom forever in the Paradise of God.

On Journey

Pacifism

So long as conflicting interests are the ruling principle of the economic order, it is hopeless to expect the political order to escape the curse of war. To
point this out, to link war into the whole causal circle where it belongs —
here is the great opportunity of the pacifist. He will deserve the nobler
name peacemaker if he can press this truth home to the world.

The Privilege of Age (1939)

Church history

Within the church, as I watch its history, two forces persist in constant tension: continuity and revolution. Struggle between them often threatens destruction of ecclesiastical unity. Did either prevail, excluding the other,
Christianity would, I think, lose all dynamic power; the church . . . would
either fade into a formal relic or lose all general communal importance to
be reckoned with. Would you like me to substitute the word "progress" for
"revolution"? I stubbornly refuse.

My Quest for Reality (1952)

Evil

My attitude toward evil? I welcome it. For I think it is waking us up.

My Quest for Reality

Old age

During one's active decades, life proceeds mostly on assumptions, made in
youth and probably based on authority, that final certainties have been
reached. One moves on solid ground. As old age gradually comes, the assumptions disappear. One draws a long breath; earth has vanished under
one's feet, and one takes a fresh view over the landscape. It is an amazing,
an awesome moment; horizons recede as if one were flying in an airplane.

Do one's old beliefs endure? Yes, I think so, but one has to look farther and search deeper for them, as the angle of vision changes.

My Quest for Reality

FOR REFLECTION AND DISCUSSION

What can be said for and against the three responses to poverty discussed by Scudder in *Socialism and Character?*

What was Scudder's understanding of Christian stewardship? What is yours?

What do the teachings of Jesus have in common with socialist principles? With capitalist principles?

Discuss the relationship of the life of prayer to the life of action.

Where in the scriptures and in your experience do you find evidence for or against the understanding of "catastrophe, no less than growth, as a normal and necessary element in human advance"?

Do you agree that church history is the story of the tension between continuity and revolution? What is the value of each?

Respond to the statement that it is by living, not by thinking, that certitude is achieved.

Chapter 21

ROLAND ALLEN

1868-1947

Missionary to the Missionaries

A T FIRST GLANCE, there would seem nothing extraordinary about Roland Allen. Ordained a priest in the Church of England in 1893, he served a curacy for two years, then went to China as a missionary, but left China seven years later due to ill health. He was then appointed vicar of a rural English parish, Chalfont St. Peter in Buckinghamshire, a position he resigned after three years, and was never employed by the church again. For the next forty years, the bookish and somewhat reclusive Allen taught school and worked for government agencies, occasionally led worship services, wrote articles and books which few people read, and traveled to promote his unorthodox views about missionary work. He and his wife spent their last years in Nairobi, where Allen learned Swahili, translating several classic Swahili texts into English. He is buried in Nairobi.

Allen's grandson and biographer Hubert Allen recalls asking his grandfather towards the end of the latter's life whether he might read the books his grandfather had written. "Oh, yes, you can read them by all means," the old man replied, "but you won't understand them. I don't think *anyone* is going to understand them until I've been dead ten years." It was, in fact, about ten years after Roland Allen's death that his works began to be "rediscovered." Today he is revered as a prophet, not only by Anglicans, but by Protestants, Roman Catholics, and Pentecostals as well.

Allen's first and most influential book, published in 1912 and revised in 1927, bore a curious but telling title: *Missionary Methods: St. Paul's or Ours?* In it Allen dissected the Book of Acts and the epistles of Paul, seeking to discover how the apostle had carried out his astoundingly successful missionary endeavors and whether his methods might produce similar results today.

Allen noted several things about the way Paul planted churches. Paul devised no plan or strategy in advance, but preached the gospel anywhere, to anyone, regardless of position or social status. After a small group had accepted the gospel, Paul appointed local leaders, or "elders," entrusted them with the responsibility of pastoral care and spreading the word to others, assured them of his continued prayers and supervision if needed, and moved on. The new congregation became indigenous almost immediately. Paul was flexible about most matters, trusting each congregation to deal with differences that might arise. Congregations were to be self-supporting financially, providing for the poor in their midst and contributing as they were able to the needs of congregations elsewhere. Unity was not promoted, but assumed, and maintained through regular celebrations of the eucharist and frequent communication among the congregations and with Paul himself.

Paul's teaching was simple and brief, Allen said. He appealed to beliefs and experiences already familiar to his hearers, assuring them that Christian faith was consistent with the truth they already acknowledged. He then told of the death and resurrection of Christ, applied it to the spiritual needs of his hearers, and warned them of the dangers of rejecting the truth. He was conciliatory and sympathetic, honest in meeting objections, always respectful of his hearers.

How did early-twentieth-century missionary methods stack up against those of Paul? Not very well, Allen observed — and moreover, they were largely ineffective. Missionary societies in Allen's day began with an elaborate plan, including fund raising, recruitment and training of missionaries, purchase of property, and the construction of mission compounds, schools, and hospitals in places chosen for their political or cultural importance. Authority was retained by educated Western professionals, who made every decision and answered every question. Fund raising and recruitment of new missionaries continued at home, even after two or three generations, because new converts were thought unable to provide financial support or leadership. Native religions were totally rejected. Unity within each mission was maintained by strict adherence to doctrinal and moral norms like those of the churches from which the missionaries had come, and which often differed from one denomination or missionary organization to another. A mission was a complex organization, maintained on foreign soil by money and manpower from far away. Missionaries were paternalistic, controlling, and untrusting in their dealings with native peoples. As a result, the Christian church was seen as an alien presence — and there were almost no lasting conversions among native peoples.

What could be done? Allen had plenty of suggestions:

- When starting new mission work, he said, give the people the basics — and just the basics: a tradition or simple creed, the sacraments of baptism and the eucharist, an ordained ministry, and the Bible. Teach them how to use these gifts, and then get out of the way. Native people must learn what these things mean in the context of their own culture. Do not create institutions which will soak up time, money, and energy that could be better spent in other ways. The missionary, Allen said, "should remember that he is the least permanent element in the church. He may fall sick and go home, or he may die, or he may be called elsewhere. He disappears, the church remains. The native Christians are the permanent element."

- No group of Christians should be without regular eucharist, so ordain lots of priests, Allen said. Priests should arise out of the Christian communities they are to serve. They should be respected leaders of those communities, but a sophisticated theological education should not be required for ordination since it would limit the number of priests and require a huge financial investment. Allen advocated "voluntary clergy," who would earn their living in some other way and carry out their priestly vocations without pay.

- All financial arrangements for the support of the church and the spread of the gospel should be controlled and managed at the local level, Allen said. To continue to support mission work by means of outside appeals would pauperize the new church and make it dependent on others. Committed Christians need to support their churches, and can always do so, even in the poorest areas.

- Continue to support new congregations through prayer and counsel, but give them the freedom to develop their own expressions of the faith. These expressions, including details of doctrine, morality, and polity, may vary from one place to another. Converts must be responsible for maintaining their own spiritual life, which will often differ from that of the missionary who converted them.

David M. Paton, editor of an anthology of Allen's writings, summarized Allen's basic doctrines at a 1984 conference on Allen held in Hawaii. He identified these six doctrines: (1) A Christian community which has come into being as the result of the preaching of the gospel should have *handed over to it* the Bible, creed, ministry, and sacraments. (2) It is then responsible with its bishop for recognizing the spiritual gifts and needs in its membership and for calling into service priests who will preside at the eucharist and be responsible for teaching and for pastoral care. (3) It is also required to share the message and the life with its neighboring communities not yet evangelized. (4) The Holy Spirit working on the human endowment of the community's leaders is sufficient for its life. Don't "train" them too much; don't import from outside. (5) A Christian community that cannot do these things is not yet a *church:* it is a mission field. (6) The local bishop and his staff are crucial.

Such, Allen felt, were the methods of St. Paul. They resulted in thriving indigenous churches when Paul employed them, and they will result in thriving indigenous churches whenever and wherever they are employed, he said.

Faith in the power of the Holy Spirit undergirded everything Roland Allen believed. His little book *Pentecost and the World*, published in 1917, dealt with the Holy Spirit, particularly as manifested in the Book of Acts. It was his favorite among all his writings. Allen saw the Holy Spirit as the power of Christ energizing the Christian community. This is not the same thing as the Spirit of the Lord inspiring the Old Testament prophets, nor is it the gradual realization of conscience or some generalized life-giving principle in all people. Rather, to receive the Holy Spirit is to receive Jesus Christ. It is a definite gift — at one time the disciples did not have it; after the Day of Pentecost, they did. And they were never again the same.

The result of receiving the Holy Spirit is missionary activity, Allen says. When reading about the Day of Pentecost in Acts 2, modern readers often become distracted trying to analyze the gift of tongues and how it operated. The important thing, Allen says, is not how the disciples were able to speak in other tongues, but that they began to preach and people began to understand. The disciples stopped responding to a merely intellectual belief and began responding to the power of Christ in them. The modern church, as Allen saw it, had ceased to obey the Holy Spirit. Identifying ministry and mission with a small professional class and acting on the basis of policy and expediency, it had abandoned its sure foundation.

Since Allen's day, some things have changed: "Worker priests" and lay people have begun to take leadership in many areas. Missionary efforts in Africa, Latin America, and elsewhere have been largely freed of Western domination, resulting in independent, energetic, growing churches. These churches have developed their own expressions of the gospel and often challenge their Western progenitors, seeking to hold them accountable to the gospel as the newer churches understand it. The Pentecostal or charismatic movement has injected a new awareness of the Holy Spirit into many Western churches. As with many prophets, the voice of Roland Allen is being heard only after the speaker himself has fallen silent.

IN HIS OWN WORDS

"I have resigned"

We see the strange and painful sight of men and women who habitually neglect their religious duties, or who openly deny the truth of the creeds, or who by the immorality of their lives openly defy the laws of God, standing up as sponsors in a Christian church, before a Christian minister, in the presence of a Christian congregation and as representatives of the church on behalf of a new-born child solemnly professing their desire for Holy Baptism, their determination to renounce the world, the flesh and the devil, their steadfast faith in the Creed and their willingness to obey God's holy will, whilst they know, and everyone in the church knows, that they themselves neither do, nor intend to do, any of these things. . . . No one can justify these things. . . . They bring the services of the church into disrepute and make them an open scorn. . . . God is not mocked. . . . A passive resistance which costs little or nothing is a passive resistance which I despise and dread. . . . One form of protest, and only one, remains open to me, and that is to decline to hold an office in which I am liable to be called upon to do what I feel to be wrong. I have chosen that. I have resigned.

letter of resignation from Chalfont St. Peter (1907)

Institution not central

Christianity is not an institution, but a principle of life. By imposing an institution we tend to obscure the truly spiritual character of our work. We take the externals first and so we make it easy for new converts to put the external in the place of the internal. Attendance at a house of prayer may take the place of prayer. It is easy to mistake the provision of the ornaments of worship for the duty of worship.

Missionary Methods (1913)

The source of strength

The fatal mistake has been made of teaching the converts to rely upon the wrong source of strength. Instead of seeking it in the working of the Holy

Spirit in themselves, they seek it in the missionary. They put him in the place of Christ, they depend upon him.

Missionary Methods

Ordination

St. Paul ordained as elders members of the church to which they belonged. He did not establish a provincial school to which all candidates for ordination must go, and from which they might be sent to minister to congregations in any part of the province, at the bidding of a central committee or at his own. The elders were really *of* the church to which they ministered. They were at home. They were known to the members of their flock. If they received any pecuniary support, they received it from men who supported them because they felt the need of their undivided and uninterrupted care. Thus the bond between the elders and the church to which they ministered was extremely close. This was of utmost importance. . . . The elders so appointed were not young. They were apparently selected because they were men of high moral character, sober, grave, men of weight and reputation. . . . They were not necessarily highly educated men; they cannot have had any profound knowledge of Christian doctrine. . . . St. Paul was not content with ordaining one elder for each church. In every place he ordained several. This insured that all authority should not be concentrated in the hands of one man.

Missionary Methods

Nature or grace?

We look too much at our converts as they are by nature: St. Paul looked at his converts as they were by grace.

Missionary Methods

What the missions have not done

Our missions are in different countries amongst people of the most diverse characteristics, but all bear a most astonishing resemblance one to another. . . . We have approached them as superior beings, moved by charity to impart of our wealth to destitute and perishing souls. We have used that argument at home to wring grudging and pitiful doles for the propagation of our faith, and abroad we have adopted that attitude as missionaries of a superior religion. . . . We have done everything for them, but very little with them. We have done everything for them except give place to them. We have treated them as "dear children", but not as "brethren." . . . We believe that it is the Holy Spirit of Christ which inspires and guides us: we cannot believe that the same Spirit will guide and inspire them.

Missionary Methods

Missionary as educator

Slavery is not the best training for liberty. It is only by exercise that powers grow. To do things for people does not train them to do them for themselves. . . . The work of the missionary is education in this sense: it is the use of means to reveal to his converts a spiritual power which they actually possess and of which they are dimly conscious.

Missionary Methods

Christ as private luxury

If we allow the consideration of heathen morality and heathen religion to absolve us from the duty of preaching the gospel we are really deposing Christ from his throne in our own souls. If we admit that men can do very well without Christ, we accept the Savior only as a luxury for ourselves. If they can do very well without Christ, then so could we. This is to turn our backs upon the Christ of the gospels and the Christ of Acts and to turn our faces towards law, morality, philosophy, natural religion.

Pentecost and the World (1917)

Obedience to the Spirit

To calculate consequences and to act solely with a view to consequences is worldly wisdom. The apostles were not guided in their action by worldly wisdom. They were guided by the Spirit. . . . They did not consider consequences so much as sources. The important question was not what result would follow, but from what source did the action spring.

Pentecost and the World

Apostolic ministry

To leave new-born churches to learn by experience is apostolic, to abandon them is not apostolic: to watch over them is apostolic, to be always nursing them is not apostolic: to guide their education is apostolic, to provide it for them is not apostolic. . . . The man then who would guide such a church . . . must obviously get out of the way to give it room; because if he stays, or if he leaves someone from outside in charge, it will plainly not have room to move. But he must watch over it and warn it by instruction when it is in danger of going seriously astray, or of falling heavily.

The Spontaneous Expansion of the Church (1927)

A new kind of episcopate

I am, indeed, sure that to consecrate native village bishops is the true way of expansion. I believe that it would be far safer for the present Bishop of Honan or S. Rhodesia, for instance, to establish a hundred, or two hundred, unpaid native bishops, not assistant bishops, but diocesan bishops ruling over small dioceses consisting of a village or a group of villages, because in ruling such dioceses men would learn the meaning of episcopal authority in its simplest form.

The Spontaneous Expansion of the Church

What is needed

The spontaneous expansion of the church . . . asks for no elaborate organization, no large finances, no great numbers of paid missionaries. . . . What is necessary is faith. What is needed is the kind of faith which, uniting a man to Christ, sets him on fire. Such a man can believe that others finding Christ will be set on fire also. Such a man can see that there is no need of money to fill a continent with the knowledge of Christ. Such a man can see that all that is required to consolidate and establish that expansion is the simple application of the simple organization of the church. It is to men who know that faith, who see that vision, that I appeal.

The Spontaneous Expansion of the Church

Truth must win its own way

It is impossible to say what effect my being in these parts is having. . . . I never ask anyone to *do* anything, and consequently I do not get a "yes" or "no". I say what seems to me obviously true. . . . If I were out to organize and lead that would be different, but . . . I long ago determined that was not the way of the Spirit for me. . . . I hold that truth must win its own way, and I stand aside when I have pointed to the truth. To me, "He must increase and I must decrease" [John 3:30] is a lively word. . . . Whether I have done anything at all, or shall do anything at all is known only to God. The day will declare it.

letter from Kenya (1932)

Which one?

I went one day into a synod office in Canada. I found there two men: the one was a young theological student, the other a man of about fifty years of age who told me that for fifteen years, when he was farming on the prairie, he held services in his own house for his neighbors. At first some six or seven Anglicans came, but later some of the other people came also. They had a celebration of the Holy Communion two or three times a year when a priest passed that way. I looked at those two men and I could not help asking myself why the bishop was going to ordain the one and why he had not ordained the other. If spiritual experience is desirable for a priest, which of those two men had the largest spiritual experience?

The Case for Voluntary Clergy (1940)

FOR REFLECTION AND DISCUSSION

Allen resigned his position as vicar of Chalfont St. Peter in 1907 because English law at that time required him to baptize children of anyone who presented a child for baptism. Do you agree with his decision? See the Baptismal Covenant on pages 304-305 in the 1979 Book of Common Prayer.

What do you think Allen would say were he writing today?

What in Allen's description of the mission work in his day do you feel could also be a description of your parish church?

How would the life of your congregation or diocese be affected if Allen's ideas were implemented? Which, if any, of Allen's ideas do you feel should be considered?

How should the role of the ordained person differ from that of the lay person?

What or who do you understand the Holy Spirit to be?

"Christianity is not an institution, but a principle of life," Allen said. How is Christianity as principle of life related to church as institution?

Chapter 22

EVELYN UNDERHILL

1875-1941

Guide in the Life of Prayer

HILDA OF WHITBY, Hildegard of Bingen, Julian of Norwich, Catherine of Siena, Teresa of Avila — women of great stature have helped shape Christian spirituality. But their home was almost always the convent or the hermitage. Of women fully in the secular world, Madame Guyon in seventeenth-century France was perhaps the only one widely recognized as a spiritual guide — until the appearance of Evelyn Underhill early in the twentieth century.

Underhill would seem an unlikely candidate for such distinction. Her well-to-do parents had a stable marriage, but were not religious. They educated their only child in languages, botany, philosophy, and history — but not theology. At thirty-two, Underhill married Hubert Stuart Moore, a childhood friend and attorney, with whom she lived comfortably and enjoyed traveling abroad. She often entertained for her husband in their London home, located a short walk from her parents' home. Underhill led a quiet, uneventful life, enjoying hobbies such as yachting, gardening, and bookbinding. None of this would seem to denote a person of uncommon spiritual aptitude. But during her lifetime, Underhill published 40 books and over 350 articles and reviews on the life of the spirit, including two major ground-breaking studies. She was in constant demand as a retreat leader and was both the first woman to lecture in religion at Oxford University, in 1921, and the first woman to lead a diocesan retreat for priests in the Church of England, in 1926.

Underhill's ministry falls into two clearly defined periods. Although she had published a few lighthearted poems, three novels, and a dozen or so articles prior to 1911, the first period begins with the publication in that year of *Mysticism: A Study of the Nature and Development of Man's Spiritual Consciousness*. The word mysticism was, then as now, often misunderstood. At the time, it carried largely negative overtones, suggesting superstition, the occult, and the erotic. At best, it was seen as a private, passive drifting of the soul into a vague, foggy union with God. Underhill sought in the opening pages of her book to establish mysticism as the foundational experience of all genuine religion, leading to a life of active holiness. She called it "the expression of the innate tendency of the human spirit towards complete harmony with the transcendental order," "the movement of the heart, seeking to transcend the limitations of the individual standpoint and to surrender itself to ultimate Reality," and "an organic process which involves the perfect consummation of the love of God." Although it is fully realized by only the great saints, Underhill believed the mystical experience is within reach of every human being.

In the first part of *Mysticism,* Underhill lays to rest various misunderstandings of mysticism and identifies its four essential characteristics: First, it is practical, not theoretical. Mysticism is "experience in its most intense form," and it leads not to speculation, but to action. Second, it is "an entirely spiritual activity." Its purpose is not to solve a problem, answer a question, or achieve a goal, but to experience God. The mystic "possesses God, and needs nothing more." Third, the method of mysticism is love. This love is no "superficial affection or emotion," but "a total dedication of the will." The mystic's outlook is that of the lover — wild and passionate, humble and rapturous. Fourth, mysticism is a definite psychological experience, involving heart and mind, conscious and unconscious, the whole self. It remakes the entire person.

In the second part of her book, Underhill seeks to draw the reader into the mystical experience itself. She quotes mystical writers through the ages — an astounding 133 of them in all — and her language is passionate, engaging, and colorful. In what is perhaps the book's most original section, she delineates five stages in the soul's journey to God (as distinguished from the three outlined by St. John of the Cross in the sixteenth century). These are (1) awakening, the first stirrings of the soul's desire for God; (2) purification, the usually painful stripping away of false values and attachments that separate the soul from God; (3) illumination, a clear and joyful vision of God, occasionally accompanied by visions and ecstasies; (4) dark night, when the exhausted soul battles against a sense of forlorn abandonment, and — finally — (5) union with God, the end and goal of the mystic way, reached only by the greatest of the saints. God is present at every stage of this journey, wooing the soul, as a lover seeks to win over his beloved.

Mysticism was a great and immediate success. A second printing was out within a year, and although Underhill wrote several books in the following decade expanding on themes first addressed in *Mysticism,* it remains to this day the classic treatment of the subject. Her book made Evelyn Underhill a person of note in the theological world. But notoriety did not bring contentment. Something seemed missing; Underhill felt adrift — she lacked a church. In her early years, she had been drawn to the Roman Catholic Church with its rich sense of the transcendent. But when in 1907 a papal encyclical condemned modern science and biblical interpretation, Underhill realized Rome could never become her spiritual home. She resisted affiliating with the Church of England for several years, but by the time of her Oxford lectures in 1921, she had come to feel at home there, a commitment which matured through the years. Taking part in a parish church with everyday Christians gave Underhill a new sense of community and a new this-worldly focus.

She also sought counsel from Baron Friedrich von Hügel, England's leading Roman Catholic thinker and one well schooled in classic mystical writers. Von Hügel became Underhill's spiritual director, and for three years, until his death in 1925, he and Underhill saw one another occasionally and corresponded frequently. Von Hügel suggested that Underhill's understanding of mysticism had also contributed to her feeling adrift: She had often quoted the third-century mystic philosopher Plotinus, who referred to the spiritual life as "the flight of the Alone to the Alone." Such a spirituality, von Hügel said, lacked grounding. It was disembodied and had little to do with historical events or the lives of human beings in this world. Underhill needed to "come down to earth." Von Hügel suggested she spend two mornings a week working among the poor in the London slums — which she did from that time until her death. He encouraged her to continue thinking and writing, but to focus on the Incarnation of Christ, Word *become flesh.*

And so it was that Underhill came to the second period of her ministry. Her interest in mysticism continued, but after 1925, she wrote no more books about it. She was now fifty years old, and her primary concerns lay elsewhere: in leading retreats, writing books and articles, delivering radio addresses (these were immensely popular), and serving as a mentor — all to guide the ordinary Christian into the life of prayer. This she would do within the institutional church, which she now saw as the body which mysticism required, just as the human soul requires a body.

In 1922, Underhill had made a retreat at Pleshey, an Anglican retreat house in rural England, where she experienced a deep joy in the sense of community among the retreatants. Two years later, she was invited to conduct a retreat at the same place. It was the first of many. Twelve sets of her retreat addresses were later published in book form. She also maintained an active correspondence with both friends and strangers who wrote to her for guidance on the life of prayer.

Underhill's other major book was *Worship,* published in 1936. It is instructive to compare it to *Mysticism,* published twenty-five years earlier.

A warm vitality flows through both books; the two works are similarly structured; and both seek to cover a broad subject thoroughly. But whereas the earlier book deals with individual mystics and their inner journeys, making little reference to the historical context of their lives, the latter book focuses on the Christian church gathering to pray, week in and week out. It is institutional, sacramental, and incarnational. In *Worship,* Underhill discusses the components of worship in general — ritual, symbol, sacrament, sacrifice — and then surveys eleven forms of worship, mostly Christian but including Jewish worship, treating each generously and appreciatively. She says in the preface that she regards them "as chapels of various types of one Cathedral of the Spirit." What characterizes each of these forms of worship is the need and longing of the human spirit to adore its Maker, she says, and each succeeds in expressing this adoration in its own way.

Underhill died on June 15, 1941, during the dark days when the United Kingdom stood alone against a ravenous Nazi war machine. Pacifism was not a popular position, but Underhill opposed the war on Christian grounds. Faith in the face of heinous evil, boundless love, acceptance of all, selfless giving, and a willingness to embrace and share the suffering of others, to the point of death if necessary — these are the requirements of Christian witness, she said. Anything less would be to strike a bargain with the devil. There is no just war; war is pure evil and therefore must be resisted — but never with anger, bitterness, or self-righteousness. The church is called to create pockets of peace, harmony, and faithfulness, even when the world goes mad, Underhill felt. This stand, taken at the end of her life when her health was failing, was the most provocative thing Evelyn Underhill ever did. But she did not waver. As she had lived her life, so she departed it, during the "times that try men's souls," full of faith, hope, and charity for all.

IN HER OWN WORDS

Mystical experience

Those who suppose mystical experience to be merely a pleasing consciousness of the divine in the world, a sense of the "otherness" of things, a basking in the beams of the uncreated light, are only playing with Reality. True mystical achievement is the most complete and most difficult expression of life which is as yet possible to man. It is at once an act of love, an act of surrender, and an act of supreme perception. . . . [Mysticism] is the eager, outgoing activity whose driving power is generous love. . . . Mystic love is a total dedication of the will; the deep-seated desire and tendency of the soul towards its Source.

Mysticism (1911)

Jesus

Now the character of Jesus . . . represents, at the very least, a personality of transcendent spiritual genius. . . . But this human nature, this personality, is placed in time: is immersed in the stream of becoming. If, then, it be really human, really alive, it will share . . . the regnant characteristic of all living things. It will move and grow. . . . the life of Jesus exhibits in absolute perfection . . . that psychological growth towards God, that movement and direction, which is found in varying degrees of perfection in the lives of the great mystics.

The Mystic Way (1913)

Mysticism and morality

The true mystical life, far from being a short cut, has been well described as an "heroic super-naturalism." It is not easy. Its moments of rapturous certitude are paid for by hard struggles and sacrifices. It flourishes best in alliance with a lofty moral code, a strong sense of duty, a definite religious faith capable of upholding the mystic during the many periods in which his vision fails him. . . . True mysticism is the soul of religion, but like the soul of man, it needs a body if it is to fulfill its mighty destiny.

"The Future of Mysticism" (1918)

Developing a spiritual life

The mystics put spiritual interests in the center of the field, and by attending to that aspect of reality enter more and more deeply into it; coming at last to the perfect and conscious harmony with the spiritual order which some of them call the "practice of the presence of God." How do they do this? First by that quiet, steady attention to the spiritual which is the essence of prayer: an art which any one may practice who chooses to open his door to the eternal world waiting on the fringes of the common life. Next by a drastic reordering of their whole natures in conformity with the perfection they have seen and loved. Last, by energetic work in harmony with their ideals; for nothing is truly ours till we have expressed it in our deeds. These are the three elements of that discipline which the spiritual life demands of those who really want it — steady contemplation, drastic self-conquest, eager service; and this, I believe, is their true order of importance.

"Sources of Power in Human Life" (1921)

Institutional religion

When we look into history we see the life of the Spirit, even from its crudest beginnings, closely associated with two movements. First with the tendency to organize it in communities or churches, living under special sanctions and rules. Next, with the tendency of its greatest, most arresting personalities either to revolt from these organisms or to reform, rekindle them from within. So that the institutional life of religion persists through or in spite of its own constant tendency to stiffen and lose fervor, and the secessions, protests, or renewals which are occasioned by its greatest sons. . . . Are [these institutions] then, in spite of these adverse characters, to be looked on as essential, inevitable, or merely desirable expressions of the spiritual life in man; or can this spiritual life flourish in pure freedom?

The Life of the Spirit (1922)

The two essentials

Love then, which is a willed tendency to God; prayer, which is willed communion with and experience of him; are the two prime essentials in the personal life of the Spirit. They represent, of course, only our side of it and our obligation. This love is the outflowing response to another inflowing love, and this prayer the appropriation of a transcendental energy and grace.

The Life of the Spirit

What next?

If anyone who has followed these arguments, and now desires to bring them from idea into practice, asks: "What next?" the answer simply is — Begin. Begin with ourselves; and if possible, do not begin in solitude.

The Life of the Spirit

Religious controversy

It seems to be implicit in the very nature of religious controversy, that it so easily persuades those engaging in it to adopt an even lower and more limited standpoint. Like persons sliding down the opposite sides of a mountain they steadily recede from those summits where they might be at one; and each new shower of stones announces a constantly accelerated retreat, which inevitably drives them further and further apart. . . .

"The Hill of the Lord" (1927)

The spiritual life

Some people appear to think that the "spiritual life" is a peculiar condition mainly supported by cream ices and corrected by powders. But the solid norm of the spiritual life should be like that of the natural life: a matter of porridge, bread and butter, and a cut off the joint.

The House of the Soul and Concerning the Inner Life (1927)

The church

The church is an "essential service" like the post office, but there will always be some narrow, irritating and inadequate officials behind the counter and you will always be tempted to exasperation by them.

Personal letter (1932)

Choosing a church

The Church of Rome must always have a sort of attraction for those who love prayer because it *does* understand and emphasize worship. But the whole question of course is not "What attracts and would help me?" but "Where can I serve God best?" — and usually the answer to that is, "Where he has put me." . . . There is a great deal still to be done [in the Church of England] and a great deal to put up with, and the diet is often none too good — but we are here to feed his sheep where we find them, not to look for comfy quarters!

Personal letter (1933)

Where all are at one

This double orientation to the natural and the supernatural, testifying at once to the unspeakable otherness of God transcendent and the intimate nearness of God incarnate, is felt in all the various expressions of genuine Christian worship. The monk or nun rising to recite the night office that the church's praise of God may never cease, and the Quaker waiting in silent assurance on the Spirit given at Pentecost; the ritualist, ordering with care every detail of a complicated ceremonial that God may be glorified thereby, and the old woman content to boil her potatoes in the same sacred intention; the Catholic burning a candle before the symbolic image of the Sacred Heart or confidently seeking the same divine presence in the tabernacle, and the Methodist or Lutheran pouring out his devotion in hymns to the name of Jesus; the Orthodox bowed down in speechless adoration at the culminating moment of the divine mysteries, and the Salvationist marching to drum and tambourine behind the banner of the cross — all these are here at one. Their worship is conditioned by a concrete fact; the stooping down of the Absolute to disclose himself within the narrow human radius, the historical incarnation of the eternal Word within time. The primary declaration of Christianity is not "This do" but "This happened" — indeed, is happening still, since the path of incarnation remains open, and Christ lives and acts in his body, the church, and gives himself in its sacraments.

Worship (1937)

Worship and holiness

Christian worship, then, is to be judged by the degree in which it tends to holiness; since this is the response to the pressure of the Holy which is asked of the church and of the soul. The Christian is required to use the whole of his existence as sacramental material; offer it and consecrate it at every point, so that it may contribute to the glory of God.

Worship

Anglicanism

The peculiar character of Anglicanism arises in part from the operation of history; the conflict . . . of Puritan and Catholic ideals. But it is also a true expression of certain paradoxical attributes of the English mind: its tendency to conservatism in respect of the past, and passion for freedom in respect of the present, its law-abiding faithfulness to established custom, but recoil from an expressed dominance; its reverence for the institutions which incorporate its life, and inveterate individualism in the living of that life; its moral and practical bent.

Worship

War

Since all Christians are now agreed on the wrongfulness and wastefulness of war, even though they may in particular instances believe themselves compelled to wage it, acquiescence in this supposed necessity can only mean capitulation to expediency and defective confidence in God. . . . War is sin worked out to its inevitable conclusion in violence, hatred, greed and mutual mistrust. . . . Thus even the most just of wars implies a movement away from Christ. . . . Its causes are rooted in possessiveness, in inordinate desire — the frenzied clutch on what we have, the desperate grab at what we have not. But Christianity, considered as a clue to life's meaning, has no more interest in the clutch than in the grab.

"Postscript" (1940)

The true pacifist

The pacifist, then, must be content to begin where he is; not by large general denunciations of war, convincing "proofs" of its folly and sin, but rather by quietly accepting his own place in a sinful order and there creating around himself a little pool of harmony and love. The home, the street, the workplace, the city should be his first, perhaps his only sphere.

"Postscript" (1940)

FOR REFLECTION AND DISCUSSION

Have you had a mystical experience or an experience with mystical overtones? If so, what parts of Underhill's description of mysticism apply to your experience?

Do you agree that every person is a potential mystic?

What contemporary expressions of spirituality run the risk of being the sort that are "supported by cream ices and corrected by powders"?

On what basis do you choose a church? How does your method of choosing compare to Underhill's?

If worship "is to be judged by the degree in which it tends to holiness," how would you evaluate the worship of your parish church? What would increase its tending to holiness?

On what grounds would you agree or disagree with Underhill's pacifism?

Make a list of suggestions from Underhill that could elevate your own prayer life.

Chapter 23

WILLIAM TEMPLE

1881-1944

Philosopher Prelate

PHILOSOPHER, THEOLOGIAN, apologist, teacher, evangelist, ecumenist, reformer, archbishop, and friend to hundreds of men and women of every social class and point of view — no other Christian exercised so wide or varied a ministry during the first half of the twentieth century as William Temple.

The son of an archbishop of Canterbury, Temple learned of Jesus Christ at the same time he learned to speak and take his first steps, and he never looked back. He was rarely troubled by serious doubts; he had no conversion experience because he had no need of one. The question for Temple was never "Shall I follow Christ?" but rather, "*How* shall I follow Christ?"

Temple studied philosophy at Balliol College, Oxford, where he engaged in lively debates with atheist and agnostic students, completing his course of study in 1903. He then lectured in philosophy for six years at Queen's College, Oxford, but soon began to think of ordination. Turned down in 1906 by the bishop of Oxford because of his unorthodox views on the virgin birth and the resurrection, Temple was ordained three years later by Archbishop of Canterbury Randall Davidson, who perhaps guessed — correctly — that the young Temple's unusual theological opinions would moderate in later years.

Following ordination, Temple served as a parish priest at St. James's Church, Piccadilly, then as headmaster at Repton School. He edited a theological journal, married, and served as canon at Westminster Abbey. In 1921, Temple became bishop of Manchester, a sprawling industrialized diocese with sharp social divisions. He was elevated to archbishop of York in 1929 and became the ninety-ninth archbishop of Canterbury in 1942, a post which he held for two and a half years until his untimely death in 1944. During all this time, Temple worked on a variety of fronts with Christian leaders from England and beyond, becoming the most influential and respected Christian leader in the Protestant world. His contributions in four areas are particularly notable:

Life and Liberty Movement. As an officially established church, the Church of England had functioned, for much of its history, almost as a department of the state. Although the clergy made day-to-day decisions, Parliament, which often included persons who were not church members, still spoke the final word on church budgets and appointments. In 1917, Temple resigned his position at St. James's, Piccadilly — taking a two-thirds cut in pay — to devote full time to heading the Life and Liberty Movement, seeking a measure of autonomy for the church and a greater role for the laity.

For the next eighteen months he traveled up and down the length of England, organizing groups to push for reform. On November 7, 1919, Parliament passed the Enabling Act. "For the first time, at least since almost primitive ages, the laity in every parish throughout the land are offered vote and voice in the management of their church," said Cosmo Lang, archbishop of York. There was still much to be done to change entrenched attitudes, among both the laity and the clergy, but the Enabling Act was the first step in validating and empowering the laity as full partners in the ministry of the Church of England.

University missions. Temple ventured often onto university campuses, where a sophisticated philosophical skepticism was much in vogue. He would preach every night for a week or longer. Attendance normally increased each night. Temple's intellectual vigor and spiritual passion revived the church on many campuses. In one memorable incident at Oxford in 1931, reported by his biographer F. A. Iremonger, Temple challenged his hearers on the final night of the mission with the words of a familiar hymn. "They are tremendous words," Temple said. "If you mean them with all your hearts, sing them as loud as you can. If you don't mean them at all, keep silent. If you mean them even a little, and want to mean them more, sing them very softly." Silence filled the room as every eye looked at the text of the hymn. Then two thousand voices sang, in a whisper:

> Were the whole realm of nature mine,
> That were an offering far too small;
> Love so amazing, so divine,
> Demands my soul, my life, my all.

Ecumenism. Temple's interest in Christian unity began as early as 1910, when he attended the Faith and Order Conference in Edinburgh which began addressing divisive matters of doctrine and polity among the world's Protestant churches. In 1929 he assumed the chairmanship of the Faith and Order Continuation Committee, and in 1937 chaired the effort which merged that movement with the Life and Work movement, a separate endeavor to unite Christians in addressing the great social and political questions of the day. Temple also launched discussions with the Roman Catholic and Russian Orthodox Churches and supported the formation of the Church of South India, a ground-breaking merger of four Protestant denominations. These efforts continued even during the Second World

War, leading eventually to the formation of the World Council of Churches in 1948.

Temple's role in bringing the Christians of the world together was pivotal right up until his death. Believers with different backgrounds, temperaments, and opinions all trusted him. His patience, humor, charity, common sense, openness to others, and above all his hunger for a unified Christian witness made Temple *the* acknowledged head of the ecumenical movement during his lifetime. He occupies among Protestant and Orthodox Christians a place comparable to that of Pope John XXIII among Roman Catholics.

World War II. As archbishop of Canterbury, Temple was second only to Winston Churchill in his influence upon the English people during the war years. He worked for famine relief in war-ravaged countries and pleaded with the British government to make the safety of European Jews a primary concern. In his writings, sermons, and broadcast addresses to the nation, he denounced Nazism as idolatry, but maintained that while the use of force to resist evil might be necessary, the English were to bear no ill will towards the Germans and resist thoughts of revenge. He advocated humane treatment for German prisoners of war. Sin, he reminded his listeners, was universal, and both sides in the war had cause for repentance. Even as German bombs were falling on English cities, Temple urged the nation to look beyond the war to a time of forgiveness and reconciliation. Although Temple was not a pacifist, even pacifists trusted him.

Temple was also a prolific writer. He had the uncanny ability to stand at a podium and deliver polished lectures from brief notes. Many of his thirty-five books are transcriptions of such lectures. His most philosophical work was his Gifford Lectures, published in 1934 as *Nature, Man and God.* Temple did not seek to prove the existence of God, but wrote that if one starts from a stance of faith, modern science and human experience make more sense than if one begins with any other presupposition. He viewed the world as an evolving process in which different "strata" of being emerge over time, from the merely mechanical, through the living and the mental, to the spiritual, finally culminating in the Incarnation of the Son of God, which he called an "enrichment of the divine life." The higher strata do not negate the lower, but incorporate and use them; the lower find their fulfillment in the higher — and *all* things reveal something of God. This open-ended philosophical scheme invited dialogue with scientific and secular thinkers.

Temple wrote that events are more revealing than nature, and some events are particularly revealing. Do not look for God's revelation in books or doctrines, Temple said, but in events interpreted by human beings, the "intercourse of mind and event." And since God is personal, revelation must also be personal, and the "fullness of revelation" comes in the Person who is "one in essence with the Being whom he reveals." It is in the Incarnation of the Son of God, Temple wrote, that we have the fullest presentation of God in the world; it is in Christ that all the strata of existence are seen to be part of God's plan.

Temple's most widely-read book is his *Readings in St. John's Gospel,* published in 1939 and reissued many times. The Gospel of John was Temple's favorite biblical book. In the *Readings,* he accepts everything in the gospel at face value, leading some to criticize him for ignoring the insights of modern biblical criticism. It was not Temple's intention, however, to write a scholarly commentary, but a nontechnical devotional work. The book gains new readers with each generation and remains a staple of the devotional genre.

Christianity and Social Order, published in 1942, was Temple's last and perhaps his most provocative book. He had often involved himself in political controversies, from mediating a coal strike in 1926 to the conduct of the war against Germany. In this little book he articulated the principles which had guided his political activity and challenged many popular assumptions. The church is not a department of life concerned only with personal beliefs and devotional practices, he wrote. From earliest times, the church has spoken out on public matters, and it is only in recent years that this right has been questioned. When the economic order fails to build Christian character, the church must seek to change it. "The church may tell the politician what ends the social order should promote; but it must leave to the politician the devising of the precise means to those ends," Temple wrote. Society should be structured to give each person the widest opportunity to become what God has placed it in that person to become, Temple said. He saw personal freedom (maximum individual choice), social fellowship (strengthening family, national, and international ties), and service (wider loyalties taking priority over narrow ones) as the key principles leading to such a society.

William Temple

IN HIS OWN WORDS

The love of God

We are not left to conceive the all-embracing love of God as a general idea: we can call to mind the agony and the cross. There we see what selfishness in us means to God; and if evil means that to God, then God is not indifferent to evil. He displays his utter alienation from evil by showing us the pain that it inflicts on him. So more than in any other way he rouses us from acquiescence in our own selfishness.

Christus Veritas (1924)

The desolate cry

It is a system which is foul and rotten. Producer, capitalist, consumer — all are entangled in the meshes of its net. While we prate about the spread of refinement; and while we pride ourselves on the spread of education; while we glory in the empire whose flag is said to stand for justice — we are convicted by the facts at our own doors, of stupid coarseness, of ignorant insensibility, and of wanton oppression. . . . if we listen, there is still the desolate cry of the Son of Man: "I am hungry and ye gave me no meat."

Address to the Christian Social Union (1924)

Christ reigns

While we deliberate, he reigns; when we decide, he reigns; when we decide foolishly, he reigns; when we serve him in humble loyalty, he reigns; when we serve him self-assertively, he reigns; when we rebel and seek to withhold our service, he reigns — the Alpha and the Omega, which is, and which was, and which is to come, the Almighty.

Sermon at Lambeth Conference (1930)

The Incarnation

The doctrine of the Incarnation is not first and foremost of importance because of what it says about somebody who lived in Palestine; it is of fundamental importance because of what it tells us about the eternal and unchanging God, who is and always will be himself; and if he . . . has given perfect expression of his character in terms of human life, then as we look at that life we see the eternal God.

Oxford University Mission (1931)

Anglicanism

The Anglican Communion . . . has as its special characteristic and contribution to the life of the whole church not any one element in specially conspicuous development, but precisely a combination of the elements which elsewhere tend to exist in separation. . . . We have to hold together these three elements — catholic, evangelical, and what is commonly called liberal. [Anglicanism is] solidly catholic, as in its doctrine, so also in its affirmation of continuity in time and unity through space, expressed by outward observances. . . . But we are also in the fullest sense heirs of . . . the Reformation, with its perpetual stress upon the immediacy of access to God which is, in Christ, offered to all his children. And in quite a peculiar degree we are free . . . free as a federation of willing units . . . [and free as to] the individual inquiry and individual response to the leading of the Spirit.

Thoughts on Some Problems of the Day (1931)

The essence of revelation

[God] guides the process; he guides the minds of men; the interaction of the process and the minds which are alike guided by him is the essence of revelation.

Nature, Man and God (1933)

Revealed truth

From all this it follows that there is no such thing as revealed truth. There are truths of revelation, that is to say, propositions which express the results of correct thinking concerning revelation; but they are not themselves directly revealed. On the other hand, this does not involve the result that there need be anything vague or indefinite about revelation itself.

Nature, Man and God

Heaven and hell

For the reward that is offered is one that a selfish man would not enjoy. Heaven, which is fellowship with God, is only joy for those to whom love is the supreme treasure. Indeed, objectively regarded, heaven and hell may well be identical. Each is the realization that man is utterly subject to the purpose of Another — of God who is love. To the godly and unselfish soul that is joy unspeakable; to the selfish soul it is a misery against which he rebels in vain. Heaven and hell are the two extreme terms of our possible reactions to the gospel of the love of God.

Nature, Man and God

Science and religion

Truth is one, and the progress towards truth in religion and in science follows converging lines. We serve truth as a whole most effectively, not when we seek to impose religious ideas upon science, nor when we seek to impose scientific ideas upon religion, but when studying both religion and the physical world with open and unprejudiced minds we seek to read their lesson.

Nature, Man and God

War

No positive good can be done by force; that is true. But evil can be checked and held back by force, and it is precisely for this that we may be called upon to use it. If it be so, let us do it in calm but unshakable resolution, trying, in spite of all the agony, to bear no ill-will to those whom we must resist, seeking to inflict no more suffering than is inevitably involved in the resistance that we must offer, bearing with patient courage the suffering that comes to ourselves. And while we do our utmost to secure the triumph of right as it has been given us to see the right, let us steadily look beyond the conflict to the restoration of peace, and dedicate ourselves to the creation of a world order which shall be fair to the generations yet unborn.

Radio broadcast (1939)

The darkness and the light

As we look forwards, we peer into darkness, and none can say with certainty what course the true progress of the future should follow. But as we look back, the truth is marked by beacon-lights, which are the lives of saints and pioneers; and these in their turn are not originators of light, but rather reflectors which give light to us, because they themselves are turned to the source of light. . . . The redemption of man is part, even if the crowning part, of a greater thing, the redemption, or conquest, of the universe. Till that be accomplished the darkness abides, pierced but unilluminated by the beam of divine light. And the one great question for everyone is whether he will "walk in darkness" or "walk in the light."

Readings in St. John's Gospel (1939)

Becoming worthy

Thou canst do all things. I have nothing. I am not fit to offer the meanest service. Surely God will first require and help me to form a character worthy to serve him, and then appoint me my task. No; in point of fact it is only through service that such a character could be formed.

Readings in St. John's Gospel

Only two centers

There are only two possible centers for life — God and self. If we are not
becoming centered upon God, we are becoming centered upon self; and
self-centeredness is the essence of sin.

Readings in St. John's Gospel

The most materialist religion

Christianity is the most materialistic of all great religions. The others hope
to achieve spiritual reality by ignoring matter — calling it illusion or saying that it does not exist; the result is a failure to control the physical side
of life, a lofty religious philosophy side by side with sensual indulgence,
not indeed in the same persons but in the same religious tradition. Christianity, based as it is on the Incarnation, regards matter as destined to be
the vehicle and instrument of spirit, and spirit as fully actual so far as it
controls and directs matter.

Readings in St. John's Gospel

God's concern

It is a great mistake to suppose that God is only, or even chiefly, concerned
with religion.

The Hope of a New World (1940)

The evil of unemployment

The worst evil of such unemployment . . . is its creating in the unemployed
a sense that they have fallen out of the common life. . . . That is the thing
that has power to corrupt the soul of any man not already far advanced in
saintliness. Because the man has no opportunity of service, he is turned in
upon himself and becomes, according to his temperament, a contented
loafer or an embittered self-seeker.

Christianity and Social Order (1942)

Charity as blood money

If the present order is taken for granted or assumed to be sacrosanct, charity from the more or less fortunate would seem virtuous and commendable; to those for whom the order itself is suspect or worse, such charity is blood-money. Why should some be in the position to dispense and others to need that kind of charity?

Christianity and Social Order

The question to ask

We are obliged to ask concerning every field of human activity what is the purpose of God for it.

Christianity and Social Order

What is best for my country?

I am to do what is best for my country? Very well. There is an opportunity to acquire for it additional wealth and power by merely expropriating some small state whose citizens are happy in their independence, or again by some successful diplomatic deception. Is it "good" for my country to gain power or wealth by those means? Is it "good" for a country to gain the whole world and to lose its own soul?

Christianity and Social Order

The art of government

The art of government in fact is the art of so ordering life that self-interest prompts what justice demands.

Christianity and Social Order

Freedom

Freedom is a great word, and like other great words is often superficially understood. It has been said that to those who have enough of this world's goods the claim to freedom means "Leave us alone," while to those who have not enough it means "Give us a chance."

Christianity and Social Order

Love and justice

Love, in fact, finds its primary expression through justice.

Christianity and Social Order

Christian social order

The aim of a Christian social order is the fullest possible development of individual personality in the widest and deepest possible fellowship.

Christianity and Social Order

FOR REFLECTION AND DISCUSSION

In a sentence, state why the Incarnation of the Son of God was important for Temple.

What problems in the life of Anglican churches does the attempt to hold together the catholic, evangelical, and liberal elements of Christian faith create?

In Temple's view, with what is God chiefly concerned?

How does Temple think God is revealed? How does this square with your own experience of God's revelation?

Temple's most famous remark is that Christianity is "the most avowedly materialist of all the great religions." What did he mean by this? Do you agree?

Does the church have the right to take a stand on a political or economic issue? On what basis is the decision made?

How do Temple's views on the social order compare with the actual social order where you live?

Chapter 24

DOROTHY L. SAYERS

1893-1957

Whimsical Apologist

266

D OROTHY SAYERS adopted porcupines at the zoo and raised a pig
named Francis Bacon. She drove a motorcycle, knitted her own
stockings, and wore gloppy earrings and exotic strings of pearls. She chain-
smoked, usually cigarettes, sometimes cigars. She was nearly bald (due to
an adolescent illness) and sometimes didn't comb what hair she had. She
sang loud in church and favored hymns that "prowl around, good swing-
ing thick stuff." She wore baggy coats with lots of pockets because she
wouldn't carry a purse. People called her precocious, capricious, and —
most often — whimsical. No one called her conventional.

Dorothy Sayers was an only child, the daughter of an Anglican clergyman. She spent her childhood roaming through drafty old rectories and
studying Latin. Her keen intellect, apparent from an early age, took her to
Oxford University, where she was among the first group of women to be
granted degrees. She took a job as an advertising copywriter (she designed
a hugely successful campaign boosting a brand of mustard), but it didn't
pay well, so she turned to the detective novel because, as she said later, it
seemed a quick route to fame and fortune. That it was — Sayers not only
edited anthologies of detective stories and wrote essays on the genre, but
also created a stylish, urbane sleuth in Lord Peter Wimsey. Royalties
streamed in as Dorothy Sayers took her place alongside Conan Doyle and
Agatha Christie as one of Britain's most popular detective writers.

Even in her detective stories, a religious and moral dimension is evident. Although Lord Peter Wimsey was not a Christian — he was more like
an eighteenth-century rationalist, with a dose of self-doubt thrown in —
many of Sayers' characters show genuine Christian commitment. The
truth always emerges in her fiction, pride leads to disaster, and goodness
triumphs, but religion and morality are never dwelt upon. They are more
of a backdrop, an implied presence, and Sayers would never have wanted
her novels labeled "religious books." She was passionate in her faith, however, and with her reputation and income secure from her detective stories,
she turned to writing explicitly theological works. Serious as she was about
religion, she often wrote about it in a humorous, tongue-in-cheek vein
that entertained while it drove home her points. Dorothy Sayers proved
herself a fervent, intellectually rigorous — and often funny — spokes-
woman for doctrinal orthodoxy.

Christian dogma was her passion. She experienced it as a gripping, exciting story. One of her peeves was the dullness of much of what she saw going on in church — the pedantic sermons, the listless singing, the obsession

with decorum, socials and bazaars. Was no one paying attention to what was being said? "We may call [Christian] doctrine exhilarating, or we may call it devastating; we may call it revelation, or we may call it rubbish; but if we call it dull, then words have no meaning," she wrote. It was not the teaching of Christian dogma that made for dullness, but the neglect of it. Moreover, she felt that classical Christian doctrine was "hammered out under pressure of urgent practical necessity" and contained the key to life and meaning. She recognized that many biblical statements are not literal facts, but saw no need to restate or "demythologize" such language. At the heart of the Christian story lay one riveting, astounding historic fact: In the person of a particular first-century Jewish carpenter, the Creator of the universe had become human. That fact was the key to everything else for Sayers. The Western world faced a choice, she felt, not between civilization and barbarism, but between the Christian creed and chaos. Christianity provided the sound understanding of human nature and authority without which the noblest intentions would prove worthless. Heresies, she felt, were not merely mistaken ideas, but blind alleys, dead-end roads, paths to disaster.

Sayers' explicitly religious works consist of essays, plays, one book-length study, and a translation of Dante's *The Divine Comedy*. Several themes recur in her essays: the vitality of Christian doctrine, the centrality of the Incarnation as a historic fact, the danger of high-minded pride, the importance of moral living in every area of human life, a plea for intellectual honesty, the sacredness of work done for the glory of God, and the blandness of much of what passes for Christian witness.

Her essays are full of fresh metaphors and wry humor, but the humor is not there merely to elicit a laugh. Sayers' humor makes a point. She is never vicious or disloyal, and her love for the church is never in doubt, but her wit often points to ways the church's behavior contradicts the Christian gospel, and her humor can be sharp: She says the church gives the impression that the seven Christian virtues are "respectability, childishness, mental timidity, dullness, sentimentality, censoriousness, and depression of spirits." Or, regarding saints, she says that they "come in all varieties. The only kind that seems to be rare in real life is the spineless and 'goody-goody' figure familiar to us in the feebler sort of pious fiction and stained-glass windows of the more regrettable sort." Or, observing that the word immorality has come to mean sexual promiscuity and nothing more, she says that a "man may be greedy and selfish; spiteful, cruel, jealous, and unjust; violent and brutal; grasping, unscrupulous, and a liar; stubborn and arrogant; stupid, morose, and dead to every noble instinct — and still we are ready to say of him that he is not an immoral man. I am reminded of a young man who once said to me with perfect simplicity: 'I did not know there were seven deadly sins; please tell me the names of the other six.'"

Sayers' greatest dramatic success was a series of twelve plays called *The Man Born to Be King*, based on the life of Christ, written for radio and broadcast over the B.B.C. in December, 1941. It was a ground-breaking use of a then new electronic medium for religious purposes, and the series was immensely popular. Sayers' goal was to bring the biblical text to life for the mid-twentieth century, to make the familiar sayings and incidents in the life of Jesus sound like *real* events, things said and done in *this* world, at a *particular* time and place not unlike mid-twentieth-century Britain. In an age when the lofty but archaic cadences of the Great Bible and the King James Bible were what most people thought of as "biblical" language, Sayers' characters spoke contemporary English, even slang. From Judas to Jesus, she gave them personal histories and believable psychological profiles. "For the Christian affirmation is that a number of quite commonplace human beings, in an obscure province of the Roman Empire, killed and murdered God Almighty — quite casually, almost as a matter of religious and political routine, and certainly with no notion that they were doing anything out of the way. Their motives, on the whole, were defensible, and in some respects praiseworthy," she wrote in her introduction to *The Man Born to Be King*. "We, the audience, know what they were doing; the whole point and poignancy of the tragedy is lost unless we realize that they did not." Many of her B.B.C. listeners, whose homes were being threatened nightly by German bombs, experienced the story of Jesus as if they were hearing it for the first time, and most of them liked what they heard, although some felt Sayers had treated the sacred text irreverently.

Dorothy Sayers' most original work was her book *The Mind of the Maker*, published in 1941, at the same time she was working on *The Man Born to Be King*. She looks at the Creation story in Genesis, then examines the creative instinct in human beings and speculates that the capacity to create is the "image of God," the human quality which mirrors the character of God. She then moves to the Trinity, often a perplexing bit of doctrine, and suggests a bold analogy: A writer has an *idea*. Then the writer exerts *energy* that results in a book — the incarnation of the idea. Then comes the *creative power* by which the idea, expressed in the book, enters into and influences those who read the book and who, by reading it, enter into a relationship with the author. Idea, energy, and creative power, though distinguishable from one another, are not three things, but three aspects of a single thing. The notion that God is one in three and three in one, then, is not so foreign to human experience as is sometimes thought, Sayers says.

The Mind of the Maker also offers an analogy about free will: From the creative imagination of a playwright comes a script. It includes characters who have lines to say. The playwright has an idea about how these lines should be delivered on stage. But when a gifted actor reads the lines, he imbues the lines with additional layers of meaning, coming from his own creative imagination. This does not negate what the playwright intended, but enlarges it. Similarly, a bad actor can diminish a play, even destroy the meaning the playwright intended. Yet if the playwright jumps on stage in the midst of the play, the meaning and direction of the play are radically and irreversibly altered. A playwright virtually never does this, even when the acting is awful. God also virtually never intervenes in history. Christians believe that God has, in fact, done it only once — and the meaning and direction of history were radically and irreversibly altered.

In the final decade of her life, Sayers learned Italian, then translated and wrote essays on Dante's *The Divine Comedy*. Her work on Dante has become a classic. Dorothy Sayers died in her home, suddenly, of a massive coronary, after a day of Christmas shopping, on December 17, 1957. C. S. Lewis wrote a eulogy read at her funeral. She is buried beneath the tower of St. Anne's Church in London, where she had served as churchwarden. A marker bears the words, "The only Christian work is good work well done."

IN HER OWN WORDS

If God set right every wrong

"Why doesn't God smite this dictator dead?" is a question a little remote from us. Why, madam, did he not strike you dumb and imbecile before you uttered that baseless and unkind slander the day before yesterday? Or me, before I behaved with such cruel lack of consideration to that well-meaning friend? And why, sir, did he not cause your hand to rot off at the wrist before you signed your name to that dirty little bit of financial trickery?

The Greatest Drama Ever Staged (1938)

Creeds and omelettes

A regulation that allowed a cook to make omelettes only on condition of first putting on a top hat might conceivably be given the force of law, and penalties might be inflicted for disobedience; but the condition would remain arbitrary and irrational. The law that omelettes can be made only on condition that there shall be a preliminary breaking of eggs is one with which we are sadly familiar. The efforts of idealists to make omelettes without observing that condition are foredoomed to failure by the nature of things. The Christian creeds are too frequently assumed to be in the top-hat category; this is an error; they belong to the category of egg-breaking.

The Mind of the Maker (1941)

The image of God

The expression "in his own image" [Genesis 1:27] has occasioned a good deal of controversy. . . . How then can [man] be said to resemble God? Is it his immortal soul, his rationality, his self-consciousness, his free will, or what, that gives him a claim to this rather startling distinction? A case may be argued for all these elements in the complex nature of man. But had the author of Genesis anything particular in his mind when he wrote? It is observable that in the passage leading up to the statement about man, he has given no detailed information about God. Looking at man, he sees in him something essentially divine, but when we turn back to see what he says about the original upon which the "image" of God was modeled, we find only the single assertion, "God created." The characteristic common to God and man is apparently that: the desire and ability to make things.

The Mind of the Maker

Metaphor and reality

Sometimes we speak of [God] as a king, and use metaphors drawn from that analogy. We talk, for instance, of his kingdom, laws, dominion, service and soldiers. Still more frequently, we speak of him as a father, and think it quite legitimate to argue from the analogy of human fatherhood to the "fatherhood" of God. . . . When we use these expressions, we know perfectly well that they are metaphors and analogies. . . . we need not allow ourselves to be abashed by any suggestion that the old metaphors are out of date and ought to be superceded. We have only to remember that they are, and always were, metaphors, and that they are still "living" metaphors so long as we use them to interpret direct experience. Metaphors become dead only when the metaphor is substituted for the experience, and the argument carried on in a sphere of abstraction without being at every point related to life.

The Mind of the Maker

Incarnation

There is, of course, no reason why an infinite Mind should not reveal itself in an infinite number of forms, each being subject to the nature of that particular form. It was said, sneeringly, by someone that if a clam could conceive of God, it would conceive of him in the shape of a great, big clam. Naturally. And if God has revealed himself to clams, it could be only under conditions of perfect clamhood, since any other manifestation would be wholly irrelevant to clam nature.

The Mind of the Maker

The world's a stage

The whole of existence is held to be the work of the divine Creator — everything that there is. . . . Consequently, whereas the human writer obtains his response from other minds, outside and independent of his own, God's response comes only from his own creatures. This is as though a book were written to be read by the characters within it. And further: the universe is not a finished work. Every mind within it is in the position of the audience sitting in the theater and seeing the play for the first time. Or rather, every one of us is on the stage, performing a part in a play, of which we have not seen either the script or any synopsis of the ensuing acts. . . . There is one episode in particular to which Christianity draws [our] attention. The leading part in this was played, it is alleged, by the Author, who presents it as a brief epitome of the plan of the whole work. If we ask, "What *kind* of play is this that we are acting?" the answer put forward is: "Well, it is *this* kind of play." And examining the plot of it, we observe at once that if anybody in this play has his feelings spared, it is certainly not the Author.

The Mind of the Maker

Why no indignation?

It is curious that people who are filled with horrified indignation whenever a cat kills a sparrow can hear that story of the killing of God told Sunday after Sunday and not experience any shock at all.

The Man Born to Be King, Introduction (1943)

Crucifying him afresh

Not Herod, not Caiaphas, not Pilate, not Judas ever contrived to fasten upon Jesus Christ the reproach of insipidity; that final indignity was left for pious hands to inflict. To make of his story something that could neither startle, nor shock, nor terrify, nor excite, nor inspire a living soul is to crucify the Son of God afresh and put him to an open shame.

The Man Born to Be King, Introduction

"The dogma is the drama"

We are constantly assured that the churches are empty because preachers insist too much upon doctrine — dull dogma as people call it. The fact is the precise opposite. It is the neglect of dogma that makes for dullness. The Christian faith is the most exciting drama that ever staggered the imagination of man — and the dogma is the drama.

Creed or Chaos? (1949)

Worship

Christ, in his divine innocence, said to the woman of Samaria, "Ye worship ye know not what" [John 4:22] — being apparently under the impression that it might be desirable, on the whole, to know what one was worshiping. He thus showed himself sadly out of touch with the 20th century mind, for the cry today is: "Away with the tedious complexities of dogma — let us have the simple spirit of worship; just worship, no matter of what!" The only drawback to this demand for a generalized and undirected worship is the practical difficulty of arousing any sort of enthusiasm for the worship of nothing in particular.

Creed or Chaos?

What people think the church teaches

Q. What does the church think of God the Father?

A. He is omnipotent and holy. He created the world and imposed on man conditions impossible of fulfilment; he is very angry if these are not carried out. He sometimes interferes by means of arbitrary judgments and miracles, distributed with a good deal of favoritism. He likes to be truckled to and is always ready to pounce on anybody who trips up over a difficulty in the law or is having a bit of fun. He is rather like a dictator, only larger and more arbitrary.

Q. What does the church think of God the Son?

A. He is in some way to be identified with Jesus of Nazareth. It was not his fault that the world was made like this, and, unlike God the Father, he is friendly to man and did his best to reconcile man to God (see *atonement*). He has a good deal of influence with God, and if you want anything done, it is best to apply to him.

Q. What does the church think of God the Holy Ghost?

A. I don't know exactly. He was never seen or heard of till Whitsunday. There is a sin against him that damns you for ever, but nobody knows what it is.

Creed or Chaos?

Offensive Christianity

I believe it is a grave mistake to present Christianity as something charming and popular with no offense in it. Seeing that Christ went about the world giving the most violent offense to all kinds of people, it would seem absurd to expect that the doctrine of his person can be so presented as to offend nobody. We cannot blink at the fact that gentle Jesus, meek and mild, was so stiff in his opinions and so inflammatory in his language that he was thrown out of church, stoned, hunted from place to place, and finally gibbeted as a firebrand and a public danger. Whatever his peace was, it was not the peace of an amiable indifference. . . .

Creed or Chaos?

Justice

When we demand justice, it is always justice on our behalf against other people. Nobody, I imagine, would ever ask for justice to be done *upon* him for every thing he ever did wrong. We do not want justice — we want revenge: and that is why, when justice is done upon us, we cry out that God is vindictive.

Introductory Papers on Dante (1954)

FOR REFLECTION AND DISCUSSION

What is exciting in the historic Christian creeds?

Why did Sayers believe doctrine was important? How do you feel about the importance of doctrine?

Do you appreciate Sayers' humor? Why do you feel there is little laughter in some church gatherings?

If you were writing a drama on the life of Christ, how closely would you stick to the biblical text and where would you take liberties with it?

Do you find Sayers' analogy of the Trinity helpful? Can you think of any other analogy? How would you explain the Trinity?

Chapter 25

C. S. LEWIS
1898-1963

Mere Christian

C. S. LEWIS was the most popular Christian writer of the latter half of the twentieth century, and his popularity continues. Total sales of Lewis's books, forty years after his death, are approaching one hundred million copies. History may judge him the most important person to have died on November 22, 1963, the same day author Aldous Huxley died and President John F. Kennedy was assassinated.

Lewis lived two lives. Outwardly, his life was usually settled and routine. He was born in Belfast, Ireland, and his mother died of cancer when he was nine years old. His father then sent him off to boarding school in England, which he hated, and then to Oxford, which he loved. Lewis eventually became a professor of English literature at Oxford, and later at Cambridge. He wrote several academic texts in his field, including an introduction to Milton's "Paradise Lost" and *English Literature in the Sixteenth Century,* published in 1954, which includes as clear and succinct a discussion of Richard Hooker and the Puritans as one is likely to find anywhere. Lewis was known on campus for his robust lectures and for his unpressed trousers, threadbare jackets, and scuffed shoes. A typical day included reading and writing, a long walk, and conversation with friends. "I like monotony," he once said. Lewis was generous, although he never talked about it and the extent of his generosity was not discovered until after his death. When an Oxford roommate was killed in World War I, Lewis assumed the care of his obstreperous and demanding mother until her death in 1951, and when Lewis's early financial concerns eased as the result of his book sales, he refused to change his simple lifestyle, giving away two-thirds of his income. Long regarded as a confirmed bachelor, Lewis startled his friends by marrying a divorced American woman, Joy Davidman Gresham, in 1956. Their happy marriage was cut short by her death from cancer in 1960. The story of their romance has been popularized in the movie "Shadowlands."

Inwardly, however, Lewis's life was anything but settled and routine. Not only did he wrestle with perplexing religious questions, but he invented fantastic new worlds in his mind. It was in the context of these imaginary worlds that Lewis explored the supernatural and probed the nature of sin and redemption. His fantasy novels are among his most popular titles.

Lewis had no formal theological training and did not regard himself as a theologian, yet he wrote about theology in a way that made its meaning and importance clear to the common reader. He had an extraordinary ability to find an image, illustration, or analogy to bring into focus even the most foggy and complex theological idea. Besides his fantasy novels, Lewis wrote explicitly theological books and articles, addressing every major area of Christian teaching. Lewis was not, however, a theological innovator, seeking instead to clarify and defend classical Christian understandings. He said of one of his books that if anything in it was original, novel, or unorthodox, it was so "against my will and as a result of my ignorance."

Lewis had not been a Christian as a young man, but following his gradual conversion in the 1920s and 1930s (which he discusses in his autobiographical *Surprised by Joy*, published in 1955), Lewis came to an understanding of Christian faith that he held consistently throughout his life. Themes recur in book after book, often with surprising twists. Undergirding all Lewis's work is the conviction of a reality unseen, another world over and beyond the world of time and space, in which good and evil conflict, and with which our lives are entwined, whether we know it or not. This conviction is winsomely propounded in one of Lewis's earliest and most popular books, *The Screwtape Letters*, published in 1942. It purports to be the correspondence of the devil (Screwtape) offering guidance and advice to his nephew (Wormwood) as the latter devises temptation after temptation, seeking to win the soul of a particular "patient" on earth for damnation. But God is also at work in the patient's life, and the patient eventually makes a Christian commitment. At the end of the book, we see that what happens in this world is of life-or-death significance when Screwtape reveals that, as a result of Wormwood's failure, he intends to devour his nephew.

Lewis discusses the reality of the supernatural world most explicitly in *Miracles* (1947), where he challenges "naturalism," the belief that the visible universe is a self-contained entity within which events occur due solely to natural causes, never influenced by anything from beyond, because there is no beyond. *Miracles* is Lewis's longest and most demanding theological book.

Lewis is known for his incisive logic. He had no patience with sloppy or sentimental thinking. *The Guardian* newspaper once wrote that following Lewis's line of thought was "like watching a master chess player who makes a seemingly trivial and unimportant move which ten minutes later turns out to be stroke of genius." We observe Lewis's use of logic both in *Miracles* and in his other extended study of a single theological question, *The Problem of Pain* (1940). There Lewis tackles that thorniest of theological dilemmas — if God is infinitely good and infinitely powerful, why is there so much pain and evil in the world?

Nowhere is Lewis's gift for logic more evident than in his classic *Mere Christianity*, published in 1952, but based on a series of radio addresses delivered a decade earlier. Lewis here seeks to demonstrate the coherence and reasonableness of "mere" Christianity — basic, traditional Christian faith, shorn of peculiar denominational twists. Conversational and down-to-earth in tone, *Mere Christianity* appeals to the common reader through homespun images and lucid analogies. Written for the searching nonbeliever, it speaks to longtime Christians as well. Lewis begins not with revealed truth but with human experience. His discussions of the Incarnation, the Trinity, human nature, and Christian morality are models of clarity and precision. *Mere Christianity* remains immensely popular today.

It is perhaps for his fantasy works, however, that Lewis will be chiefly remembered. Best known of these are his seven children's novels, *The Chronicles of Narnia*, published between 1950 and 1956. These books have earned Lewis a place alongside Lewis Carroll, Beatrix Potter, and A. A. Milne in the top rank of British children's writers. The tales relate the adventures of a group of children in a mythical land called Narnia, where they meet talking animals, dwarfs, dragons, witches, and surrealistic creatures such as — my favorite — a "marsh-wiggle" named Puddleglum. Christian content is never blatant, but each tale concerns the battle between good and evil in a supernatural world, and the lion Aslan is an unmistakable Christ figure.

The human need for transformation and redemption is a recurring theme in *The Chronicles of Narnia*. A graphic example is found in *The Voyage of the Dawn Treader*. Here a nasty little boy named Eustace Clarence Scrubb is lost on a strange island. He finds himself in the cave of a dragon where he discovers gold treasure. As Eustace selfishly begins plotting how to spend this treasure, he falls asleep, and when he awakens, he discovers that having entertained dragon thoughts, he has become a dragon, complete with scales and webbed feet. Eustace cannot scrape off his dragon skin. Then Aslan mysteriously appears and, with Eustace's consent, "undresses" him, removing his dragon skin and restoring him to the body of a boy. A similar scene occurs in *The Lion, the Witch, and the Wardrobe*, where the boy Edmund becomes the slave of the White Witch by gluttonously devouring huge quantities of Turkish delight which she offers him to lure him under her control. The rest of the book relates the adventures of Edmund's brother and sisters as they seek to free him from the witch. Both tales include clear but unstated connections to Christian teachings.

The adult counterpart to *The Chronicles of Narnia* is Lewis's "space trilogy," published between 1938 and 1945. The trilogy concerns the adventures of a philologist named Elwin Ransom who is kidnaped and taken to Mars and Venus, where he takes part in a cosmic struggle. Particularly suggestive are Ransom's experiences among the Malacandrians, a race of intelligent creatures who, unlike human beings on earth, are not "fallen," but voluntarily and happily obey a benevolent deity whom they call Maleldil.

Heaven and hell are frequent Lewis themes. In addition to *The Screwtape Letters,* he explores the afterlife in his short novel *The Great Divorce* (1945), concerning a group of people with unsettlingly familiar attitudes who live in purgatory or hell (it is the same place). They travel by bus to heaven, where they are invited to remain — if they so choose. Only one person chooses to remain in heaven, and the reasons why the others elect to return to hell reveal the gripping power of spiritual pride, envy, and selfishness over the human soul.

A new tone appears in Lewis's last writings. *Letters to Malcolm: Chiefly on Prayer,* published in 1964, contradicts nothing Lewis had written earlier, but seems less buoyant, more tentative and exploratory. By far his most personal book is *A Grief Observed* (1961), first published under a pseudonym, lest it shake the faith of those who had embraced his earlier writings. This is a no-holds-barred account of Lewis's searing, lacerating grief over the death of his wife. Gone are the confident analogies and appeals to logic. Here Lewis stares at unanswerable questions about the afterlife and the presumed goodness of God. His faith is shaken to its roots, and when he finally finds it again, it is changed. It was perhaps in these last years, as he groped for a faith that would transcend the arguments he had earlier championed with such assurance, that Lewis's courage and integrity are most manifest and that he rose to his greatest stature.

IN HIS OWN WORDS

Acceptable actions

All our merely natural activities will be accepted, if they are offered to God, even the humblest: and all of them, even the noblest, will be sinful if they are not.

"Learning in War-time" (1939)

God's governance

We want, in fact, not so much a Father in heaven as a grandfather in heaven — a senile benevolence who, as they say, "liked to see young people enjoying themselves," and whose plan for the universe was simply that it might be truly said at the end of each day, "a good time was had by all." Not many people, I admit, would formulate a theology in precisely those terms: but a conception not very different lurks at the back of many minds. I do not claim to be an exception: I should very much like to live in a universe which was governed on such lines. But since it is abundantly clear that I don't, and since I have reason to believe, nevertheless, that God is love, I conclude that my conception of love needs correction.

The Problem of Pain (1940)

The love of God

To ask that God's love should be content with us as we are is to ask that God should cease to be God: because he is what he is, his love must, in the nature of things, be impeded and repelled by certain stains in our present character, and because he already loves us he must labor to make us lovable.

The Problem of Pain

Sin

A recovery of the old sense of sin is essential to Christianity. Christ takes it for granted that men are bad. Until we really feel this assumption of his to be true, though we are part of the world he came to save, we are not part of the audience to whom his words are addressed.

The Problem of Pain

No ordinary people

There are no *ordinary* people. You have never talked to a mere mortal.

"The Weight of Glory" (1942)

Attending church

If there is anything in the teaching of the New Testament which is in the nature of a command, it is that you are obliged to take the sacrament, and you can't do it without going to church. I disliked very much their hymns, which I considered to be fifth-rate poems set to sixth-rate music. But as I went on I saw the great merit of it. I came up against different people of quite different outlooks and different education, and then gradually my conceit just began peeling off. I realized that the hymns (which were just sixth-rate music) were, nevertheless, being sung with devotion and benefit by an old saint in elastic-side boots in the opposite pew, and then you realize that you aren't fit to clean those boots. It gets you out of your solitary conceit.

"Answers to Questions on Christianity" (1944)

"A good life"

The idea of reaching "a good life" without Christ is based on a double error. Firstly, we cannot do it. And secondly, in setting up "a good life" as our final goal, we have missed the very point of our existence.

"Man or Rabbit?" (1946)

The popular God

We who defend Christianity find ourselves constantly opposed not by the irreligion of our hearers but by their real religion. Speak about beauty, truth and goodness, or about a God who is simply the indwelling principle of those three, speak about a great spiritual force pervading all things, a common mind of which we are all parts, a pool of generalized spirituality to which we can all flow, and you will command friendly interest. But the temperature drops as soon as you mention a God who has purposes and performs particular actions, who does one thing and not another, a concrete, choosing, commanding, prohibiting God with a determinate character. People become embarrassed or angry. Such a conception seems to them primitive and crude and even irreverent. The popular "religion" excludes miracles because it excludes the "living God" of Christianity and believes instead in a kind of God who obviously would not do miracles, or indeed anything else.

Miracles (1947)

The grand miracle

. . . the Christian story is precisely the story of one grand miracle, the Christian assertion being that what is beyond all space and time, what is uncreated, eternal, came into nature, into human nature, descended into his own universe, and rose again, bringing nature up with him. It is precisely one great miracle. If you take that away there is nothing specifically Christian left.

"The Grand Miracle" (1947)

Preaching

Our business is to present that which is timeless (the same yesterday, today, and tomorrow) in the particular language of our own age. The bad preacher does exactly the opposite: he takes the ideas of our own age and tricks them out in the traditional language of Christianity.

"Christian Apologetics" (1947)

The devil

Enemy-occupied territory — that is what this world is. Christianity is the story of how the rightful king has landed, you might say landed in disguise, and is calling us all to take part in a great campaign of sabotage. When you go to church you are really listening in to the secret wireless from our friends: that is why the enemy is so anxious to prevent us from going. He does it by playing on our conceit and laziness and intellectual snobbery. I know someone will ask me, "Do you really mean . . . to re-introduce our old friend the devil — hoofs and horns and all?" Well . . . I am not particular about the hoofs and horns. But in other respects my answer is "Yes, I do." I do not claim to know anything about his personal appearance. If anybody really wants to know him better I would say to that person, "Don't worry. If you really want to, you will. Whether you'll like it when you do is another question."

Mere Christianity (1952)

Pride

In God you come up against something which is in every respect immeasurably superior to yourself. Unless you know God as that — and, therefore, know yourself as nothing in comparison — you do not know God at all. As long as you are proud you cannot know God. A proud man is always looking down on things and people: and, of course, as long as you are looking down, you cannot see something that is above you.

Mere Christianity

Theology

I remember once when I had been giving a talk to the R.A.F., an old, hard-bitten officer got up and said, "I've no use for all that stuff. But, mind you, I'm a religious man too. I *know* there's a God. I've *felt* him, out alone in the desert at night, the tremendous mystery. And that's just why I don't believe all your neat little dogmas and formulas about him. To anyone who's met the real thing they all seem so petty and pedantic and unreal!" Now in a sense I quite agreed with that man. I think he had probably had a real experience of God in the desert. And when he turned from that experience to the Christian creeds, I think he really was turning from something real to something less real. In the same way, if a man has once looked at the Atlantic from the beach, and then goes and looks at a map of the Atlantic, he also will be turning from something real to something less real. . . . but there are two things you have to remember about [the map]. In the first place, it is based on what hundreds and thousands of people have found out by sailing the real Atlantic. In that way it has behind it masses of experience just as real as the one you could have from the beach. . . . In the second place, if you want to go anywhere, the map is absolutely necessary. As long as you are content with walks on the beach, your own glimpses are far more fun than looking at a map. But the map is going to be more use than walks on the beach if you want to get to America.

Mere Christianity

The Trinity

An ordinary simple Christian kneels down to say his prayers. He is trying to get into touch with God. But if he is a Christian he knows that what is prompting him to pray is also God: God, so to speak, inside him. But he also knows that all his real knowledge of God comes through Christ, the man who was God — that Christ is standing beside him, helping him to pray, praying for him. You see what is happening. God is the thing to which he is praying — the goal he is trying to reach. God is also the thing inside him which is pushing him on — the motive power. God is also the road or bridge along which he is being pushed to that goal. So that the whole threefold life of the three-personal Being is actually going on in that ordinary little bedroom where an ordinary man is saying his prayers.

Mere Christianity

What kind of God?

Not that I am (I think) in much danger of ceasing to believe in God. The real danger is of coming to believe such dreadful things about him. The conclusion I dread is not, "So there's no God after all," but, "So this is what God's really like. Deceive yourself no longer."

A Grief Observed (1961)

Faith

You never know how much you really believe anything until its truth or falsehood becomes a matter of life and death to you. It is easy to say you believe a rope to be strong and sound as long as you are merely using it to cord a box. But suppose you had to hang by that rope over a precipice. Wouldn't you then first discover how much you really trusted it? . . . Only a real risk tests the reality of a belief. Apparently the faith — I thought it faith — which enables me to pray for the other dead has seemed strong only because I have never really cared, not desperately, whether they existed or not. Yet I thought I did.

A Grief Observed

Religion

Talk to me about the truth of religion and I'll listen gladly. Talk to me about the duty of religion and I'll listen submissively. But don't come talking to me about the consolations of religion or I shall suspect that you don't understand.

A Grief Observed

FOR REFLECTION AND DISCUSSION

If you were writing a book on theology, would you avoid anything "original, novel, or unorthodox"? Why?

What has led to the widespread "naturalism" in the modern world? What would you say to a naturalist?

Write a statement defining "mere" (basic) Christianity as you understand it.

Is religious truth better expressed in fantasy and myth than in factual statements?

Does the early Lewis or the Lewis after 1960 speak more tellingly to you?

What is the difference between believing in a "Father in heaven" and believing in a "grandfather in heaven"?

Do you believe the devil is an actual being? What difference does it make?

Chapter 26

VERNA J. DOZIER

B. 1917

Re-envisioning the Laity

W HEN I BEGAN to list the great Anglican thinkers I wanted to include in this book, most of the names that first came to mind were of ordained English men. Ordained English men have indeed made substantial contributions — but 99 percent of Christians have always been *lay* people; most congregations consist of more *women* than men; and over half of Anglicans today reside in *Africa*. A book purporting to be about Anglican spirituality that focused solely on ordained English men would be incomplete at best, and totally misleading at worst. I suppose this would have dawned on me eventually even without Verna Dozier. But it was through her that this anomaly came to my attention. One reason is that Dozier herself is a black lay woman who has never lived in England, but the main reason is what she says. When I first heard her speak and read what she wrote, she impacted me like a splash of cold water in the face. I said to myself, "Wake *up!* Where *have* you been?"

Dozier (she pronounces it do-ZEER) has spent all her life in Washington, D.C. Reared by two loving parents, an agnostic father and a Baptist mother, she inherited both a questioning mind and a deep faith. As a young girl she went with her father to Howard University to hear the preaching of the great black theologian Howard Thurman. "I was spellbound," she says. "It was the first time I had heard anyone question the divinity of Jesus, and the chapel did not fall down. . . . My father and I just drank it in."

As an adult, Dozier taught English to junior and senior high students in the District of Columbia public schools for thirty-two years. When she retired, she began to lead Bible study groups for her parish. To those who say that she "began her ministry" then, she quickly replies, "No, I *continued* my ministry!" Christian ministry was once seen as something the clergy do, Dozier says, with lay people expected to pay their pledges, show up on Sundays, and otherwise support the ministry of the clergy. The laity were to remain essentially passive, and if anyone spoke of the "ministry" of a lay person, it was something churchy, like singing in the choir or teaching Sunday school. Dozier feels ministry is for *all* the baptized and that most of it takes place outside the church. What happens on Monday is more important than what happens on Sunday, and if what happens on Sunday has no impact on Monday, then Sunday's activities are a waste of time. "The call to ministry," Dozier says, "is the call to be a citizen of the kingdom of God, in a new way, the daring, free, accepting, compassionate way Jesus modeled. It means being bound by no yesterday, fearing no tomorrow, drawing no lines between friend and foe, the acceptable ones and the out-casts. Ministry is commitment to the dream of God." Teaching in the public schools is one of countless ways lay people carry out this ministry, she says.

Dozier had already traveled widely to teach lay people to use the Bible as a resource for ministry when she published her first book, *Equipping the Saints,* in 1981. It is a short book on how to develop a lay-led Bible study group. To be effective ministers, lay people must know who they are, Dozier says, and Christians learn who they are when they know "the Story" — the story of the Bible. Her Bible study method is simple and easy to use. Although intended for groups, it can be adapted for individuals as well. It has been used all over the world. Taking a passage of scripture, in several translations and with the aid of a few commentaries, the group moves through three steps: (1) Clarify what the passage is saying. What do the words mean? What are the key concepts? (2) Clarify why the passage was preserved. What did it mean to the early Christian community? What issues were they dealing with? How did the passage help them make sense of their lives? (3) Reflect on what the passage means to you and to the church today. Each student's reflection will be different. There will be right and wrong answers in steps one and two, but every reflection in step three has value and complements those of others in the group.

The Bible is not a book of rules or a "guide for every hour and every day of our life," Dozier says. That would produce a static, lifeless faith, eliminating the challenge to keep probing and growing. When we read the Bible, we should say, "So that's how they saw it." It should come as no surprise to discover differences among the biblical authors, she says. Biblical authors were unique individuals, living over a period of a thousand years, and each saw God at work in the world and responded faithfully in his or her own way. By learning how the biblical authors saw God acting in their lives and reflecting upon their response, we learn to see the hand of God in our lives and to determine our response — but the biblical viewpoint can never be our viewpoint. To absolutize biblical perspectives as if they were eternally binding doctrines or laws is to make an idol out of the Bible, Dozier says.

So just what is "the Story" about? What does the Bible say? Freedom is the heart of the biblical story, Dozier says. God freely created human beings and freely chooses to love us — and God gives us freedom and the choice to love him in return. It is because God loves us that human beings are free. God's love is not in question. Dozier says: "When I hear someone talking about people being damned and going to hell, I feel sorry because they don't know anything about the God that I know something about — because that God is not saving me on the basis of my saying the right thing or doing the right thing or being in the right place or connected to the right group. . . . I believe God loves me and loves every single creature and the whole creation. I don't know any other way to talk about it."

"The Story" could, of course, be wrong. Faith cannot be proven and always includes the risk that we could be mistaken. Dozier likes to illustrate this with something she heard from a friend: "Can you imagine what story would have been told by the lone Egyptian who escaped from the Red Sea debacle? He would have reported to Pharaoh, 'Pharaoh, O King, we didn't plan that expedition very well. We should have been able to calculate the tides better and to have planned our pursuit more expeditiously. Also we should have known that wooden chariot wheels would bog down in that mud. We didn't plan very well.'" That is as reasonable an explanation of the Red Sea incident as to say that "the Lord has triumphed gloriously." It may even be that, within their own terms, both explanations are true. Faith is always ambiguous, Dozier says. In fact, God is an ambiguous symbol, pointing to a reality we cannot comprehend. Ambiguity is going in two directions at the same time. We are called to acknowledge both sides — or all sides — of an issue and to abandon our need to be right. What we see today by the light of faith may not be what we see tomorrow by the light of faith because all our sight is limited and partial. "I will know more and different things tomorrow than I know today, and I can be open to the new possibility I cannot even imagine today," Dozier says.

Over the centuries, the church has usually denied this faith, Dozier feels. She speaks of two churches. "A funny thing happened on the way to the Kingdom," she says in the opening lines of *The Authority of the Laity.* "The church, the people of God, became the church, the institution." God calls the church, the people of God, to live God's dream, to take the risk of faith in a world that denies faith. Very quickly, though, the church becomes an institution, and like every institution, soon focuses its energy on perpetuating itself and maintaining its power. Ambiguity and risk are covered over by rules, dogmas, and unbending structures. The church comes to be seen as the clergy — those with the answers — and Christian living as deferring to the clergy and accepting the answers they offer. Dozier sees three moments — three "falls" — when the people of God visibly became the institution. The first is *the* Fall in traditional thinking, when Adam and Eve disobeyed God, as told in Genesis. The second is the fall in I Samuel when the people of Israel asked for a king that they might become like other nations. The third is the fall in the fourth century A.D. when the church aligned itself with imperial power under Constantine. In each of these incidents, the people of God turned their back on faith, risk, and ambiguity, in favor of rules, safety, and certainty. For all this, however, Dozier would not abolish the institutional church. Even when it acts unfaithfully, the institution preserves the story and the record of those who have lived by it, thereby challenging each new generation.

IN HER OWN WORDS

Bible study

The point of lay Bible study is to help lay people reclaim their authority as the people of God.

Equipping the Saints (1981)

Two churches

There are two churches: the church, the institution, and the church, the people of God. In the church, the institution, there are two orders, clergy and lay. In the church, the people of God, there are varieties of gifts and functions. The two are *not* identical. The institution is the earthen vessel in which the treasure is kept. It is *not* the treasure.

The Calling of the Laity (1988)

The institutional church

The institutional church is subject to all the sin of any other institution: pride and arrogance and ordering and counting its life more important than anything else. Someone has said you can tell the purpose of an organization by looking at what it measures. What does the institutional church measure? The number of people on the rolls. The number of baptisms. The size of the collection. The number of services. The number ordained. And it thinks these figures are an expression of its concern for spreading the gospel. . . . [The institutional church rarely questions its] investment in slum properties, silence in the face of nuclear destruction, exploitation of the helpless. The institutional church today as in the time of Jesus rushes to the precipice him who would proclaim deliverance to captives and liberty to the bruised.

The Calling of the Laity

The church as people

If the church is the people and not the institution, it seems to me some significant implications follow at once: (1) What happens on Sunday morning is not half so important as what happens on Monday morning. . . . (2) It is the lay people who are the key agents in the ministry of reconciliation. The clergy are the support system. . . . (3) There are no second-class citizens in the household of God. . . . Indicative of the tragic confusion of the two churches, for me, is that as clergy assumed institutional power, . . . lay people gave up to them religious authority as well. . . . (4) The clergy are also part of the church, the people of God; and therefore their first, their prime loyalty should be to the church, the people of God. Everything they do for the church, the institution, must clearly be in the service of the church, the people of God.

The Calling of the Laity

The church's business

What is the church's business? . . . Not soul saving. God has already done that, and nothing can be added to God's almighty work. Not legislating morality. That's shifting sand and lures us away from the biblical call to repent. Not social service. The need for the church to do social service is eloquent testimony, to me, that we have failed in our business. So what is our business? Ministry.

The Calling of the Laity

The church's vision

God came into history to create a people who would change the world, who would make the world a place where every person knew that he or she was loved, was valued, had a contribution to make, and had just as much right to the riches of the world as every other person. That is what the church is all about, to bring into being that vision, that ideal community of love in which we all are equally valuable and in which we equally share. Every structure of life comes under the judgment of that vision: our politics, our economics, our education, our social structures. Even the church!

The Authority of the Laity (1982)

Living religiously

If you tell most people that the whole of life is religious, they think of somebody who gets up in the morning and says prayers, stops in the afternoon and says prayers, says prayers again at night, wears a cross, and says the Jesus prayer. We seldom recall that being religious means that our whole life is so ordered that every moment we are aware that we are not the final explanation for ourselves. It means that the ethics that control our work are the ethics of a servant, because we are not our own masters. It means that our relationships to our fellow human beings are under the lordship of our Creator — whether we're married to those fellow humans or whether we are their parents, or are their friends or co-workers. We do not have to stop and think about being religious because that is the way our lives are lived.

The Authority of the Laity

Faith

Faith is something I live by. It is a decision to risk that this is the way God meant the world to be. In a world that exalts whiteness, maleness, youth, I live by the faith that whiteness, maleness, youth is not the best part of reality — nor the worst, either — but only part of reality, and indeed, without blackness, femaleness, age, a very incomplete part. In strange ways that only the faithful know — and I cannot articulate — faith is not only the decision to risk; it is also the power to make that decision.

from an interview (1990)

God still calls

Christians are not the first chosen people to lose the way. I think that is what the biblical story is all about — the people of God losing the way and a God who will not give up calling them back. Again and again God calls us to return. I think the calling still goes on today, but I believe the Christian church has distorted the call, narrowed it from a call to transform the world to a call to save the souls of individuals who hear and heed a specific message, narrowed it from a present possibility to a future fulfillment.

The Dream of God (1991)

Faith and risk

The Bible is the testimony of two worshiping communities, Hebrew and Christian, about their faith. It speaks most profoundly to us as we step into that faith view of reality. The opposite of faith is not doubt, but fear. Faith implies risk. I will cast my life on this possibility that God is for me. I do not have to have any proof except my commitment. I do not have to claim complete understanding — that is idolatry. The faith view of reality is frightening in its openness, and so institutions are always trying to control reality with dictums and laws and creeds.

The Dream of God

Love and justice

We wax dewy-eyed over love in the New Testament, but we ignore justice in the Old so we don't know what we are talking about when we talk about love. Love is justice in action.

The Dream of God

The Incarnation

It is comforting for the church to declare the Bible as the Word of God instead of taking seriously what the Bible says — that Jesus himself is the Word of God. . . . How troubling if God came as a person and not a book! And if that Person is eternally living, eternally in communication with God's people, one age can eternally say to another, "Your understanding is not my understanding. God has a new word to say to us."

The Dream of God

Religion and God

Jesus did not come to bring a new religion. As religions go, Judaism was as good as any, and Jesus practiced it up to the end. . . . Religion is always "about" God: intellectual formulations, institutional orderings, liturgical expressions. All, over time, run the danger of solidifying into "God." Instead, Jesus came as the Way, a new possibility for encountering God ever anew in the fluid, changing experience of life.

The Dream of God

Worship or follow?

The church missed its high calling to be the new thing in the world when it decided to worship Jesus instead of following him. . . . Worship is setting Jesus on a pedestal, distancing him, enshrining (enshrouding) him in liturgies, stained glass windows, biblical translations, medallions, pilgrimages to places where he walked — the whole nine yards. Following him is doing what he did, weeping over a situation that was so far removed from the dream of God and spending his life to make it different. Following is discipleship.

The Dream of God

The question

The important question to ask is not, "What do you believe?" but "What difference does it make that you believe?"

The Dream of God

Biblical morality

I think that the basic thrust of the Bible has very little to do with private and personal morality. The Bible is directed to a *people* and to the issue of a *people's* morality. We play up individual morality. I think that if you love your neighbor and love God you *will* have a personal morality — but I don't think that is the thrust of the biblical story. One of the problems we have with the biblical story is that we go at it by bits and pieces and we don't get the whole sweep. So we concentrate on certain items, but I think they have to be played against the whole story. In one way *that* is a definition of sin because that's what we do — we cut God down to our size, so that's not loving the Lord God.

from an interview (1995)

No standing

There's no place where a human being can stand. Standing somewhere implies a permanence, a finite position. And I don't think there is any finite position. When I was a little child we used to sing a hymn, "On Christ the solid rock I stand. All other ground is sinking sand." I found that very meaningful, but the thing about it is, what does it mean? *Where* is Christ the solid rock? Because I think the minute you stand on it, it shifts. You have to be able to live perpetually without answers and that's the trouble — we want some certitude. I call that *faithlessness*. Faith is risking that God is for you — Abraham went out from everything he had known.

from an interview (1995)

A possibility

It is important to keep open to the possibility that we may be wrong. . . .
I need to understand that where I stand is not necessarily the totality of
where God stands.

from an interview (1997)

Saintliness and madness

Q. How does somebody follow Jesus?

A. Become as nutty as he was! Throw all caution to the winds. Run
contrary to every system, every status symbol that we have. I think that the
followers of Jesus are considered mad by their time. We have a tendency to
romanticize our saints, but we only do that after they are dead.

from an interview (1998)

FOR REFLECTION AND DISCUSSION

Define "ministry." You might consult the catechism in the Book of Common Prayer in forming your definition.

Look up the baptism and ordination services in the Prayer Book. How do
the responsibilities of the laity and the clergy compare?

Do you concur with Dozier's largely negative assessment of the institutional church? What steps might be taken to bring the church as institution closer to the church as people of God?

Do you agree that the opposite of faith is not doubt but fear? How does
what we define as its opposite influence our understanding of faith?

How does Dozier's understanding of faith as risk, living without answers
and with no place to stand, square with your understanding of faith?
Is Dozier's understanding compatible with the metaphor of Christ as
"sure foundation"?

What is your answer to the question, "How does somebody follow Jesus?"

Chapter 27

MADELEINE L'ENGLE

B. 1918

Teller of Tales

IF YOU GO to a library or bookstore to collect all of Madeleine L'Engle's fifty or so books, you will do a lot of walking before you find them all. You might start in the section for children's books — she made her name as a children's author with *A Wrinkle in Time*, published in 1962. Then you might go to adult fiction. Then look under fantasy or science fiction, and then autobiography, poetry, and finally, spirituality. You still might miss a few of her titles. Like Dorothy Sayers and C. S. Lewis before her, L'Engle defies categorizing. Many of her books could be filed in several sections. L'Engle's readers include children and adults, Christians and skeptics, and people who simply like a good story.

Above all, L'Engle is a storyteller. Unlike propositional statements, stories are multidimensional. If asked what a story means, ten people may give ten different answers — and all will be correct. A story draws the listener into it and appeals to the imagination, and its "meaning" therefore depends on who the listener is and how the listener connects with the narrative. L'Engle's books exude faith, but in many of them, particularly her fiction, the religion is not stated, but enfleshed in the characters. L'Engle's stories also contain things that seem impossible to a closed mind, but she feels God and truth are not limited by what closed minds believe possible. A story can "tell the truth" in ways more subtle — and more "true" — than propositional statements. L'Engle points out that this approach to truth is biblical — the Bible contains few propositions (God "is") but hundreds of stories (God "did" or "is doing"), and Jesus in particular told stories and refused to define their "meaning."

L'Engle draws some of her most compelling stories from her own life. She was an only child. Her well-to-do parents were delighted at her birth, having experienced several failed pregnancies. They provided a secure, loving home for young Madeleine, but they had already developed a routine when their daughter was born and did not greatly alter it on her account. L'Engle grew up moving between New York City (her place of birth) and Jacksonville, Florida (her mother's home), with extended periods abroad. She was often alone as a young child and spent several of her adolescent years in a boarding school, where her creativity was not appreciated. During her youth, L'Engle's best friends were books. She spent long hours reading and writing, including a personal journal and short works of fiction.

After graduating from Smith College in 1941, L'Engle settled in New York City, where she pursued her writing and a career in the theater. Her first published book was a novel, *The Small Rain*, in 1945. A year later, she married actor Hugh Franklin (Dr. Charles Tyler in the television show "All My Children"). The couple bought Crosswicks, an old farmhouse in northwestern Connecticut, where they reared a family and where L'Engle spent many of her happiest years. Her four autobiographical works, known as the Crosswicks Journals, published between 1972 and 1988, are like a fabric weaving together different threads — childhood reminiscences, events taking place at the time of writing, reflections on the Bible and other literature, struggles with faith and doubt, homespun wisdom, and humor. I found the two volumes dealing with death particularly powerful. *The Summer of the Great-Grandmother,* published in 1974, tells of the death of L'Engle's aged mother, who had come to Crosswicks to live her final years, and *Two-Part Invention,* published in 1988, is the story of L'Engle's happy marriage to Franklin and his illness and death in 1986.

Families figure prominently in many of L'Engle's works, both fiction and nonfiction — healthy, multi-generational families in which each member is encouraged to become all that he or she can become. L'Engle says that when she was young, her parents encouraged her to pursue any goal she envisioned, even though she was often left to pursue such goals alone. It may have been the limited time spent with her family as a child, L'Engle says, that led her to place such importance on family as an adult. She remained at home and did little writing during the time her own children were young, and most of the women in her novels are secure, self-confident professional people who are also faithful wives and mothers. Her male characters are also strong and self-motivated. Feminists have embraced L'Engle as one of their own — and she has embraced them in return — but her feminism is not the sort that demeans either men or stay-at-home mothers, and like her Christian faith, it is rarely stated outright, but is unmistakable in the characters she creates.

L'Engle is best known for her children's fantasies, although she resists being pigeonholed as a "children's author" and says when she has an idea she suspects will be too difficult for adults, she puts it into a "children's book." Her best-selling time trilogy, beginning with *A Wrinkle in Time,* has captivated thousands of readers, adults as well as children. It concerns a healthy, loving family, with children who travel through time and deep space, becoming involved in a cosmic struggle between good and evil. Supernatural characters, servants of God, appear as whimsical, sometimes befuddled beings. Christians believe in supernatural realities, L'Engle says, so she introduces them into her books in a seemingly offhand, unselfconscious way. As in several of her adult books, the mysterious and illogical notions of reality found in the "new physics" of Einstein and Planck inform her children's books. She sees everything in the universe as interrelated and says the sense of rapture and glory she discovered in scientific writings helped restore her faith after, as a young adult, she had abandoned the church.

L'Engle's adult fiction includes several novels, of which the best known is *A Severed Wasp,* published in 1982. Uncharacteristically for L'Engle, it contains a lot of overt religion, centering around the Cathedral of St. John the Divine in New York, where she worships and maintains an office. But characteristically, its characters are complex, with both strengths and weaknesses, at the same time noble and petty.

The Bible itself is also a mine from which L'Engle extracts good stories. Several of her books are in the tradition of the Jewish *midrash,* which takes a biblical story and enlarges it, adding color, detail, and additional voices to bring the story to life in the minds of the listeners. In her *midrash* tales of Hebrew women and the sons of Jacob, she weaves into the biblical narrative incidents from her own life and commentary on contemporary issues, imparting to old stories a new vitality. L'Engle uses the Bible in other ways as well. Mrs. Whatsit and Aunt Beast, angelic beings in *A Wrinkle in Time,* quote scripture at unexpected moments, and biblical references are sprinkled, often subtly, through her adult fiction and autobiographical books. L'Engle's view of the proper use of scripture is perhaps most explicit when she gives a priest or bishop in one of her novels the opportunity to preach.

Biblical literalists have not always appreciated L'Engle. She sees the Bible as profoundly true, but not as a literal, factual statement of events. The mistaking of story, drama, and poetry for factual history is, she says, "one of Satan's cleverest devices," which constricts our understanding of God, gutting it of its power and glory. By reducing God to a concept we can understand, literalism leads to idolatry, L'Engle says. She never tries to explain God or justify the ways of God to her readers, nor does she hesitate to learn from skeptics and nonbelievers, often appropriating their ideas in her work. The reality of God, and especially the Incarnation of God in the person of Jesus, she says, is neither rational nor comprehensible. The only way to enter into relationship with God is through poetry, symbol, and myth.

Christians who are uncomfortable with ambiguity and theological loose ends will be uncomfortable with Madeleine L'Engle (unless they read her solely for a good story). She is not a systematic theologian who seeks to

301

express Christian understandings in an all-encompassing system. Ambiguity and theological loose ends, in fact, become in her work an essential part of the human relationship to God. Perhaps this is one reason her voice speaks so powerfully to an age when, as in the fifth and the fifteenth centuries of the Christian era, the scientific, ethical, and religious conventions of the past are being vigorously challenged.

IN HER OWN WORDS

A holy death

"I think I would like to die a holy death, Stella. Does that give me away as being hopelessly old-fashioned? I suppose I am. But perhaps our death is the one strange, holy, and unique thing about us, the one thing we can *do*, as *ourselves*. Maybe in dying I will at least become me." She held one of the footposts of the bed to support herself. "I've always been a coward — " She gave a small gasp of pain. "I'll get into bed now."

The Other Side of the Sun (1971)

Humility

The moment humility becomes self-conscious, it becomes hubris. One cannot be humble and aware of oneself at the same time. . . . Humility is throwing oneself away in complete concentration on something or someone else.

A Circle of Quiet (1972)

The intellect

We do not go around, or discard the intellect, but we must go through and beyond it. If we are given minds we are required to use them, but not limit ourselves by them.

A Circle of Quiet

Structure and fun

The amoeba has a minimum of structure, but I doubt if it has much fun.

A Circle of Quiet

Compassion

Compassion is nothing one feels with the intellect alone. Compassion is particular; it is never general.

A Circle of Quiet

The mysterious

If we accept the mysterious as the "fairest thing in life," we must also accept the fact that there are rules to it. A rule is not necessarily rigid and unbending; it can even have a question mark at the end of it. I wish that we worried more about asking the right questions instead of being so hung up on finding answers. . . . One of the reasons my generation has mucked up the world to such an extent is our loss of the sense of the mysterious.

A Circle of Quiet

Guilt

It is only by accepting real guilt that I am able to feel free of guilt. . . . If all my mistakes are excused, if there's an alibi, a rationalization for every blunder, then I am not free at all. I have become subhuman.

The Summer of the Great-Grandmother (1974)

The Creed

You can't understand the Creed like your Baedeker guide to Athens. It's in the language of poetry. It's trying to talk about things that can't be pinned down by words, and it has to try to break words apart and thrust beyond them.

The Summer of the Great-Grandmother

Myth

Myth is the closest approximation to truth available to the finite human being. And the truth of myth is not limited by time or place. A myth tells of that which was true, is true, and will be true. If we will allow it, myth will integrate intellect and intuition, night and day; our warring opposites are reconciled, male and female, spirit and flesh, desire and will, pain and joy, life and death.

The Irrational Season (1977)

This is the irrational season
when love blooms bright and wild.
Had Mary been filled with reason
there'd have been no room for the child.

The Irrational Season

How shall we sing our love's song now
In this strange land where all are born to die?
Each tree and leaf and star show how
The universe is part of this one cry,
That every life is noted and is cherished,
And nothing loved is ever lost or perished.

A Ring of Endless Light (1980)

Angels

I believe in angels; guardian angels; the angel who came to Gideon and told a shy, not very brave young man that he was a man of valor who was going to free his people; the angels who came to Jesus in the agony of the Garden. And, what is less comforting, avenging angels, destroying angels, angels who come bringing terror when any part of God's creation becomes too rebellious, too full of pride to remember that they are God's creatures. And, most fearful of all, fallen angels, angels who have left God and followed Lucifer, and daily offer us their seductive and reasonable temptations.

Walking on Water (1980)

Faith

My faith in a loving Creator of the galaxies, so loving that the very hairs of my head are counted, is stronger in my work than in my life, and often it is the work that pulls me back from the precipice of faithlessness. It is not necessarily an unmixed blessing to be a well-educated person in a secular society. [Someone once] wrote, "God must be very great to have created a world which carries so many arguments against his existence."

Walking on Water

Evangelism

We do not draw people to Christ by loudly discrediting what they believe, by telling them how wrong they are and how right we are, but by showing them a light that is so lovely that they want with all their hearts to know the source of it.

Walking on Water

Inspiration

To work on a book is for me very much the same thing as to pray. Both involve discipline. If the artist works only when he feels like it, he's not apt to build up much of a body of work. Inspiration far more often comes during the work than before it, because the largest part of the job of the artist is to listen to the work, and to go where it tells him to go. Ultimately, when you are writing, you stop thinking and write what you hear.

Walking on Water

In the end

I am convinced that not only is our planet ultimately to be freed from bondage to Satan, but with it the whole universe — all the singing, dancing

305

suns and stars and galaxies — will one day join unhindered in the great joyous festival. The glorious triumph of Easter will encompass the whole of God's handiwork. The praise for the primal goodness of God's creation in the beginning will be rounded out with the final worship, as John has expressed it in the Revelation: "Worthy art thou our Lord God. . . . To him who sits upon the throne and to the Lamb be blessing and honor and glory and might for ever and ever. Amen!"

And It Was Good (1983)

Answered prayer

Like a human parent, God will help us when we ask for help, but in a way that will make us more mature, more real, not in a way that will diminish us. And God does not wave a magic wand. . . .

Two-Part Invention (1988)

Moments close to God

It is when things go wrong, when the good things do not happen, when our prayers seem to have been lost, that God is most present. We do not need the sheltering wings when things go smoothly. We are closest to God in the darkness, stumbling along blindly.

Two-Part Invention

Pattern?

There are many times when the idea that there is indeed a pattern seems absurd wishful thinking. Random events abound. There is much in life that seems meaningless. And then, when I can see no evidence of meaning, some glimpse is given which reveals the strange weaving of purposefulness and beauty.

Two-Part Invention

Word made flesh

I have long felt that the sacrifice of the mystery of the Word made flesh was a far greater sacrifice than the crucifixion. That was bad, yes. Terrible, yes. But it was three hours on the cross. Three hours . . . there are worse deaths. And these deaths make no sense at all unless the mystery of the Word made flesh is present in them too; death makes no sense at all if the God who is in it with us is not in the dying body of the young man down the hall; the people killed, burned, in the most recent air crash, in my husband, in me, our children.

Two-Part Invention

Scripture

So what do I believe about Scripture? I believe that it is true. What is true is alive and capable of movement and growth. Scripture is full of paradox and contradiction, but it is true, and if we fallible human creatures look regularly and humbly at the great pages and people of Scripture, if we are willing to accept truth rather than rigidly infallible statements, we will be given life, and life more abundantly. And we, like Joseph, will make progress towards becoming human.

Sold Into Egypt (1989)

Change

To be human is to be able to change, knowing full well that some change is good and some change is bad; some change is progressive and some is regressive, and we often cannot discern which is which. But if we lose the ability to change we stultify, we turn to stone, we die. Remember, yesterday's heresy is tomorrow's dogma.

Sold Into Egypt

Judgmentalism

Too many answers lead to judgmentalism and to human beings (rather than God) deciding who can and who cannot go to heaven.

The Rock That Is Higher (1992)

How to spot a true Christian

Virtue is not the sign of a Christian. Joy is.

The Rock That Is Higher

Stories and *the* Story

We've heard the story of Jesus so often that our ears have become blunted. Story reawakens us to truth, the truth that will set us free. Jesus, the Story, taught by telling stories, quite a few of which on the surface would appear to be pretty secular, but all of which lead us, if we will listen, to a deeper truth than we have been willing to hear before.

The Rock That Is Higher

What would Jesus do?

When I am in a quandary about something, I usually ask, "What would Jesus do?" And often I don't know the answer. Life is very different at the end of the twentieth century than it was two thousand years ago. But I know that whatever Jesus' answer would be, it would be the loving answer. And love, like Jesus, is seldom easy. When it's easy, it's sentimentality, not love. Love often says *no* when we would like the answer to be *yes*. Jesus did not allow all the people he had cured to follow him as one of his disciples. He told them to stay where they were and spread the word of love, and often they were disbelieved. He didn't let the rich young man come to him, keeping all his riches. Whenever Jesus calls us, something has to be given away.

Our self will. Our eagerness to make judgments about other people's sins. Whenever I do that, I can almost hear Jesus telling me to look at my own sins, instead.

Penguins and Golden Calves (1996)

Incarnation

In my mind's ear I can hear God saying to God, "Can I do it? Do I love them that much? Can I leave my galaxies, my solar systems, can I leave the hydrogen clouds and the birthing of stars and the journeyings of comets, can I leave all that I have made, give it all up, and become a tiny, unknowing seed in the belly of a young girl? Do I love them that much? Do I have to do that in order to show them what it is to be human?" Yes! The answer on our part is a grateful Alleluia! Amen! God so *loved* the world that he sent his only begotten son . . .

Penguins and Golden Calves

FOR REFLECTION AND DISCUSSION

What would you say to someone who, after being told a story, said, "What does that mean?"

Think of an experience in your own life which "tells the truth" about God. Write it down and show it to a friend, or tell it to the group, and then ask for response. Is it possible to derive a propositional teaching about God from your experience?

Do you agree that "myth is the closest approximation to truth available to the finite human being"? What does that statement mean?

How do you feel L'Engle would respond to someone who said, "The Bible is the infallible Word of God"?

Do you believe that God reveals new truth through science and other secular disciplines?

Chapter 28

FESTO KIVENGERE

1921?-1988

World Evangelist

CHRISTIAN MISSIONARIES first arrived in Uganda in 1877 and quickly met opposition — the first Anglican bishop of the area, James Hannington, and a number of native converts were martyred by a native prince in 1885. But the church had been planted and it began to grow. Within fifty years, however, a crusty lethargy seemed to threaten its vitality. Whites were often condescending to blacks; blacks often resented whites. Then, on September 22, 1929, a white Christian physician, Joe Church, and a prominent black Christian, Simeon Nsibambi, met one another in Kampala. Nsibambi told Church that he knew something was missing in the Ugandan church and in himself. "Then I had the great joy of telling him about the filling of the Spirit and the victorious life," Church recalled years later. The pair began to pray for a new spirit in the church in Uganda, and so began the East African revival, one of the most enduring revival movements in the history of the Christian church. It spread to half a dozen other neighboring countries, centered in Anglican churches but affecting other churches as well.

Like the Wesleyan revival in eighteenth-century England, the East African revival was not initially embraced by the established church leadership. The *balokole* (or "saved ones," as the movement came to be known) preached a practical Christianity, emphasizing personal conversion and a life of sobriety, honesty, and marital fidelity — and calling for specific acts of contrition and reconciliation where needed. The *balokole* could be aggressive in their missionary tactics and were sometimes perceived as a self-appointed spiritual elite. But the movement was motivated by a shared experience of the love of Christ which proved contagious. It aimed to revitalize the church, not set up a new church, and its fruits included hundreds of thousands of adult baptisms, restored personal relationships, renewed prayer and Bible study, and the sending of African Christian missionaries to England, America, Brazil, India, and elsewhere. Membership in the Anglican Church of Uganda numbered in the tens of thousands in 1929; by 2000, it had grown to eight million. Today one out of nine Anglican Christians in the world is a Ugandan. The East African revival is a major factor in this vitality, and the most popular and renowned spokesman for the revival has been Festo Kivengere.

Kivengere (pronounced ki-VEN-je-re) did not set out to become a hot gospeler. Baptized at the age of ten, he later drifted away, becoming a teacher by day and a "serious" sinner by night. "I was really trying to get away from God," he said. But he couldn't. As a teacher in a missionary school in Kigezi province, in the remote southwest of Uganda, Kivengere was expected to attend church every Sunday, and after 1935, the speakers there were usually people who had experienced life-changing conversions as part of the revival, experiences they were eager to share. Kivengere saw them as "fanatics" and steeled himself against becoming one of them. "I was hating God because the awareness of him embarrassed me continually," he later wrote. "I was running away from 'churchianity,' from the Bible and from clergy. I wanted to escape this business of being 'holy.' I simply wanted to be my own manager. My life was turning round itself like a spinning top. A top has a big head and a thin base, so it can't stand up unless it is spinning round and round. If it slows down, it topples over. It depends on spinning to keep going. My spinning cycle was work-play-eat-drink-sleep-work-play-eat-drink, and so on, round and round. I thought that the faster I went, the livelier life would be."

It didn't work. One day in October of 1941, Kivengere was seated in the back of the church (so he could leave if things got too "hot") when his niece asked to speak. She told the congregation that the Lord had assured her two days earlier that her uncle Festo "is going to come back to the Lord today." Embarrassed and enraged, Kivengere walked out of the church, intending to get drunk. But a friend and fellow teacher approached him and said, "Festo! Three hours ago Jesus became a living reality to me. I know my sins are forgiven!" The friend then asked Kivengere's forgiveness for three specific things they had done together. "I am sorry, Festo. I will no longer live like that. Jesus has given me something much better." Kivengere went home and knelt beside his bed. "God! If you happen to be there, as my friend says, I am miserable. If you can do anything for me, then please do it now. If I'm not too far gone . . . *Help!*"

Then it was as if heaven opened and Jesus himself stood in front of Kivengere. Suddenly he knew it was his own badness that had crucified the King of life. He thought he was going to hell and that he deserved it. He told Jesus to go away. But Jesus didn't go away. Kivengere looked into Jesus' eyes and heard Jesus say, "This is how much I love you, Festo!" Kivengere shook his head and said, "No, I am your enemy. . . . How can you love me like that?" Fifty years later, after traveling the world to preach the love of Jesus, Kivengere still could not answer that question. "There is no reason in me for his love."

In the years that followed, Kivengere continued to teach school, first in Uganda and later in Tanganyika. He also married. He and his wife Mera sought to model their relationship on Christian lines of mutual love, kindness, and respect. Many African men treated their wives like slaves and some grew angry when Kivengere spoke of mutuality in marriage. One young African man actually hid in a mango tree next to the Kivengere bungalow one night and eavesdropped. He was amazed to hear Kivengere apologize to Mera for having aggrieved her and then offer to put their young daughters to bed. He climbed down from the tree and banged on the door. That night he became a Christian.

In addition to teaching, Kivengere also became an immensely popular lay preacher. He told Bible stories in a way that made them seem like events happening to the listeners themselves, adding color, humor, and a personal dimension. He freely revealed his own vulnerability, often illustrating his sermons with examples of his own sins and failures and the redemption that came from confessing them and laying them at the foot of the cross. Kivengere organized small home groups for prayer and Bible study and himself took part in such a group every week. He also mediated conflicts within the revival movement, counseling against an overly rigorist approach that cast out persons deemed unworthy — citing, in typical fashion, his own early rigorist tendencies and how the Lord had taught him that this was not the way of humility.

Kivengere resigned his teaching position in 1961 to become a full-time evangelist. He often teamed with Michael Cassidy, a white South African, with whom he formed an organization which sponsored evangelistic campaigns that crossed racial, national, and denominational lines. A black African sharing a podium with a white South African sent a message of reconciliation stronger than mere words. Kivengere was ordained priest in 1967. A strong believer in lay ministry, he saw ordination in largely pragmatic terms, as a means — particularly among Anglicans — to open doors. Kivengere soon gained an international reputation and received invitations to address mission conferences in Europe and America. He crossed the world repeatedly, preaching on every continent. He often shared the podium with the American evangelist Billy Graham and was offered a position as staff evangelist both by Graham and by World Vision, neither of which he accepted.

Kivengere had been conducting a mission in Papua, New Guinea, on January 25, 1971, when he heard on the radio of a military coup in Uganda. The unpopular government of President Milton Obote had been overthrown. The new ruler, Idi Amin, a Muslim, urged Christians and Muslims alike to be faithful in worship and promised free elections. There was dancing in the streets of Kampala. In September 1972, however, neighboring Tanzania invaded Uganda. Amin's forces turned back the invaders, but he grew suspicious of anyone not closely tied to him, began praising Adolf Hitler in his speeches, and expelled 50,000 legal residents from the country. Amin's army began plundering and killing in the countryside; a reign of terror ensued. Increasingly irrational, Amin accused Christians of planning his overthrow, concocted false evidence against them, and held public executions. Anglicans in particular were singled out. Police broke into and vandalized churches and the homes of Anglican leaders. Church services were disrupted — but church attendance soared.

When Amin summoned a group of Anglican bishops to "talk it all over" on February 16, 1977, they cautiously obeyed. Kivengere, having been made bishop of Kigezi in December, 1972, was among them. Unbeknownst to the bishops, Amin had gathered a mob of his supporters outside the meeting hall and primed them to shout on cue, "Kill them! Kill them!" Then he dismissed the bishops — all but archbishop Janani Luwum. The other bishops remained for hours, awaiting their archbishop's return, but eventually departed without word of him. The next day the government announced that Luwum had died in a car accident. Newspapers carried a photo of the accident — the same photo they had run two weeks earlier of another purported accident. Amin had murdered the archbishop. On February 20, despite government threats, 4,500 people packed the Anglican cathedral in Kampala for Luwum's memorial service. His body was never returned.

Festo Kivengere did not attend the memorial service. Friends had urged him to leave the country — "One dead bishop is enough," one of them said — and despite a keen desire to remain with the people of his diocese, Kivengere and his wife, whose home was being watched by police awaiting their return, drove along back roads into the mountains in the middle of the night of February 20, then walked when the roads gave out. Assisted by loyal church people in the hills, they slipped across the border into Rwanda at dawn on February 21.

For the next two years, Kivengere spoke all over the world, using the story of the East African revival and the invincible Church of Uganda to tell of the love and power of Jesus Christ, refusing to blame Idi Amin, insisting that he loved Amin as a fellow child of God. But from the day of Janani Luwum's murder, Amin's days were numbered. He had lost what respect he still retained among world leaders, and in May of 1979, Amin himself was ousted by a coup. Kivengere and other exiled Anglican bishops returned to a relieved but devastated Uganda. The remaining nine years of his life Kivengere devoted to working for reconciliation in his native land. In 1987, a year before his death from leukemia, he said, "For me, the heart of spiritual liberation is Jesus and him crucified, risen and reigning among his people. But spiritual liberation never takes place in a spirit without the rest of what makes you and me human. It embraces the whole of me — my rights, dignity, property, security, and freedom. Mere political and social liberation do not go far enough. They need a greater dynamic . . . the preaching of Christ."

IN HIS OWN WORDS

The crucified Christ

It is Christ, the one crucified, who wins rebellious lives, melts stony hearts, brings life to the dead, and inspires stagnant lives into unsparing activity. It is the crucified who makes us see the world alive with need for forgiveness. It is the crucified who crosses out our fancies and introduces us to the inestimable value of people. It is the crucified Christ who destroys our prejudiced evaluations of our fellow men as racial cases, tribal specimens, social outcasts or aristocrats, sinful characters, and religious misfits, by giving us the fresh evaluation of all men as redeemable persons "on whose behalf Christ died." Evangelism fails miserably when its purpose becomes to draw people to its programs of preaching or social concern. Men are to be drawn by the power of the self-sacrificing love of God in Christ into new life in him. The cross gives flesh and bones to evangelism.

to the Lausanne Congress on World Evangelism (1974)

Resurrection

Resurrection is not for upright people. It's for brokenhearted people, the defeated and shattered. . . . Before Christ died and rose again, suffering was meaningless, empty, a shattering experience which made life bitter. Then

315

Jesus died in suffering and pain, and he covered suffering with love — victorious, holy love. This kind of love will never be conquered!

Easter sermon (1977)

The power of Christ

Several times I shared in public [in 1973] that when a man uses force, he confesses that he cannot change the situation which threatens him, and so, being weak and insecure, he turns to methods of elimination. . . . How can One who hung on a cross, who couldn't even drive a fly from his face, be the power of God? Because in love he prayed for the men who drove the nails into his hands to kill him. . . . He who hung on the cross in blood and sweat is the One who can embrace humanity, change, and re-create it. I know, because one day I opened my poor heart to Jesus Christ, and the cross did a miracle. God set me free, sending me through the fields to ask people's forgiveness. I remember the day I bicycled 50 miles to a white man whom I had hated. I stood there in his house, telling him what Christ had done for me, and that now I was free and saw him as my brother. English as he was, he stood there weeping, and we were in each other's arms. I used no weapon, but Christ's love had won. This is victory! This is the power which the world is desperately in need of.

I Love Idi Amin (1977)

The effect of persecution

Persecution of Christians broke out immediately [after the assassination of Janani Luwum], but far from destroying the church, people were crowding into churches more than ever. Many were being born again. People who had taken Christianity lightly became serious. Backsliders were being restored. People said, "There is no time to waste, maybe you'll be the next!"

I Love Idi Amin

Embracing our Judases

If there is a Judas, love him. Do you know what Jesus did to Judas who betrayed him? He . . . washed his feet as he did the other disciples. Although Judas did not change, he made a confession when he died: "I am guilty because I rejected innocent love." Jesus died for him. So can we not embrace our Judases?

from a speech to Ugandan clergy (1983)

Reconciliation

No one ever forgives without suffering. It costs to forgive! And costs dearly. That God forgives is a divine miracle. The power of his justice and his mercy working in harmony, restoring the alienated wrongdoer, is the heart of "the good news of God." Mercy is not the opposite of justice; *injustice* is, and God has nothing to do with injustice in his central work of liberating the guilty through his reconciling love. The price of reconciliation is full identification with the guilty in order to arouse hope for liberation and restoration.

to the Amsterdam conference on evangelism (1983)

A dream

I seemed to be standing in a courtroom before a severe judge and I was afraid. From one side and another there were voices accusing me. My own conscience was the prosecutor, presenting a pile of claims. They were like IOUs I had to pay. Witnesses were gazing at me reproachfully — I knew their faces. "You were not honest here. . . . You acted in a mean way. . . . You failed morally." I had nowhere to look. On and on it went. When you buy, you have to pay. When you sin, you have to suffer. That is what my heart told me. . . . Then, oh, the wonder! God himself stepped into the courtroom. Steadily, firmly, he picked up all the things which had wrecked my humanity, all the nasty experiences of my sinful nature, all my accumulated guilt, all the accusations against me, and put them on the shoulders of his God-Man. Jesus voluntarily chose to take on himself the responsibility for all I owed.

Revolutionary Love (1983)

Jesus fills the empties

I am not always full of love, not always seeing [Jesus] clearly. Self-indulgence has a way of creeping in. Sometimes I am thoroughly empty and have to say so in public. But what I have discovered is that *Jesus loves to fill the empties!* All I need to do is to keep open to him and to admit frankly what's wrong. He does the rest.

Revolutionary Love

God as organist

[God] is the organist and we are the keys on his keyboard. The time for a key to go down is only when it is touched by the finger of the organist. An organist would be entirely frustrated if the keys of the organ kept going up and down of their own accord without being touched. They would make a jarring discord. On the other hand, if a key was stuck and would not go down at his touch, or remained down after his touch, he would have to stop and say, "It is impossible for me to play until this key is fixed." Or what if one key should speak up and say to the organist, "Wait a minute. Don't touch me, touch this one first"? Again the organist would give up and say, "These keys are in rebellion. I know the piece I want to play and how to produce the harmony. Please, *leave it to me.*"

Revolutionary Love

Christian fellowship

I have seen many methods devised in attempting to produce a love-fellowship. But the only known power for keeping together a group of believers — intact in love, fruitful and not ingrown — is the presence of the Author in the midst who is listened to and obeyed. It is not a product of man's desire for socializing. It is a fruit of Christ's self-giving love, which always draws us together and creates a community wherever people have opened their hearts to him.

Revolutionary Love

God and ball bearings

Any group that is committed to walking and working together in love is in God's workshop. The Holy Spirit has tools and equipment to bring each important part into shape. There are those who think they are big, who suffer from a superiority complex. These, along with the ones who think they are little, who suffer from an inferiority complex, all need to be made one size — his size. You know that if the ball bearings in the hub of a bicycle wheel are exactly the same size, the wheel runs smoothly. If you put unequal bearings in the wheel, there is a crunching sound and you go no where on that bicycle. The Lord is continually in the process of filing and building up his "ball bearings."

Revolutionary Love

Living in danger

We learned that living in danger, when the Lord Jesus is the focus of your life, can be liberating. For one thing, you are no longer imprisoned by your own security, because there is none. So the important security that people sought was to be anchored in God.

Revolutionary Love

Revival and humility

In America there is a feeling that God revives people when churches are sound in doctrine, teaching is biblical, and preaching is good. Isaiah was a good preacher. But when he looked to the Lord, he saw in himself things he had never seen before. So too must the church see itself. It is easy to say we should be humble. But when the church is humbled, it's a tough experience. Revival is not full churches and good feelings. These are accompaniments. Revival is the living Lord working among his people. When this happens, people see things they don't like to see. Repentance begins not only when a sinner comes, but when a saint is growing.

from an interview (1986)

What God does

One day a little girl sat watching her mother working in the kitchen. She asked her mummy, "What does God do all day long?" For a while, her mother was stumped, but then she said, "Darling, I'll tell you what God does all day long. He spends his whole day mending broken things."

a favorite story, often told by Kivengere

FOR REFLECTION AND DISCUSSION

What caused the East African revival?

Why do many people feel uncomfortable when talking with a Christian evangelist?

What accounts for the persecution of Christians?

Imagine your response if you lived in an area where to profess Christ was to risk your life.

Comment on the saying, "The blood of martyrs is the seed of the church."

How would you answer the question, "What does God do all day long?"

Chapter 29

DESMOND TUTU

B. 1931

Prophet of Forgiveness

CHRISTIAN THEOLOGY does not arise in a vacuum, but out of the hearts and minds, the fears and hopes of real people, living in specific places, at particular moments.

The place was South Africa, the time 1948. Racial barriers were beginning to fall in America and native peoples were challenging colonial governments elsewhere in the world, but in South Africa the Nationalist Party was elected to power on a platform of racial apartheid (apartness). Only whites, comprising just twenty percent of the population, were allowed to vote.

The Nationalists held power for nearly a half century, enacting a series of laws to keep races strictly separate and to perpetuate white control of South Africa's government and economy. Every citizen was required to register by race. Homes of black families were bulldozed under, their land appropriated for white residences, and the black former owners "dumped like a sack of potatoes" (the words are Desmond Tutu's), often hundreds of miles away, into one of ten "homelands" or "reserves." These areas encompassed a mere thirteen percent of the country's land, most of it in the least desirable places. Black people were forbidden to travel elsewhere without a government-issued pass.

Christian missionary schools for the blacks were taken over by the government, which designed a curriculum to prepare blacks to work only as manual laborers and domestic servants in white homes. Black men were required to spend eleven months each year working on white-owned farms or in mines, far from their wives and children, who lived in vast slums consisting of cardboard shacks with no sanitation. Meanwhile, white families enjoyed commodious homes surrounded by green lawns in tree-shaded suburbs. In a program eerily reminiscent of Nazi Germany and Stalinist Russia, the South African government conducted scientific experiments to introduce cholera, botulism, anthrax, drug addictions, and chemical poisons into black communities. Anyone who protested ran the risk of being arrested by the police, beaten up, tortured, and murdered.

Desmond Tutu was a teenager in 1948, but he remembers as a young child, even before the Nationalists assumed power, the humiliation his father endured at having to produce his passbook and at being called "boy" by whites with far less education. As a youngster, Tutu looked upon his black skin as a badge of dishonor: "You come to believe what others have determined about you, filling you with self-disgust, self-contempt, and self-hatred," he said years later.

Tutu became a school teacher and was known in the classroom for his energetic, vigorous personality, a reputation he would retain all his life. When the Bantu Education Act of 1955 restricted the academic subjects that could be taught to black students, Tutu saw that he could no longer help black people expand their horizons through teaching. He turned to the church and was ordained priest in 1961, at the age of thirty.

With the help of white friends, Tutu, along with his wife Leah and their two children, traveled to London the next year, where Tutu began studies at King's College. It was in London that the Tutu family first experienced the freedom to do, speak, and travel as they pleased. When they returned to South Africa in 1967, it was not easy to become second-class citizens again. Tutu taught theology, then worked for the World Council of Churches, and was named dean of St. Mary's Cathedral, Johannesburg, in 1975.

All this time, Tutu had taken no prominent role in politics or the resistance to apartheid. The turning point came in 1976 when he wrote an open letter to South African Prime Minister John Vorster warning of "bloodshed and violence" if the suffering and injustice endured by South African blacks was not addressed. He appealed to the prime minister as a family man and one who sought to do the right thing. Vorster replied, accusing Tutu of political propaganda. Tutu's fears came true just one month later, when 15,000 children from the black neighborhood of Soweto organized a peaceful demonstration and were fired on by police. One was killed. Tutu rushed to Soweto to calm parents and children. The struggle for freedom had begun in earnest, and Desmond Tutu would be at the heart of it.

Tutu was named General Secretary of the South African Council of Churches (SACC) in 1978, a highly visible position in which he became a leader in the movement for peaceful resistance and reform. Since most black leaders had been either murdered or imprisoned, Tutu's public voice became crucial. In the years that followed, the government sought to undermine his reputation, denied him permission to travel abroad, and threatened his life, but they dared not arrest him.

The confrontation between Tutu and the government climaxed in 1982 with his testimony before the Eloff Commission, a government-appointed body, consisting entirely of white people, charged to investigate the alleged Communist infiltration of the SACC. Tutu's speech to the commission was electrifying. He quoted the Bible. He prayed. He said it was not the SACC that was on trial, but the Christian faith, and that a Christian's loyalty was to Jesus Christ, not to any earthly prince. "Where there is injustice, exploitation and oppression, then the Bible and the God of the Bible are subversive. . . . Our God, unlike the pagan nature gods, is not God sanctifying the status quo. He is a God of surprises, uprooting the powerful and unjust to establish his Kingdom."

In 1984, Tutu received the Nobel Peace Prize, which made him a world celebrity but was not acknowledged by the South African government. In 1985 he was made bishop of Johannesburg, and a year later, archbishop of Cape Town.

Finally, on February 2, 1990, South African President F. W. de Klerk announced to a stunned world the end of apartheid. A new constitution, guaranteeing the freedom of all the nation's citizens, was written, and on April 27, 1994, Nelson Mandela, released after twenty-seven years in prison, was inaugurated as South Africa's first freely elected president.

Many of Tutu's sermons, addresses, and short articles have been collected and published. They reveal a faith with the Bible as its source, fed by three theological streams: *African theology* grows from the spiritual roots of the African people which antedate the arrival of Christianity. These roots (unlike much of Western theology) are not cerebral, but are expressed in music, mystery, nature, and the interdependence of all things. "We are compelled to help the white man to correct many of the distortions that have happened to the gospel to the detriment of all," Tutu said. *Liberation theology* arose in the late 20th century out of the barrios of Latin America. It proclaims God's compassion and preference for the poor and challenges government, business, church, and any other institution that maintains itself at the expense of the powerless. *Classical Anglicanism* emphasizes God's love of the created universe, as expressed in God's act of joining himself to the creation in the person of Jesus Christ, the incarnate Son of God. These three theological streams inform and energize Desmond Tutu's biblical faith and his public witness.

Tutu's one book, *No Future Without Forgiveness,* published in 1999, is not, strictly speaking, about religion. It recounts Tutu's experiences between 1995 and 1998 as chairman of South Africa's Truth and Reconciliation Commission — but his Christian faith saturates every page. Tutu speculates that President Mandela appointed an archbishop as chairman of the commission because he "must have believed that our work would be profoundly spiritual. After all, forgiveness, reconciliation, reparation were not the normal currency in political discourse."

Although it ostensibly pertains to just four years of Tutu's ministry, *No Future Without Forgiveness* expresses the ideals and beliefs which have guided him all his life. He writes of *ubuntu,* an African word of which he had often written and spoken before, and which, perhaps more than any other word, captures the vision of Desmond Tutu. It is a vision of what it means to be human. Human beings are not isolated individuals, Tutu says, but bound together in relationship with each other, nature, and God. Co-operation (not competition, as Western culture often assumes) defines human life. A person with *ubuntu* is open, vulnerable, affirming of others. Although *ubuntu* is an African concept, Tutu says it also lies at the heart of the Christian gospel. To teach or act otherwise is to violate human nature, distort the gospel, and deny God.

There were, Tutu relates, three ways to deal with the atrocities of apartheid once the new government had been sworn in: (1) pretend they never happened; (2) identify, try, and punish the guilty; or (3) grant amnesty and forgive. Only the last option could exorcize the demons that plagued the hearts and memories of both perpetrator and the victim, Tutu writes. The perpetrators were victims of apartheid also, he says, because apartheid had hardened their hearts and numbed their souls. Justice, then, cannot be about retribution, but must be about restoration and reconciliation. This is *ubuntu* in action.

To gain amnesty, those guilty of violence and torture (including both whites and blacks) would be required only to make a full confession in a public hearing. Victims and the surviving loved ones of the murdered and missing would also be invited to tell their stories in a public forum. In the end, the Truth and Reconciliation Commission recorded the public testimony of 20,000 South Africans — blacks and whites, victims and perpetrators, the prominent and the lowly. Although unrepentant whites mocked the commission for all the tears that flowed at its hearings, calling it the "Kleenex Commission," Tutu says the commission discovered "how the act of telling one's story has a cathartic, healing effect." Thousands of South Africans will attest that having one's story listened to and taken seriously is also part of that cathartic, healing effect. And no one listened more attentively than Desmond Tutu.

IN HIS OWN WORDS

No final theology

Westerners usually call for an ecumenical, a universal theology which they often identify with their brand of theologizing. Now this is thoroughly erroneous. Western theology is no more universal than other brands of theology can ever hope to be. For theology can never properly claim a universality which rightly belongs only to the eternal gospel of Jesus Christ. Theology is a human activity possessing the limitations and the particularities of those who are theologizing. It can speak relevantly only when it speaks to a particular . . . community; and it must have the humility to accept the scandal of its particularity as well as its transience. Theology is not eternal nor can it ever hope to be perfect. There is no final theology.

"Black Theology and African Theology" (1975)

Ubuntu

I lay great stress on humaneness and being truly human. In our African understanding, part of *ubuntu* — being human — is the rare gift of sharing. This concept of sharing is exemplified at African feasts even to this day, when people eat together from a common dish, rather than from individual dishes. That means a meal is indeed to have communion with one's fellows. Blacks are beginning to lose this wonderful attribute, because we are being inveigled by the excessive individualism of the West. I loathe capitalism because it gives far too great play to our inherent selfishness. We are told to be highly competitive, and our children start learning the attitudes of the rat-race quite early. They mustn't just do well at school — they must sweep the floor with their rivals. . . . We give prizes to such persons, not so far as I know to those who know how best to get on with others, or those who can coax the best out of others. We must delight in our ulcers, the symbols of our success. (1979)

What kind of God?

By becoming a real human being through Jesus Christ, God showed that he took the whole of human history and the whole of human life seriously. He demonstrated that he was Lord of all life, spiritual and secular, sacred and profane, material and spiritual. We will show that scripture and the main stream of Christian tradition and teaching know nothing of the dichotomies so popular in our day which demand the separation of religion from politics. These I will demonstrate are deeply theological matters. . . . Our God cares that children starve in resettlement camps, the somewhat respectable name for apartheid's dumping grounds for the pathetic casualties of this vicious and evil system. The God we worship does care that people die mysteriously in detention. He is concerned that people are condemned to a twilight existence as non-persons by an arbitrary bureaucratic act of banning them without giving them the opportunity to reply to charges brought against them. I will show this from the Bible. I might add that if God did not care about these and similar matters, I would not worship him for he would be a totally useless God. Mercifully, he is not such a God.

Address to the Eloff Commission (1982)

"Totally superfluous"

I have already said we owe our ultimate loyalty and allegiance only to God. With due respect, I want to submit that no secular authority or its appointed commissions have any competence whatsoever to determine how a church is a church or what is the nature of the Gospel of Jesus Christ. When secular authority tries to do this, it is then usurping divine prerogatives and the prerogatives of the church itself. With respect, we do not recognize the right of this commission to inquire into our theological existence, and therefore into any aspect of our life as a council, since every other aspect of our existence is determined by theological facts, as I have already pointed out. Only our member churches can call us to task. If we have contravened any laws of the country, then you don't need a commission to determine that. There is an array of draconian laws at the disposal of the government and the courts of law are the proper place to determine our guilt or innocence. This commission, with respect, is totally superfluous.

to the Eloff Commission

What can they do?

There is nothing the government can do to me that will stop me from being involved in what I believe God wants me to do. I do not do it because I like doing it. I do it because I am under what I believe to be the influence of God's hand. I cannot help it. When I see injustice I cannot keep quiet, for, as Jeremiah says, when I try to keep quiet, God's word burns like a fire in my breast. But what is it that they can ultimately do? The most awful thing that they can do is to kill me, and death is not the worst thing that could happen to a Christian.

to the Eloff Commission

Biblical separation

The only separation the Bible knows is between believers on the one hand and unbelievers on the other. Any other kind of separation, division, disunity is of the devil. It is evil and from sin.

to the Eloff Commission

"No false dichotomies"

For this God, our God, no one is a nonentity. For this God, our God, everybody is a somebody. All life belongs to him. Because of him all life is religious. There are no false dichotomies so greatly loved by those especially who are comfortable in this life. Consequently, if you say you love God whom you have not seen and hate your brother whom you have, the Bible does not use delicate language; it does not say you are guilty of a terminological inexactitude. It says bluntly you are a liar. For he who would love God must love his brother also.

Sermon (1986)

The Rainbow People of God

You are very special to God. You are of infinite worth to God. God loves you not because you are lovable, but you are lovable precisely because God loves you. And that is a love that will never change. God loved you and that is why God created you, created me. God loves you now, God will always love you, for ever and ever. His is a love which will never let you go. Your name is engraved on the palms of God's hands. The very hairs on your head are numbered. You and I, all of us, are known by name. . . . There is life after April 28. We are all wounded people, traumatized, all of us, by the evil of apartheid. We all need healing and we, the church of God, must pour balm on the wounds inflicted by this evil system. Let us be channels of love, of peace, of justice, of reconciliation. Let us declare that we have been made for togetherness, we have been made for family, that, yes, now we are free, all of us, black and white together, we the Rainbow People of God!

From a sermon preached at St. George's Cathedral, Cape Town, April 24, 1994, the Sunday before Nelson Mandela was sworn in as president of South Africa

No self-sufficiency

A self-sufficient human being is subhuman. I have gifts that you do not have, so, consequently, I am unique — you have gifts that I do not have, so you are unique. God has made us so that we will need each other. We are made for a delicate network of interdependence. We see it on a macro level. Not even the most powerful nations in the world can be self-sufficient.

"God's Dream" (1992)

Is God in charge?

We prayed earnestly that God would bless our land and would confound the machinations of the children of darkness. There had been so many moments in the past, during the dark days of apartheid's vicious awfulness, when we had preached, "This is God's world and God is in charge!"

Sometimes, when evil seemed to be on the rampage and about to over-whelm goodness, one had held on to this article of faith by the skin of one's teeth. It was a kind of theological whistling in the dark and one was frequently tempted to whisper in God's ear, "For goodness' sake, why don't you make it more obvious that *you are* in charge?"

No Future Without Forgiveness (1999)

What theology does

So frequently we in the commission were quite appalled at the depth of de-pravity to which human beings could sink and we would, most of us, say that those who committed such dastardly deeds were monsters because the deeds were monstrous. But theology prevents us from doing this. Theol-ogy reminded me that, however diabolical the act, it did not turn the per-petrator into a demon. We had to distinguish between the deed and the perpetrator, between the sinner and the sin, to hate and condemn the sin while being filled with compassion for the sinner. The point is that, if per-petrators were to be despaired of as monsters and demons, then we were thereby letting accountability go out the window because we were then de-claring that they were not moral agents to be held responsible for the deeds they had committed. Much more importantly, it meant that we abandoned all hope of their being able to change for the better. Theology said they still, despite the awfulness of their deeds, remained children of God with the capacity to repent, to be able to change. . . . In this theology, we can never give up on anyone because our God was one who had a particularly soft spot for sinners. The Good Shepherd in the parable Jesus told had been quite ready to leave ninety-nine perfectly well-behaved sheep in the wilderness to look for, not an attractive, fluffy little lamb — fluffy little lambs do not usually stray from their mummies — but for the trouble-some, obstreperous old ram. This was the one on which the Good Shep-herd expended so much energy.

No Future Without Forgiveness

FOR REFLECTION AND DISCUSSION

How does the concept of *ubuntu* fit with your understanding of the Christian gospel?

How does the way Christian faith is taught and practiced in your church compare with the understanding of Christian faith as *ubuntu*?

What do you think would have happened if the South African Truth and Reconciliation Commission had decided either to pretend that no atrocities had taken place under apartheid, or to bring the perpetrators to trial?

If "death is not the worst thing that could happen to a Christian," what is?

By what principles or criteria should a Christian decide to defy the government?

How do you feel God would answer this question: "For goodness' sake, why don't you make it more obvious that *you are* in charge?"

Acknowledgments

The author and publisher gratefully acknowledge permission to include material from the following sources:

Dorothy L. Sayers, *Creed or Chaos,* © 1949, published by Methuen. Used by permission.

Dorothy L. Sayers, *The Mind of the Maker,* © 1941, published by Methuen. Used by permission.

C. S. Lewis, *God in the Dock,* copyright © C. S. Lewis Pte. Ltd. 1970. Extracts reprinted by permission.

C. S. Lewis, *The Weight of Glory,* copyright © C. S. Lewis Pte. Ltd. 1949. Extracts reprinted by permission.

C. S. Lewis, *The Problem of Pain,* copyright © C. S. Lewis Pte. Ltd. 1940. Extracts reprinted by permission.

C. S. Lewis, *Miracles,* copyright © C. S. Lewis Pte. Ltd. 1947, 1960. Extracts reprinted by permission.

C. S. Lewis, *Mere Christianity,* copyright © C. S. Lewis Pte. Ltd. 1942, 1943, 1944, 1952. Extracts reprinted by permission.

C. S. Lewis, *A Grief Observed,* copyright © C. S. Lewis Pte. Ltd. 1961. Extracts reprinted by permission.

Acknowledgments

Verna Dozier, *The Dream of God,* copyright © 1991 Verna Dozier. All rights reserved. Published by Cowley Publications, 907 Massachusetts Avenue, Cambridge, MA 02139. www.cowley.org (1-800-225-1534).

Madeleine L'Engle, excerpts from *The Other Side of the Sun.* Copyright © 1971 by Madeleine L'Engle. Reprinted by permission of Farrar, Straus and Giroux, LLC.

Madeleine L'Engle, excerpts from *A Circle of Quiet.* Copyright © 1972 by Madeleine L'Engle Franklin. Reprinted by permission of Farrar, Straus and Giroux, LLC.

Madeleine L'Engle, excerpts from *The Summer of the Great Grandmother.* Copyright © 1974 by Crosswicks, Ltd. Reprinted by permission of Farrar, Straus and Giroux, LLC.

Madeleine L'Engle, excerpts from *A Ring of Endless Light.* Copyright © 1980 by Crosswicks, Ltd. Reprinted by permission of Farrar, Straus and Giroux, LLC.

Madeleine L'Engle, excerpts from *Two-Part Invention.* Copyright © 1988 by Crosswicks Ltd. Reprinted by permission of Farrar, Straus and Giroux, LLC.

Festo Kivengere, *Revolutionary Love,* ©1983 Africa Enterprises, published by Christian Literature Crusade. Used by permission.

Desmond Tutu, *The Rainbow People of God,* edited by John Allen, copyright © 1994 by Desmond Tutu and John Allen. Used by permission of Doubleday, a division of Random House, Inc.

Desmond Tutu, *No Future Without Forgiveness,* copyright © 1999 by Desmond Tutu. U.S.: Used by permission of Doubleday, a division of Random House, Inc. U.K.: Used by permission of the Random House Group Limited.

Index